IRELAND

Art into History

IRELAND
Art into History

Edited by

Raymond Gillespie and Brian P Kennedy

TOWN HOUSE
Dublin

ROBERTS RINEHART PUBLISHERS
Niwot, Colorado

Published in Ireland and the UK by Town House & Country House, Trinity House, Charleston Road, Ranelagh, Dublin 6

ISBN: 0 948524 47 2

Published in the US and Canada by Roberts Rinehart Publishers, P.O. Box 666, Niwot, Colorado 80544

ISBN: 1 57098 005 5

Library of Congress number: 94–67455

Distributed by Publishers Group West

Acknowledgements

The editors wish to thank the following for their assistance with this book: Treasa Coady for her splendid belief in this project; Elaine Campion for excellent copy editing; Bernie Daly for helping to source illustrations; Cian Ó hÉigeartaigh for most of the captions; Anne Crookshank, Roy Foster and Kevin B Nowlan for their endorsement of the book; Michael Olohan and John Kellett for photographing some of the illustrations; Raymond Keaveney, Director, National Gallery of Ireland, for his support of this project since its inception; Marie McFeely, Rights and Reproductions Officer, National Gallery of Ireland; the National Museum of Ireland, the National Library of Ireland, the Irish Architectural Archive, the Central Bank of Ireland, the Hugh Lane Municipal Gallery of Modern Art, Dublin, the General Post Office, Dublin, the Royal Dublin Society, the Church of Ireland Representative Body Library, Dublin, St Patrick's College, Maynooth, the Cork Public Museum, the Crawford Municipal Art Gallery, Cork, the Ulster Folk and Transport Museum, Cultra, the Belfast Public Library, the Ulster Museum, Belfast, the British Museum, London, the Mitchell Wolfson Museum, Miami, Florida; last, and most importantly, the contributors, whose cooperation and endeavour, in researching, writing and accepting our editing, have made the editors' role a most stimulating and enjoyable one.

Cover illustration: *A Kitchen Interior* by John Mulvany (National Gallery of Ireland, no 1277)

Title page illustration by Birgitta Säflund from an eighth-century crucifixion plaque found at St John's, Rinnagan, Athlone, County Westmeath

Design: Jack Van Zandt and Frederick R Rinehart, Roberts Rinehart Publishers

Typesetting: Red Barn Publishing, Skeagh, Skibbereen, Co. Cork, Ireland

Printed in Hong Kong by COLORCORP–Sing Cheong

CONTENTS

Notes on the Contributors

Sighle Bhreathnach-Lynch has lectured in the history of art at University College, Dublin. Her doctoral thesis was on the life and work of Albert Power.

Marie Bourke is education officer in the National Gallery of Ireland. Her exhibition based on *The Aran Fisherman's Drowned Child* by Frederic William Burton toured a number of Irish venues in 1987–8.

Margaret Crawford is research officer in the Department of Economic and Social History, Queen's University, Belfast. She specialises in the history of diet and famine in Ireland. She edited *Famine: The Irish Experience 900–1900* (1989).

W H Crawford was formerly keeper of material culture in the Ulster Folk and Transport Museum. He is now development officer for the Federation of Ulster Local Studies. He has written extensively on the history of Ulster in the eighteenth century.

Marie Davis completed her master's thesis on childhood in eighteenth-century Ireland at Trinity College, Dublin.

P J Duffy is associate professor of geography at St Patrick's College, Maynooth. His principal research interest is the development of the Irish landscape. He is the author of *Landscapes of South Ulster* (1993).

Mairead Dunlevy is director of the Hunt Museum at the University of Limerick, and was previously on the staff of the National Museum of Ireland. She is the author of *Dress in Ireland* (1989).

Raymond Gillespie lectures in history at St Patrick's College, Maynooth. He has written widely on Ireland in the seventeenth century, including *Colonial Ulster* (1985) and *The Transformation of the Irish Economy, 1550–1700* (1991).

Brian P Kennedy is assistant director of the National Gallery of Ireland. His publications include *Alfred Chester Beatty and Ireland: A Study in Cultural Politics* (1988), *Dreams and Responsibilities* (1990), an examination of arts policy in Ireland since 1922, and *Irish Painting* (1993).

Edward McParland is a Fellow of Trinity College, Dublin, where he teaches in the Department of the History of Art. He has written extensively on eighteenth- and nineteenth-century architecture in Ireland, notably *James Gandon: Vitruvius Hibernicus* (1985).

Fergus O'Ferrall is the author of a number of studies of Daniel O'Connell, including *Catholic Emancipation: Daniel O'Connell and the Birth of Irish Democracy* (1985) and *Daniel O'Connell* (Gill's Irish Lives series).

Gary Owens teaches history at Huron College, University of Western Ontario, Canada. His main research interest is popular politics in nineteenth-century Ireland.

Alistair Rowan is principal of Edinburgh College of Art and past professor of the history of art in University College, Dublin. He has written extensively on Robert Adam and on Irish architecture. He is the editor of the Buildings of Ireland series.

PREFACE

In Ireland, historians still regard visual images as sideshows to the main task of interpreting written documents from the past. Illustrations are often incorporated into historical works only at the insistence of publishers, or at best to make large bodies of text more attractive visually. Images are rarely treated as evidence in themselves. On the other hand, several large archives of photographs have been presented to the public in book form in recent years, with almost no exploration of context. Visual images can be a powerful tool for understanding the past, and deserve to be treated not merely as illustrations or appendages to a text, but as documents, to be read as such in conjunction with other contemporary material, so that the viewer may understand not only the images, but also the cultural context that shaped them.

An opportunity to test this contention was provided during a two-day conference in the National Gallery of Ireland in December 1990, when we invited a number of Irish historians and art historians to come together to consider how best to use visual material in the exploration of Ireland's past. The essays in this volume have been written as a result of that exploration. We hope that they will serve as a stimulus to others to pursue the same approach, and that they will demonstrate the incontrovertible point that images of the past are at least as important as oral or written evidence.

Raymond Gillespie and Brian P Kennedy

INTRODUCTION

*Great nations write their autobiographies in three manuscripts — the book of their deeds, the book of their words
and the book of their art. No one of these three books can be understood unless we read the two others.*

John Ruskin

This book is not about history in the sense of exploring the public and private manuscripts of the past in an attempt to recreate something of a vanished world. Nor is it
about art as a reflection of the high culture of the past, identifying its symbols, styles
and techniques. Rather, it is about how people tried to use visual images to express ideas about
themselves, their society and the world around them. The range of images they deployed was
far wider than a traditional art historian might expect to encounter, and the impact that images
made in a society of limited literacy was much greater than many historians might suspect. The
images that appear in this volume range from the ephemeral postage stamp, through uniforms,
newspaper illustrations and sketchbooks, to more formal engravings, paintings, sculpture and
architecture. Despite their diversity, they have one feature in common: they were all created
in a specific cultural context.[1]

No image can escape the social and intellectual background or the religious or political
beliefs and patronage structure of the age in which it is created. The choice of theme by an
artist is constrained by these realities, and consequently they affect the viewer's understanding
of why images were created and their role in the society of their day. Images of all sorts can
be as important to our understanding of the world as written documents. If we can understand why certain images were created at certain times and their effect on contemporaries,
then we have a powerful analytical tool for interpreting the past. This is not an easy task. Many
of the assumptions of those who sculpted, drew, painted or printed in the past have passed out
of our cultural baggage. The language of heraldry, for example, has been lost to all but a few
specialists. Questions of patronage structure, perception, aesthetics, as well as the technical
limitations of the artist, all need to be taken into account in this exercise, but the central concern remains the cultural context of the image.

It is easy to see individual images as neatly framed slices of reality, or as a bundle of conventions, imitations or symbolic transformations of reality. We need an interpretative framework
wider than this, however, to understand their importance. No image stands by itself; it is always
related to other images and to its audience. In some cases the context might be aesthetic; col-
lectors often acquired paintings, tapestries, furniture and sculpture to beautify their houses and
to give themselves pleasure. Patrons sometimes commissioned images for utilitarian purposes,
such as the miniatures of some of his children commissioned by the Earl of Cork in 1621 to be
sent to prospective marriage partners.[2] Tourists such as Thomas Dineley and Francis Place in
the seventeenth century often kept sketchbooks to record their impressions of the countryside
and material culture.[3] In other cases the context might be politics, religion or status: landlords
tended to display pride in their estates through maps and landscapes; politicians at all stages in

Ireland's past were well aware of the effect of demonstrations, triumphal arches and commemorations in articulating and defining political consciousness. At an individual level, portraits conveyed pride in a family's past, and honours and decorations displayed status. These contexts explained and interpreted images for contemporaries.

The importance of context may be appreciated by considering the diversity of images associated with religion in Ireland. Such images and artefacts were created for a specific place, usually a church, and deployed for particular reasons, which were expressed through a liturgy. Some works of art were intended to create a sense of awe and to glorify the building in a configuration of spaces, forms and colours. To isolate individual elements from their backgrounds is to miss the experience of wonder that, for example, a place of religious worship can convey.[4] It is also to distort the significance of these works for their creators. A chalice, no matter how beautiful, is only a piece of worked silver when viewed in isolation from the ritual actions of the celebrant. To try to understand it without these actions is like attempting to read a foreign text with only the aid of a dictionary. Similarly, to examine individual statues of the Madonna and Child from fifteenth-century Ireland without some knowledge of the significance of Mary in that society, is to remove the image from the cult of the saints that flourished with extraordinary intensity during that period.[5] By so doing, we fail to appreciate the effect such images had on shaping the perceptions of ordinary people about religion and its role in the world. One woman at Shrule in County Mayo explained to a visitor in 1692 that at the Eucharist she received not the body and blood of Christ but the Virgin Mary and the baby Jesus.[6] In her own mind the ritual actions of the priest had merged with the powerful image of the Madonna and Child to create a satisfactory explanation of the events taking place. Thus, by divorcing the image from its cultural context, we can miss the functions that contemporaries assigned to it. In Ireland, from at least the fifteenth century, many statues were attributed miraculous powers, and such images thus formed a bridge between the natural world and the supernatural world. It is not simply that this religious imagery was aesthetically pleasing, for much of it was not, but it was a sign of the power of God at work in the world, a perception that had far-reaching consequences.

In the thirteen essays contained in this volume, a wide range of visual images are examined, within their cultural contexts, in order to explore aspects of Ireland's past, and so to enrich our understanding of both the past and the images. Three broad themes have been chosen: the use of images to reconstruct the material world of the past; images as a reflection of political life in the past; and images as evidence of ideas and mentalities. Of these, the material world is the most accessible through visual sources. As Marie Bourke's essay demonstrates, even when a painter is working within accepted artistic conventions, and hence distorting reality to achieve a specific effect, the eye for detail is still sharp. Costumes, social arrangements and customs can all be revealed through the details in a picture. The same sort of detail, this time preserved in a sketchbook possibly created by Samson Towgood Roche, is discussed by W H Crawford and reflects on the economic life of a particular region when seen in the wider context provided by written documents. Aspects of women's work, dress and diet at a low social level are all recoverable in these watercolours, as well as more general information on the development of marketing and transport facilities for the sale of agricultural produce. However, the essays by Edward McParland, P J Duffy and Margaret Crawford warn that this technique must be used with care. Malton's views of Dublin certainly preserved details of eigh-teenth-century life in the city, but they also contain many inaccuracies that would mislead the unwary. Images of landscape were also often composed of what observers preferred to see rather than what was there. Patronage drew artists to 'preferred landscapes', with views often uncluttered by people in an age of dramatic population growth. Similarly, during the trauma of the Famine of the 1840s, the horrors recounted in *The Illustrated London News* were often at variance with the milder images printed in its pages, representing a perceptual problem on the part of the artists.

If perception poses a problem for those trying to recreate the material world of the past through the study of visual images, it is a strength for those trying to analyse how political life is depicted. The four essays concerned with this theme try to recover the effect that a series of images was intended to have on contemporary public perceptions of the political world. In the case of Fergus O'Ferrall, the essay focuses on one individual, Daniel O'Connell, and the image he wished to create of himself through engravings, portraits and uniforms. Brian P Kennedy's essay looks at how the newly created Irish Free State tried to forge and portray an identity for itself: flags, stamps, currency, statues, architecture and paintings were all used to reinforce the sense of identity already created through the Irish language and Roman Catholicism. This same theme is approached in a different way in Sighle Bhreathnach-Lynch's essay on the art of Albert Power. Power's concern to express his own Irishness, at the same time as the Irish Free State was engaged in forging a cultural identity, encouraged him to spe-cialise in the creation of political and religious sculpture. As in recreating the material world, however, the interpretation of the evidence of political life has to be conducted with care. Public art carried a message that was often reiterated in ritual and ceremonies. It is this aspect of nineteenth-century public monuments in Ireland that forms the centrepiece of Gary Owens' essay. The centenary of the 1798 Rising provided an occasion for the erection of popular mon-uments to dead nationalist heroes, and in so doing played an important part in constructing and articulating the political culture of Irish nationalism at a time of considerable ideological flux.

The final group of essays in this volume uses both the idea of image creation and the details of the material world to explore the less tangible worlds of ideas and mentalities in the past, about which more formal written documents are often silent. Marie Davis and Raymond Gillespie use visual evidence to explore two themes that have preoccupied social historians in recent years: childhood and death. Marie Davis uses the evidence of architecture, costume and education, as depicted in the visual arts, to offer clues to the relationships between par-ents and children in the eighteenth century; Raymond Gillespie uses early modern funeral monuments to reflect not only changing ideas about death, but developments in the related areas of religious practices and senses of group identity. These interrelationships between dif-ferent identities and religious ideas and their role in creating mentalities as displayed in visual evidence are taken up in Alistair Rowan's examination of the ecclesiastical architecture of nineteenth-century Ireland. In an age of growing religious and political tensions, it is hardly surprising that the building of churches should express these tensions. What is remarkable is that nuances of differences even within Protestantism and Catholicism should each have expressed themselves architecturally, thus reinforcing the connections between images and their cultural context. The interaction of changing ideas in a cultural context also features in

Mairead Dunlevy's essay. New ideas of liberty, freedom and a sense of modernity in Dublin during the early nineteenth century changed the way the middle class and their servants lived. New styles of furniture and decoration as well as labour-saving devices all expressed the arrival of a new world.

A volume of thirteen case studies cannot hope to exhaust what is potentially such a rich field for all those concerned with Ireland's past. Works of art can capture experiences and moods that written documents with their deceptive precision cannot hope to preserve, especially in matters of religion and politics. Many areas in which images can be of crucial importance in exploring the experience of the past have hardly been touched in this collection. What this volume does is to suggest ways of approaching the visual evidence of the past by taking three broad themes as examples, and pointing to the potential of this type of study.

In a country whose official and private archives have been subject to various periods of destruction from the seventeenth century onwards, visual evidence is relatively abundant. Architectural evidence, for example, survives in some quantities in the landscape and is currently being listed by the Office of Public Works in Dublin and by the Archaeological Survey of Northern Ireland. For later periods, architectural drawings and photographs, especially the large collection held by the Irish Architectural Archive, can be especially valuable. Such evidence deserves to be treated not simply as a succession of styles or of distribution maps but, as Mairead Dunlevy and Alistair Rowan do in this volume, as reflections of people's beliefs and ways of living. The decline of the castle and the rise of the manor house in seventeenth-century Ireland is a reflection of the changing political and social perceptions, as well as the fashions and security needs of those who lived in these buildings. Such an analysis need not be confined to great houses. Vernacular dwellings also provide evidence of priorities for day-to-day living and the cultural and social norms that accompanied the various lifestyles depicted.[7] Likewise, the design and layout of churches provide evidence of changing beliefs and religious practices.[8]

Perhaps the most striking examples of visual evidence surviving in the Irish landscape are the public monuments erected throughout the nineteenth and twentieth centuries. Almost every town in Ireland has some form of monument. These span a wide range of political and religious attitudes, from the Marian grottos of the 1950s through the war memorials set up in many Irish towns after the 1914–18 war, to the sort of nationalist monuments described by Gary Owens. These are all worthy of study, not only the iconography of the monuments, but the contemporary accounts of their design, funding and erection.[9] More prosaic monuments to the dead, in the form of gravestones, deserve much greater attention than they have received. As Raymond Gillespie's essay shows, changing patterns of monument types can often be revealing of changes in the wider world. By the nineteenth century, even the poorer classes were setting up funeral monuments that are worthy of study.[10]

Perhaps the most attractive road into the past is through the archives of visual images in the collections of the National Gallery of Ireland, the Ulster Museum, the Crawford Gallery in Cork, and other galleries. To these might be added the large nineteenth- and twentieth-century photographic collections of the National Library, especially the Lawrence Collection, and the Ulster Museum's Welch Collection, as well as collections in private hands. The essays by W H Crawford and Marie Bourke suggest ways of approaching this type of material by looking at details as a way into a lost material world. The cautionary notes of Edward McParland,

Margaret Crawford and P J Duffy should be borne in mind here. Such care need be no greater, however, than that which a historian examining written documents might be expected to show in weighing and assessing evidence.[11]

These riches can also be approached through the eyes of those who originally saw them. The essays of Brian P Kennedy, Marie Davis and Sighle Bhreathnach-Lynch suggest ways of dealing with the evidence to recover lost identities or unravel the underlying ideas and affections. If we can recover the aims of the patrons of these works or the impact they had on contemporaries, we will have gone a long way to a genuine understanding of a world that we have perhaps not quite lost. We need more studies, like that of Fergus O'Ferrall, of how individuals tried to mould their images using cheap print, formal portraits and rhetoric, as well as manipulating the artistic conventions of the day. This vast array of evidence both in the landscape and galleries should not distract us from written descriptions of how buildings or pictures looked, or the most transient images of printed pamphlets, broadsheets, stamps, posters and other ephemera, all of which have their role in explaining the past.

All of this evidence will be of little value unless we are prepared to change the way in which we approach the past. We must be prepared to think visually and to reconstruct in our own minds how the past looked, both from written descriptions and visual evidence.[12] There is little historical value in collecting random images without understanding how they fitted together and the cultural context to which they belonged. A volume such as this offers suggestions as to how we might proceed. We should, however, agree on a central point, that the image is a document just as much as the more traditional state paper, government report, lease or ecclesiastical visitation. Reading the visual document requires a rather different set of skills to those of the expert in palaeography or the subtleties of diplomacy, and the results may well be more ambiguous than those provided by the apparent precision of the written word. Important though these technical skills are, they are not the crucial element in the task of using images as evidence. What is most important is the willingness to make an imaginative leap into the world of the past and to bring to bear all the available evidence in as creative a way as possible in order to understand it.

Raymond Gillespie and Brian P Kennedy

PART ONE

RECOVERING LOST WORLDS

1

Edward McParland

MALTON'S VIEWS OF DUBLIN: TOO GOOD TO BE TRUE?

A s every Dublin manufacturer of Christmas cards or table-mats knows, James Malton's views of the capital city are familiar and popular. His aquatints and watercolours are perceptive, informative and beautiful witnesses to the appearance of Dublin at the end of the eighteenth century.

The details of Malton's life are somewhat less familiar. Estimates of the date of his birth range from about 1750 to 1766, although he has been pinned down more successfully than his brother Thomas, whose birth date ranges in the literature from 1748 to 1784. The most reliable account of James Malton seems to be that found in the Knight of Glin's introduction to the Dolmen Press 1978 reprint of Malton's *Picturesque & Descriptive View of the City of Dublin*, which was originally published in volume form in 1799. According to this, James Malton (the brother of Thomas Malton junior and the son of Thomas senior) was probably born in 1764. He served in the Dublin office of James Gandon, then the city's premier architect, for three years from 1781. Malton himself confirms that he took his views of Dublin in 1791 — he could hardly have chosen a better year in which to record the splendour of the city's architecture.

AQUATINTS AND WATERCOLOURS

Malton's views fall into two categories. Firstly, there are the aquatints, serially produced in a printing press using plates prepared by James Malton from his own drawings; the fact that the drawings and plates were of his own making is indicated on each print by the words: 'James Malton del[ineavit] et fecit.'[1] The word 'aquatint' refers, not to colour, but to the technique by which tone, or a furry texture, is given to the print. On emerging from the printing press,

1.1 *Trinity College Dublin*, James Malton (*c*1764–1803), Ink and water-colour on paper; signed and dated 1796

A literal record, or 'snapshot', of what could have been seen in 1796? Not really, for the artist's viewpoint is deep within the Parliament House, now the Bank of Ireland, behind walls that were then — as they still are — windowless.

National Gallery of Ireland (no 2184)

these aquatints were monochrome, the colour of the ink used during the process. Such colour as they now sometimes carry was applied later by hand, in some cases soon after printing, in other cases long after.[2] These prints, twenty-five views in all (not counting 'extras' such as a map and coat of arms of Dublin, and not counting Malton's view of the forecourt of the Parliament House, engraved by Wilson Lowry in 1793), were published between 1792 and 1799, and were then issued in volume form in 1799.[3]

Secondly, there are the watercolour views of the city, individually drawn and painted by Malton. Of the watercolours that correspond to views found in the bound volume of 1799, ten survive in the National Gallery of Ireland (others survive elsewhere).[4] Seven of these ten are signed, seven are dated variously from 1792 to 1796, and three are undated.[5] In some cases the watercolours date from after the publication of the corresponding aquatint: the west front of *Trinity College, Dublin* in watercolour is dated 1796 (Illus 1.1), while the corresponding print was first published three years earlier. The watercolours may well have been produced independently of the print-making process. Many were exhibited at the Royal Academy: the Custom House watercolour, for example, is dated 1793, the year in which it was exhibited at the academy, but the corresponding print had been published the previous year.[6]

IRELAND: ART INTO HISTORY

It is reasonable to assume that the watercolours and prints were produced from the same set of field sketches. Malton tells us that he recorded the views on the spot in 1791. The following year he was exhibiting in London from an address near Golden Square; in 1793 he had moved to the neighbourhood of Fitzroy Square; and from 1794 to 1803, when he died, he exhibited from Norton Street, Portland Place. Perhaps he revisited Dublin during the 1790s: the introduction to the 1799 volume tells us that 'as the work was in hand till the year 1797, such alterations as occurred in each subject, between the taking and publishing of any view of it, have been attended to'. On the other hand he may have relied in making these revisions on information supplied by friends. What is important is that both the highly finished watercolours and the prints were prepared, not on the spot, but at a distance.

As is the case with many well-known images, each of Malton's views of Dublin is seen by most people as a whole, while its details are unfamiliar. With the aid of close-up photography, however, details can be isolated from the too familiar context of the entire picture and examined for their own sake. When this is done with Malton's views, the population of boatmen, fruit sellers, hod men, chairmen, beaux, soldiers, academics, clerics, beggars, butchers, drovers, tipplers (Illus 1.2), haymakers and lamplighters comes to life outside button shops, around street fountains (Illus 1.3), in lottery booths, on grave slabs, in shambles, on solid-wheel carts, in boatyards, up ladders, leaning out of windows, or lounging on the Magazine Hill, dressed in everything from secondhand coats, to *déshabillé*, to 'cardinals' (red capes worn by women) (Illus 1.4), to aprons, to trousers (only then coming into fashion), to toilettes that might have been copied from the fashion plates of Heideloff.[7]

1.2 Detail from *St Catherine's, Dublin*, James Malton (*c*1764–1803), Ink and watercolour on paper
This representation of a street scene is vivid, and the architectural details of St Catherine's Church, Thomas Street (eg the round-headed window and the blocked archway) are verifiable today. But is the name of the innkeeper — Patrick O'Murphy — too good to be true?
National Gallery of Ireland (no 2186)

1.3 Detail from *St Catherine's, Dublin*, James Malton (*c*1764–1803), Ink and watercolour on paper
The houses near this public fountain in Thomas Street may have old-fashioned roofs (high-pitched, with roof ridges running back from the street), but instead of Dutch gables they have more up-to-the-minute horizontal roof parapets.
National Gallery of Ireland (no 2186)

MALTON'S VIEWS AS HISTORICAL SOURCES

How reliable is Malton as a reporter of life in eighteenth-century Dublin? There is a good deal of evidence to show that he took great pains to be accurate. On the columns of his *Parliament House*, the joints between the individual blocks of stone are marked exactly as we see them today. He captures the unusual pattern of rusticated stone on the ground floor of the Blue Coat School (Illus 1.5). His statue of George II is a very small detail in his plate of St Stephen's Green, but its pedestal corresponds closely with what once stood there. In his view of *The Tholsel* (watercolour 1792, print published 1793), Robert Thomas's name is on the adjoining tallow chandler's shop (Illus 1.6): he is listed as tallow chandler of 1 Skinner Row in the Dublin directories only for 1791 (when Malton made his notes) and 1792, after which he disappears. This is reassuring evidence in favour of examining the Tholsel plate (Illus 1.7) for what it tells us of life in eighteenth-century Dublin: buildings that have since vanished (not just the Tholsel, but also the round-arched building at the right-hand edge of the view), the glazed shop fronts, shop window displays (eg Thomas's shop), costume, nosebags, registration numbers and curtaining of sedan chairs, street lights, wooden area railings (as crop up in other views), insurance plaques, window joinery, partially encased lead downpipes, and much more. We are left to speculate, alas, on the quality of repartee of Dublin urchins of the late eighteenth century (Illus 1.8).

1.6 Detail from *The Tholsel, Dublin,* James Malton (*c*1764–1803), Ink and watercolour on paper; signed and dated 1792

The only years in which Robert Thomas's tallow chandler's shop appears in the Dublin *Directory* are 1791 and 1792, the very years in which Malton was preparing and painting this picture. This reinforces the idea that in some of the incidental details, Malton is remarkably reliable.

National Gallery of Ireland (no 2185)

1.7 *The Tholsel, Dublin*, James Malton
(*c*1764–1803), Ink and watercolour
on paper; signed and dated 1792

This view is valuable for being the
most detailed representation of the
Tholsel that we have (it stood in
Skinner's Row, just to the south of
Christ Church Cathedral). It is fascinating, too, for its details of the sedan
chair, street lighting, wooden railings,
shop fronts, down pipes and much
besides.

National Gallery of Ireland (no 2185)

Predictably, however, if we look long enough, and hard enough, we will spot signs that we must be on our guard. In the *Parliament House* print, Robert Parke's colonnade is omitted from the building at the left-hand margin. In his *Custom House* watercolour, there is no indication, at the south-west corner (Illus 1.9), of the transition from Portland stone to granite. And although we may have to overlook his omission of the roof-top urn on this corner pavilion (per-haps not put in place until after 1793, the date of the watercolour), it was incorrect of him to omit the pediments over the upper central windows on either face of the pavilion. In the Four Courts view (Illus 1.10), his portico projects far enough from the façade to allow passage through the flanking intercolumniations (something that Gandon desired but was denied), and he shows niches on the ground floor of the projecting wings, a plausibly Gandonian idea, but not one that was executed. His watercolour shows his columns projecting much too far from the face of the drum.

There are too many differences between his central block of the Royal Infirmary, Phoenix Park, and the admittedly much altered present building, for it to be easy to believe in what Malton shows. The tower and steeple on his Blue Coat School (Illus 1.5), and the long recessed panels in the surface of the façade in either side intercolumniation, owe more to Pool and Cash's partly fictional elevation published in 1780 than to anything that was ever built. Furthermore, the Blue Coat School was never set back from the road with lawns as deep as these. In his *Rotunda and New Rooms* plate, he puts too many window bays into the façade of what is now the Gate Theatre. In the print of *St Catherine's Church*, Dennis Plunket may have purveyed rum, brandy, mead, whiskey and arrack in Thomas Street, though he is not listed in the Dublin directories, but we may well be sceptical of the name on the shop front in the cor-responding watercolour: surely Patrick O'Murphy is too good to be true (Illus 1.2)? In *Leinster House*, Malton places his top line of windows much too close to those of the main storey below.

And knowing as we do that there is a two-storey high entrance hallway here, we realise that the lady looking out the window must in fact be doing so in some alarm, as she must be perched on a cornice half-way up the wall inside.

These straightforward mistakes are not very interesting. What is worth noting, however, is a more insidious process of idealisation at work. Consider those north-facing façades — Royal Exchange, Tholsel, Royal Hospital, St Catherine's — can they ever have been illuminated by the sun as brilliantly as in these views? Was Dame Street, or Capel Street Bridge, or Cork Hill, really as uncongested with traffic as this? Did the Dublin mendicants conform as obligingly as they do here to the picturesque demands of a Thomas Gainsborough or a George Morland (Illus 1.11)? Were there no derelict sites, or building sites, in Dublin in the 1790s? We have caught Malton out here, since his watercolour of *The Four Courts* is dated 1793, five years before the laying of the foundations for the eastern ranges. And we know that he finished off the Blue Coat tower, even though the builders never did.

The idealisation becomes even more clear when we consider his graphic techniques. Where was he standing to take his view of Trinity College (Illus 1.1)? Go to College Green and you will realise that the viewpoint is within the Parliament House (now Bank of Ireland), behind walls that neither now, nor then, had windows. Where was he standing to get his view of the Custom House? In the days before Butt Bridge or Loop Line Bridge, the only answer is the impossible one: on a platform in the middle of the river. Go to South William Street to find

Below left

1.9 Detail from *The Custom House, Dublin*, James Malton (c1764–1803), Ink and watercolour on paper; signed and dated 1793

Why has Malton omitted the urn on the skyline of the west face of this pavilion? Perhaps it was not yet in place when he painted this. More surprising is his mistaken omission of the pediment over the upper central window on each face, and his failure (or refusal) to distinguish the different colours of Portland stone and granite on the different faces.

National Gallery of Ireland (no 2705)

1.10 Detail from *The Four Courts, Dublin*, James Malton (c1764–1803), Ink and watercolour on paper; signed and dated 1793

The range on the right had not even been begun when Malton painted this view. Is he reflecting an early intention of James Gandon to have niches on the ground floor of this range, which Gandon abandoned in favour of rectangular opes when he came to build it?

National Gallery of Ireland (no 7713)

the point on the pavement from which he viewed Powerscourt House (Illus 1.12). There isn't one. He has widened the street. He has heightened the colour and chiaroscuro (at least in the watercolour) of the principal object in his composition, Powerscourt House itself. He has drawn it so that the verticals of his buildings remain vertical, and do not converge. And he has enhanced the perspective further by 'swinging around' the façade of Powerscourt House so that more of it is visible.

Malton's views beguile us into believing that we are looking at snapshots of Dublin in the 1790s. In many cases we can indeed use them as we would use photographs: for an unparalleled record of details of street life. They are more artificial, however, than many photographs, not least because these perspectives were produced not on the spot but later in the studio (in London). This later process involved not just field sketches, but also other architectural drawings, such as the plans and elevations needed for the elaborate perspectival constructions. (Some of Malton's watercolours are perforated at their vanishing points by the compasses used in setting out the perspective.)

As with every other historical source, we cannot approach Malton's views naïvely, even if they are only pictures. Malton presents his evidence in a highly stylised form. What he has to tell us is absorbing and, to an unacknowledged degree, unfamiliar, but he demands an audience as sophisticated as he was himself.

1.11 Detail from *The west front of St Patrick's Cathedral, Dublin*, James Malton (*c*1764–1803), Ink and watercolour on paper; signed and dated 1793

This mendicant, subscribing to the picturesque demands of a Morland or a Gainsborough, wears a yellow coat which he has probably bought second hand: in other Malton views, such dashing coats are seeing better days on the backs of more fashionable men.

National Gallery of Ireland (no 2620)

IRELAND: ART INTO HISTORY

1.12 *Powerscourt House, Dublin*, James
Malton (*c*1764–1803), Ink and watercolour on paper; signed and dated
1796

Subtle perspectival tricks idealise this
view: Malton widens the street, and
slightly swings around the façade of
Powerscourt House to face the
viewer, in his attempt to ameliorate
the awkward situation of the building.
National Gallery of Ireland (no 3019)

2

P J Duffy

THE CHANGING RURAL LANDSCAPE 1750–1850: PICTORIAL EVIDENCE

Paintings, drawings and the work of landscape artists have been much underused as a source of evidence for historians. When they have been used it has been mainly to provide a background or context to a study — a frontispiece, for instance — often in a tangential fashion. An example of this is the inclusion of Joseph Peacock's *Pattern of Glendalough 1813* on the dust-jacket of Alfred Smyth's book on medieval Leinster.[1] Despite this neglect of visual evidence, its potential for geographers, who share an interest with historians in what might be called the 'humanised landscape' — landscapes that reflect the impact of society in the past — is enormous. The customary way of describing changing landscapes is through the use of sources such as maps, estate surveys and ranges of data relating to a given place over a period of time, which allow measurements of rates of change to be made. For the changing rural landscape of the eighteenth and nineteenth centuries, another type of source offers itself: description of the landscape in the form of paintings and drawings.

ELEMENTS OF IRISH LANDSCAPE ART

Landscape consists of a range of elements, both tangible, such as buildings and settlement patterns, and intangible, such as 'community', 'atmosphere' and 'sense of place'. The intangible elements are often best captured in imaginative records of the landscape, through literature, or in the words of one historical geographer: 'there are times when the poor interpretative hack must show proper respect for the true creative artist.'[2] Many geographers have realised

IRELAND: ART INTO HISTORY

the value of literature, for example, in analysing landscape and landscape change.[3] In the context of changing landscapes, visual art holds out greater promise than the written word: seeing the place painted or drawn is often superior to verbal representations of it. As John Berger says of painting, 'no other kind of relic or text from the past can offer such a direct testimony about the world which surrounded other people at other times'.[4]

An important characteristic of the work of artists is that things can be omitted from their depictions of a place or landscape if they are disliked for one reason or another. Aesthetic reasons might require the exclusion of some element in order to distil the essence of the place, or ideological reasons might cater for a particular social point of view. Painters or poets can do violence to topography without affecting their own integrity.[5] An artist's view, therefore, is highly subjective, reflecting the values of his class, his times, his education or his market orientation. Thomas Gainsborough's refusal to paint Lord Hardwicke's park because it 'wasn't a *real view* from Nature' reflects perhaps an exceptionally independent spirit in an eighteenth-century artist, as well as an established idea of what a landscape should look like.[6] From the point of view of the historian, therefore, the canvas as a document must be cross-checked against the often dry and tedious written record.

In view of the shortcomings of the painted or sketched record of the Irish countryside in the eighteenth century, what use can be made of it? John Barrell, for example, has used the often 'unreal' painted record of the poor in eighteenth- and nineteenth-century England to examine the social strategy implied in this artistic representation — where artist conspired with establishment to depict the poor in an acceptable manner — and Ann Bermingham similarly examines the ideological evocation of country lanes and rivers during the agrarian revolution at the end of the eighteenth century.[7] There are essential differences in Irish landscape evolution, and in English perceptions of Ireland, which make for notable contrasts in paintings and illustrations of Irish scenes.

There is a real need for a typology of landscape art that identifies images with a minimal level of 'facts' or features to give us reliable hints about changing place or landscape — such as, for example, information on fields, farms, trees, buildings and other evidence of human impact on the landscape (Illus 2.1). The art historian's standard classification of eighteenth- and nineteenth-century art — classical, pastoral, romantic, picturesque, or perhaps 'rustic' and 'antiquarian' — is a valid method of studying artistic and aesthetic theory, and reflects stages in elitist perception of changes in society and environment. It bears little relation, however, to the real changes that were taking place in eighteenth-century Ireland. The period from the classical to the picturesque saw the beginnings of a revolution in the Irish landscape, which is poorly accommodated in such a classification. English paintings, in contrast, seem to reflect changes in the English landscape more closely, often in a selective manner. Hugh Prince, writing in 1988, wondered why artists had ignored all the evidence of agrarian change in England between 1710 and 1815 — the recently enclosed fields, newly built farmsteads, newly reclaimed heaths and newly introduced crops. Indeed he wondered if a so-called 'agricultural revolution' had in fact taken place, and if historians had given too much credence to the literary evidence![8]

The images of the Irish countryside in the period from 1750 to 1850 are conveyed through the eyes of contemporary observers. These witnesses may be classified as artistic (such as

2.1 *An Irish Road Scene* c1737, Artist unknown, Pen and ink

A drawing of a farm showing the lay-out of fields and the construction of buildings and implements: but can we rely on the accuracy of the details? Has the artist drawn what he saw, or what he (and his patron) would wish to have seen? Was the road really so broad and straight?

From the Journal of George Edward Pakenham, 1737–9

writers like William Carleton or Maria Edgeworth and painters like Thomas Roberts or James A O'Connor) and topographic (with writers such as Isaac Weld and painters like George Petrie), though there is always a modicum of 'topography' in the former, if not art in the latter. All of these observers in fact distort our picture of the landscape, enlarging or obscuring different parts of the reality according to the conventions of the day. The art that offers most hope of fulfilling the needs of historians is probably topographical art. This is derived from the seventeenth-century Dutch 'landscapes of fact' and was condemned in the later eighteenth-century Royal Academy as constituting the 'tame delineation of a given spot' — a view that has continued into the twentieth century with Kenneth Clark referring to Canaletto sinking to the condition of 'an industrious topographer', with the atmosphere leaking out of his landscapes.[9]

'PREFERRED' OR 'VALUED' LANDSCAPES

In examining the observations of witnesses to the landscape in the eighteenth century, it is important to appreciate how contemporaries perceived their environment. From the point of view of the surviving record, it is clear that in different cultures and different times, certain landscapes were preferred over others. The concept of 'valued' landscape is probably useful in this regard, 'valued' landscapes being ones that were rated highly for social, economic or aesthetic reasons, and consequently were most likely to feature in the written, drawn or painted record.[10] What constituted a 'valued' landscape in eighteenth-century Ireland? For the artist, it was the sublime, romantic or picturesque landscape, though aside from Gainsborough's oft-repeated reply to Lord Hardwicke, the landscape preference among artists probably reflected the prejudices of their clients and patrons.[11] Valued landscapes tended to reflect familiar places that were accessible to the consciousness and senses of the observer, as well as the attitudes and prejudices of society in general. For the landowner, it might be romantic and fashionable landscapes (such as Killarney or Connemara or the Giant's Causeway, or an artistic *mélange* of such landscape types, suitable as decoration for his hall or saloon), as well as the romantic or picturesque elements in his local landscape. For the English visitor (or reader about Ireland), Irish landscape preferences would focus on the scenic, wild, probably natural landscapes favoured by the growing tourist market in the late eighteenth century. Valued landscapes for the farmer would be the land with agricultural utility, the 'improved land' in his home barony or parish: mountains, uplands and boglands would have no value. For the merchant and town-dweller, favoured areas would probably be the town itself, or land with investment potential in the vicinity of the town. For the small farmer and labourer, 'landscapes of survival' would constitute the main concern: the corner of an estate or townland, the edge of a bog, head of a valley, side of the road or backstreet of the town. For them, much of the landscape would be out of bounds, or distant and inaccessible.

In relation to the landscape images handed down in paint or drawings, the preferred land-scapes of the upper echelons of society have dominated. The landscapes preferred by the propertied classes or elite tourists were the ones that were painted or drawn by artists. This is the class that not only shaped landscape taste, but moulded the very landscape itself.[12] The landscapes of the poor in Ireland were seldom of interest to the buyers or painters of pictures. In contrast, in early nineteenth-century England there was a distinctive market for pic-turesque views of the landscape of the lower orders.

The legacy of landscape images in Ireland was further influenced by the backgrounds of the artists themselves: some were English, some were Irish who aspired to English standards, some were influenced by European schools, others were trenchantly Irish, some were successfully market-oriented, others were failures, some were members of the gentry, others from poorer classes, and most were men.[13] The kind of romantic milieu in which Irish artists worked and were educated is hinted at in Hugh Frazer's advice to artists in 1825 to 'follow the English school of painting … make nature the basis of your art, returning often to the antique, and particularly to the Elgin marbles or casts … using the paintings of the old Masters as guides to nature, to her simplicity and subtle beauties, and as a never failing source of poetic inspiration'.[14]

All the evidence convinces us that much of the face of the Irish countryside today owes its origins to the period from 1750 to 1850. The broad pattern of rural settlement, many of the fields and hedges, trees and plantations, buildings in country, village and town, the road network, were all laid down in this crucial century. There are probably at least 500,000 kilometres of hedgerows in Ireland, most of which were planted during this period. In many instances whole landscapes may have changed in a generation. Apart from Aodhagán Ó Rathaille's elegy on the destruction of the old world of Cill Cais, literary and especially painted comment on landscape change is comparatively silent in Ireland. On the basis of what has been said of valued landscapes, three general reasons may be suggested for this. First, much of the countryside held out little of interest to contemporary artists; spatially limited and select landscapes were painted or drawn. Secondly, the kinds of changes that took place in the eighteenth and early nineteenth centuries were not attractive to artists or were otherwise not worthy of comment. Finally, contemporary artistic taste imposed constraints on the type of landscape subject in the eighteenth century. Put another way, the 'market' shaped both subject matter and mode of presentation. Historians' use of art as a source must work within these limitations. The work of Barrell and Bermingham has, with considerable ingenuity, exploited what Bermingham calls the 'discrepancies, blindnesses and silences'[15] in English art. A much more comprehensive and in-depth analysis of Irish art than is possible in this study would be necessary to pinpoint the kinds of landscape biases present in the Irish artistic legacy.

PATTERNS OF IRISH LANDSCAPE ART

The constraint of 'preferred landscapes' may be detected in the pattern of Irish landscapes that has survived in paintings or prints. Many places are represented again and again, whether because of unique or unusual aspects of their invariably 'natural' landscape, or simply because other artists painted them before. The maps illustrated here (Illus 2.2 and 2.3) show the distribution in Ireland of paintings and drawings as listed in the National Gallery's *Catalogue* and Elmes' *Catalogue of Topographical Prints*.[16] In Illus 2.2 George Petrie's prodigious output of antiquarian drawings for the first thirty years of the nineteenth century gives a regional bias to the map in the direction of Connemara and Kerry. Without Petrie's contribution, the National Gallery's collection of drawings before 1850 is firmly based in Dublin, with outliers in east Down and the Giant's Causeway. Illus 2.3 provides a much more comprehensive list of drawings for the country. There is a clear preference shown for Leinster and Munster, with Killarney, Limerick, south Wexford, Cork and south Tipperary, the Boyne Valley, Wicklow, and especially Dublin, well represented. Ulster and Connacht were least favoured for illustration. In addition, in Illus 2.2 an attempt has been made to symbolise the type of illustration catalogued. Antiquarian drawings predominate, with illustrations of houses coming next. The 'other' category refers mainly to 'natural' views, though there are many views of some of the major towns. Powerscourt Waterfall, the Dargle River, the Sugar Loaf, the Giant's Causeway, and many views in Killarney occur most often. Scenes in Connemara begin to appear regularly as the nineteenth century progresses.

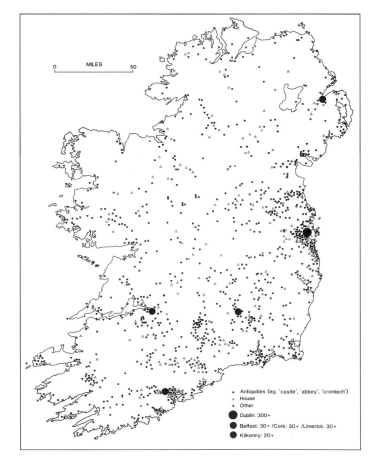

The common trend in most of these views, whether scenic or antiquarian, is that they were uninhabited by people (except for the occasional odd picturesque labourer). From the later eighteenth century, most journeys were predictably from town to town (especially those with comfortable inns), taking in well-known sights *en route*.[17] 'Artist trails' are evident in the second map, paralleling the favoured routes of tourists. Sketches and prints were dominated by this pattern — views of towns and rural tourist spots prevail. Most of the intervening countryside, which was experiencing extensive social and economic change, held little interest. It was to be got through as quickly as possible. Thomas Creswick expressed it well in 1837 when referring to the Wicklow scene around Powerscourt and Luggellaw:

> It is the desolation which has built the inns, and the loneliness of the hills and lakes in the neighbourhood which has attracted travellers to fill them. Grandeur in natural scenery is nothing if it cannot be enjoyed from a coach window; and the wilds of the Sliebh-buck would be untrodden, and the shores of Lough Dan unexplored, if the pilgrim of nature could not return to Roundwood in the sure and certain hope of a good supper and a luxurious bed…[18]

Apart from the need for comforts in the wilderness, the Romantic age continued to have a fascination for the wild and sublime up to the Great Famine. George Petrie accompanies his drawing of Gougane Barra with comments on the ' sense of desolation — the feeling of a total severance from mankind — of utter abandonment…Escape seems impossible'.[19] In the early nineteenth century English travellers were similarly revelling in 'the delightful horror and terrible joy' of the mountains of Wales and Scotland.[20] Travellers, tourists and antiquaries shaped the paint and print markets. Many travellers 'reported' on the 'intervening countrysides'; Arthur Young and the Halls did so at considerable length with accounts of poverty, often based on the view from the main road; but their 'illustrations' were dominated by views of the sublime, the scenic or antiquities. In John Carr's *Tour of Ireland* in 1805, the sixteen illustrations are principally of castles, scenic lakes, bridges (an important feature of the new roads) and 'Mrs Grattan's Cottage — an elegant and romantic little summer retreat by the Dargle River'.[21] Gabriel Beranger in the 1770s (Illus 2.4), whose drawings of the Boyne Valley were described by Sir William Wilde as 'stiff, but most faithful',[22] sketched mainly for antiquarian purposes. His cows, which certainly seem stiff, may be interesting from the social historian's point of view: like the holy cows of India, they appear everywhere! His travel descriptions were often more enlightening. For example, in June 1779 he journeyed from Kells, County Meath, by Bailieborough, County Cavan, to Clones, County Monaghan (off the beaten track for most tourists at the time) through country that 'looked poor, the land coarse, the cabins as if going to ruin, half thatched, several bogs close to the road and digging turf going on almost everywhere'.[23] His chaise broke down and he had to walk to Clones, where he spent the day sketching the old church and market cross. Occasionally, some of these detailed drawings of castles or abbeys give incidental glimpses of parts of the surrounding countryside, like Beranger's view of Holycross Abbey, County Tipperary, Tinnahinch Castle in County Carlow, or Athsigh Castle in County Meath.[24]

While the first edition of Mr and Mrs S C Hall's *Ireland*, published in 1843, contains innumerable comments on the 'human' landscape of pre-Famine Ireland, the overwhelming majority of its scores of illustrations refer to antiquities and 'natural' scenes. There are thirty illustrations for Galway, sixteen for Mayo, one for Roscommon and none for Westmeath.

2.4 *Kells on King's River, County Kilkenny* 1775, Gabriel Beranger (1729–1817), Watercolour

According to Sir William Wilde, Gabriel Beranger's work is 'stiff but most faithful'; but were the field boundaries really as regular as shown here? The artist's interest seems mainly antiquarian.

From *Beranger's Views of Ireland*

This pattern is underscored by their opinion that no country was so rich as Ireland in materials for the painter: with its 'lines of mountains…rocks of innumerable shapes…passes rugged…rivers rapid…broadest lakes…Nature abundant'.[25]

Lady Chatterton in 1839 articulated the view of many of the new tourist elite in being 'particularly struck with the rich and vivid colouring of the scenery in Ireland. When the sun shines after one of the frequent showers, the whole landscape resembles a highly finished and freshly varnished picture, not by any well-known master, for the composition, to speak technically, is totally different, though I think quite as fine as any ideal imagery of Claude, Hobbina [Hobbema] or Poussin'.[26] Like many English visitors she was accustomed to the tamed and humanised landscapes of England. W H Bartlett's *Scenery and Antiquities of Ireland Illustrated* had the object of providing 'a series of Pen and Pencil illustrations of the charms of the Green Isle of the West'.[27] The indefatigable traveller Anne Plumptre in 1817 pledged to observe the 'strictest fidelity' in her drawings, reprobating 'the too common practice among artists of rather aiming at forming a pleasing combination of objects, than delineating the spot such as it really is…'.[28] All her plates, however, with the possible exception of the view of Dublin Bay, comprise natural views, and her commentary on the Salmon Leap at Leixlip, County Kildare, epitomises the taste that artists and illustrators satisfied.

The image of Ireland held by visitors from England was dominated by poverty-stricken masses on the one hand, and empty wild landscapes profusely dotted with picturesque ruins on the other. Near Kilmallock, County Limerick, in the summer of 1838, there was a moment for one sensitive visitor when 'a few scattered sunbeams darted through the dark clouds, and cast a brilliant fleeting ray on the rugged mountains. The view was then grand and awfully beautiful, possessing a strange mixture of dismal stern gloom and vivid brilliancy'.[29] These images are probably most aptly captured in the melodrama of the period, which favoured landscapes of wildness and sublimity peopled by villainous peasants in rags. In Thomas Dibdin's *Suil Dhuv the Coiner*, the final scene was 'a druidical circle of rude stones. Lowering, low horizon all round, with flickering lightning breaking through...'.[30]

TASTE VERSUS REALITY

While there were widescale changes taking place in the Irish countryside, much of it was clearly unattractive to the eyes of artists. Contemporary taste, especially among trend-setting English visitors, despised poverty and its visible manifestations. English visitors to Wales during the late eighteenth and early nineteenth centuries were in search of wild beauty in the mountains, with their simple peasantry demanded by Romanticism, and were 'studiously blind' to the new crops and enclosures, the rural poverty and burgeoning industrial chaos in many Welsh valleys.[31]

Among many visitors to Ireland was one Thomas Reid, who described the miserable conditions of Donegal peasants: 'They are dirty, superstitious, existing on scanty and bad food. Their habitations presented if possible a still more disgusting sight. A description of them could not be attempted without offending the ears of those who have seen the cottage of the English peasant.'[32] In Aghalurcher, County Fermanagh, the Ordnance Survey Memoirs reported that while the cottages of the better class of farmers were very comfortable and clean, the cottiers and labourers 'live in a most wretched way in mud huts, without either window or chimney, with, in almost every case, an offensive heap of liquid manure at the very entrance to their miserable abodes. Still they appear happy and contented...'.[33]

The dynamic of change in this period was the surging population in the rural areas. In some places there were four hundred persons per square mile in 1841, nearly one person on every acre.[34] In landscape terms this was expressed in large huddles of thatched houses, representing a population being confined to marginal areas. The better lands were cleared for grazing or dairying, especially in western areas, and throughout the country there were mushrooming cabin clusters on the roadside or the outskirts of towns. This rural world teeming with people is almost uniquely depicted in the stories of William Carleton, not just in a topographical sense, but in the description of densely populated, dynamic communities: thronged outdoor masses, packed hedge-schools and lively pattern and fair days.[35] But Carleton's depiction of poverty was made more acceptable by giving it a gloss of humour. The illustrations in Carleton's early editions were caricatures by Phiz and others: the men had *Punch*-like visages, and the landscape context was drawn in a Dublin or London studio.

Such populated scenes and landscapes are not well represented in more formal drawings. Peacock's view of Glendalough in 1813 is exceptional, and others by Nathaniel Grogan exist for areas mainly around Cork city.[36] Drawings in Hall's *Ireland*, such as one of a cabin cluster at Dooagh in Achill, are rare (Illus 2.5). Topographical art, which actually tried to describe the reality of the rural landscape, was not popular among the patrons of artists. Thomas Black's *View of Armagh 1810*, for instance, is a typical view taken in the vicinity of a town, containing a wide

2.5 *Cabins at Dooagh, Achill, County Mayo*, F W Fairholt

Drawings like this, accurately showing the miserable hovels of the rural poor, are unusual; artists and their patrons preferred to look away from scenes of poverty.

From Hall's *Ireland: Its Scenery and Character* (1843)

variety of landscape 'facts' that one would expect to find in a topographical painting.[37] It failed to find a buyer and was raffled publicly. Everyday squalor and poverty would have offended most artistic eyes (and noses), and only the most dedicated illustrators faithfully recorded living conditions that were quite alien to their class. Occasional glimpses of what must have constituted the majority of house structures are presented, such as Henry O'Neill's *Glen of the Down* (1843) in County Wicklow, which includes a good depiction of a hipped-roofed house on the roadside; his commentary, however, reflects the tensions in the Irish artist's endeavour: 'In the foreground is a genuine Irish cabin, an object to the artist, of picturesque, to the philanthropist, of melancholy interest; adding beauty, by contrast, to the face of nature, but detracting most sadly from the prospect of national improvement.'[38]

In response to the growing population and underlying economic changes, the rural landscape was altering rapidly. Recently, historians and historical geographers have pointed to the need to revise our assessment of the changes that took place in the eighteenth century, assessments which, it is claimed, were based on exaggerated views of prevailing rural squalor and poverty as witnessed from the coach-driver's seat. While the image of Ireland conveyed in travellers' accounts emphasised the poverty and overpopulation, as Kevin Whelan points out, the small farmer's overcrowded world was a spatially restricted one.[39] More orderly and substantial changes were taking place in more extensive parts of the countryside, especially in the midlands and Munster and away from the main roads, which were largely missed by the visual

IRELAND: ART INTO HISTORY

and, often, the verbal record. So Thomas Creswick came away from pre-Famine Ireland having seen no sturdy yeomen 'distinguished from his labourers both by the respectability of his dress and the air of command with which he looks around him'.[40] In the 1770s, for example, apart from the obvious and well-represented Big House, there was a significant growth in middle-sized country housebuilding by the large farmer class. By the end of the eighteenth and into the nineteenth century, many of the large, often gaunt townland farmhouses began to appear in County Meath. John Andrews has referred to the 'modernising' landscapes, with new central farmhouses being built on the Duke of Leinster's Kildare estates and in the Duke of Devonshire's Lismore estate — very extensive changes in the countryside, all accurately portrayed in the estate maps of John Rocque (Illus 2.6) and Bernard Scalé.[41] In south Monaghan in the 1770s, Scalé portrays a landscape with dozens of house clusters, all of which had been broken up and dispersed by the 1830s.[42] In the north west, Alistair Rowan has pointed to the surge in housebuilding in the later Georgian period.[43] Many of these more substantial houses were restricted to the better lands, such as the valleys of Fermanagh, around the lakes, forming fairly extensive landscapes of country houses. Much of this building activity, which aped the more grandiose schemes of the ascendancy, was undertaken by Protestant farmers, leaseholders and middlemen; the substantial tenants of Gaelic stock in Munster and Leinster were content with more rudimentary traditional farmsteads, a factor that partly explains why they were overlooked.[44] Apart from these country houses and the vernacular farmhouses and cabins, the most important building was probably concentrated in and around the towns. These certainly feature in contemporary prints; the vicinity of Dublin is well represented in artistic views, and the edge of the city clearly presented artists and illustrators with dramatic (and convenient) locations. But the fairly distinctive rural landscapes of housebuilding are not well represented.

2.6 Extract from *A Survey of the Manor of Maynooth* 1757, John Rocque (*c*1705–62), Ink and watercolour

Rural poverty was not the whole story; this Maynooth estate map shows extensive development and suggests a well-managed landscape of strong farmers.

Department of Geography, St Patrick's College, Maynooth, County Kildare.

For Anne Plumptre, Ireland abounded everywhere with noblemen's and gentlemen's seats, 'but these did not excite my curiosity like the natural beauties and wonders of the country'.[45]

In summary, if one looks at a recent typology of changes in regional landscapes in eighteenth-century Ireland,[46] one can ask how useful is the artistic evidence in illustrating these changes? In the main the changes taking place in regional landscapes were largely unnoticed by artists or illustrators. Verbal commentators noted the obvious squalor of the roadside and the north-west farm regions as they journeyed from one tourist or antiquarian high point to another. But such views were underrepresented in illustrations, with the possible exception of Nathaniel Grogan's late eighteenth-century landscapes for the Cork region; few of these have survived and most are in the category of genre interiors. 'The real "hidden Ireland" of the eighteenth century,' says Kevin Whelan, 'was the comfortable, Catholic strong farm class of south Leinster and east Munster' — a very extensive part of the Irish rural landscape. And as the second map illustrated here shows, south Leinster and east Munster were most commonly illustrated in eighteenth- and nineteenth-century prints and publications. But the places and buildings illustrated had little link with the real changes occurring in the landscape. In these regions were the nearest equivalents to the yeomen of England, who were truly 'hidden' and largely unnoticed by the artists as they scrambled to the gates of the Big House to paint the lord or his house and demesne.

MARKET AND PATRONAGE INFLUENCES

Contemporary artistic fashion was partly a response to market constraints: artists painted or drew subject matter that would sell (either as paintings or book illustrations). Patrons or clients were interested in a world of wild and romantic landscapes, like Barret's (Illus 2.7) or O'Connor's,[47] or the picturesque or antiquarian of Nicholl or Petrie. Indeed Carleton's stories were popular because they appealed to an interest in remote and exotic places. From the fairly narrow viewpoint of the historian, the market for paintings or printed pictures of landscape was primarily interested in comparatively empty lands — at a time when the country was densely populated and experiencing a landscape revolution at the hands of a huge rural population. In successfully responding to the market, the artist had to ignore what was happening in most of the countryside. Arthur Young, the sharpest observer of what was happening in the real world of eighteenth-century Ireland, put it well:

> What passes daily, even hourly, before our eyes, we are very apt entirely to overlook; hence the surprising inattention of various people to the food, clothing, possessions and state of the poor, even in their own neighbourhood; many a question have I put to gentlemen upon these points, which were not answered without having recourse to the next cabin...[48]

What seems to be missing is an Irish equivalent of the English picturesque, which detailed and prettified the changes taking place in the English countryside, whether for nostalgia for a fast-vanishing world or justification of the oppression of the labouring classes. Conditions in Ireland (or the perception of conditions in Ireland) were different. Bermingham's 'cult of ruins'[49] certainly took root in Ireland. It is possible, however, that the romanticism that influenced landscape preference in England also shaped prevailing views of Ireland: just as it shaped images of the poor in England, so it shaped images of poor Ireland. Much of the workaday Irish landscape, apparently squalid and teeming with paupers, had little of the

2.7 *A View near Avoca*, George Barret
(1728/32–84), Oil on canvas

A romantic landscape near Arklow,
County Wicklow, typical of what popular taste required of the artist,
though the water-wheel is an interesting and unusual detail.

National Gallery of Ireland (no 175)

romantic or picturesque about it; if it could not be concealed or removed, it was ignored, like the paupers in it. Though Lady Chatterton represents a minority of distinguished women travellers, and though she made some astute observations on landscape and society in Munster, her first impression of Ireland betrays her class and its delicate English taste for the picturesque, where cows grazed on 'lawns':

> Some cows were gently grazing on my favourite green lawn. A young girl, with milk-pail and stool, approaches one of them. No, not a young girl; I forget that I am in Ireland, and that I have been told that youthful creature, apparently not seventeen, is married. How picturesque she looks, tripping along, her scarlet kerchief folded over her well-turned shoulders, her bright green dress gathered up in graceful drapery. Her boyish-looking husband bounds across the lawn to meet her, from under the trees on the right. He holds the cow by the horns, while she seats herself and begins milking — gazing up into his face all the while with looks of fond and grateful affection...[50]

The importance of patronage is well shown in the predominance of park landscapes in Irish paintings and illustrations, proportionately more than in England.[51] The creation of parklands and country mansions represents one of the most important changes in the landscape of eighteenth and early nineteenth-century Ireland. This is probably the only instance where there was a correspondence between the real changes taking place in the landscape and the market demand for paintings and drawings of them.[52] Examples abound, such as the anonymously executed views of Stradbally in County Laois and Kilruddery in Wicklow, Thomas Roberts' views of Lucan in Dublin and Carton in Kildare, James Arthur O'Connor's portraits of Westport, Ballinrobe (Illus 2.11) and Rockingham Houses in County Mayo.

In many ways the dominance of park landscapes in artistic endeavour up to the 1820s is a mirror of the attitudes of the property-owning classes to the landscape as a whole. Some Irish landowners are estimated to have invested significantly less than their English counterparts in their estates.[53] Most of their conspicuous spending was on their persons, their houses and their parklands — all of which featured prominently in oil paintings! Their demesne walls, which had no equivalent in England, insulated the owner from his tenants' landscape, and a demesne like Carton in Kildare, for example, had the fashionable perimeter belt of beech trees, which even blocked out the sight of the estate lands beyond. Ann Bermingham has pointed out that late eighteenth-century landscape gardening taste in England was increasingly leaning towards the creation of picturesque landscapes, with strategies designed to conceal natural defects or to remove mundane objects, such as unsightly poverty, which could not be integrated into the garden scenery.[54]

In most cases, the popular views of demesnes and houses concentrated on showing the parklands with little or nothing of the surrounding estate land (Illus 2.8). Even the surveyors and map-makers who provided one of the most reliable views of the changing rural landscape, often offered to provide special demesne maps, framed and glazed, as an attractive wall decoration for the proud owner. As Andrews suggests, landowners were generally fairly disinterested in maps of the internal arrangements of farms, and slow enough to commit themselves to detailed surveys of the landscape outside the demesne walls.[55]

Indeed when one looks at landholding and population patterns between 1750 and 1850, probably the most telling contrast with England in the context of the present discussion was the fact that a significant proportion of the labouring or cottier population and small tenant population did not tenurially exist for the landowner, and their presence in the landscape of the estate might be seen as an affront to him and his visitors. In addition, in terms of preferred landscapes that might find themselves recorded in sketches or paintings, if proud ownership is accepted as a measure of preference, it might be worthwhile to examine the incidence of non-resident landowners in Ireland between 1750 and 1850. There were extensive tracts of countryside that were not lived on by their owners, either because they had more valuable estates elsewhere in Ireland or England, or because they represented small property speculations by merchant or professional classes in town or city. Large parts of Counties Monaghan and Cavan, for example, had no resident proprietor in the mid nineteenth century.[56] Clearly, unless such landscapes had outstanding scenic qualities, they did not rate very highly in their owners' regard. There are few Irish equivalents of Gainsborough's portrait of Mr and Mrs Andrews presiding over their well-managed estate.[57] Wheatley's 1782 portrait of the Marquess and Marchioness of Antrim

shows them in well-appointed finery and carriage in an anonymous but romantic-type background, with a hint of the town in the distance (Illus 2.9). The portrait of the Duke and Duchess of Leinster shows them in 1753 appropriately laying out the new demesne of Carton[58] (which entailed a fairly radical transformation of the pre-existing farmed landscape).

CATEGORIES OF RURAL LANDSCAPE

We might, on the basis of the preceding discussion, refer broadly to the following types of rural landscape as the most commonly illustrated, but which in actual fact referred to a very limited area of the countryside. These included: pictures of *wild country*, 'natural' landscapes devoid of human impact; *Romantic landscapes*, also generally uninhabited, except possibly for a couple of picturesque labourers and a tastefully arranged windmill or castle; *tourist scenes* of established locations like the Giant's Causeway or Killarney (Illus 2.10); *antiquarian views* of monastic ruins, castles and archaeological remains; *town views*, showing prospects of the capital city and larger country towns; *industrial landscapes*, depicting examples of productive changes in the environment, such as new mills or bleaching greens, and finally, and most importantly, *park landscapes* (Illus 2.11). Almost all of these landscapes might be characterised as landscapes of convenience, since most of the drawings would have needed some field study. Accessibility was important for travellers in eighteenth-century Ireland and, as Illus 2.2 and Illus 2.3 show, a great many illustrations reflected the significance of the beaten track.[59] The artistic criteria that would entice an artist to travel far from the capital must have grown more rigorous with distance from Dublin: only places of strikingly fashionable beauty — or with

2.8 *A Landscape with Curragh Chase House, County Limerick* 1834, Jeremiah Mulcahy (*fl c*1830–89), Oil on canvas An empty parkland; the owner would not have welcomed a depiction of the rural poor, by whose efforts this tranquillity was probably maintained. National Gallery of Ireland (no 1795)

2.9 *The Marquess and Marchioness of Antrim* 1782, Francis Wheatley (1747–1801), Oil on canvas

An attractive portrait of the marquess with his lady, his carriage and his servants: but where was it painted? The landscape is curiously anonymous, the location apparently unimportant.

National Gallery of Ireland (no 4339)

extremely salubrious lodgings in a country mansion — would persuade an artist to leave the environs of Dublin or Wicklow.

CONCLUSION

Much of the above discussion is based on the work of well-known and 'successful' landscape artists, whether measured by their place in gallery catalogues or their mass publication in topographical prints. The observations of the judges in the art section of the Dublin Exhibition of 1853 sum up the standards by which landscape art continued to be measured, and reveal its limitations for historians:

> The specimens of Ashford, of Roberts, of Barrett of the last century and of the late James A O'Connor, small but able pictures of sweet and lovely scenes, only made us regret the want of grander and nobler efforts on the part of men who appear even from these to have been filled with the character of their native landscape. We can but hope that the examples of other countries may stir up some of our aspiring students ... The taste of our next neighbours tends peculiarly towards the cultivation of that branch of Art which employs itself in giving expression to the sweet scenes of quiet nature in a country which possesses abundant beauty of a soft and homely character ... many a beautiful stretch of truly poetic nature may be confidently sought ... [60]

From the point of view of the historian working in a place or examining the changing landscape, the evidence of artists and illustrators clearly has certain deficiencies, arising from the

IRELAND: ART INTO HISTORY

2.10 *A View of the Eagle's Nest, Killarney*, Jonathan Fisher (*fl* 1763–1809), Oil on canvas

A frequently painted scene in Killarney, attractive but untypical of the countryside; the figures are of secondary interest, and are included mainly to indicate scale.

National Gallery of Ireland (no 1813)

2.11 *Pleasure Grounds, Ballinrobe, County Mayo*, James Arthur O'Connor (*c*1792–1841), Oil on canvas

Another fine parkland scene shows the efforts of an improving landlord: but where is the teeming tenantry of Mayo? For the artist, as for his patron, they are not in the picture.

National Gallery of Ireland (no 4012)

social, economic and aesthetic influences on their products. One important qualification in any use of visual, and indeed literary, images is an awareness that the evidence was not produced to provide answers for historians or geographers in the 1990s! From a strictly utilitarian viewpoint, more fruitful results might be obtained from more obscure artists, who by virtue of their 'obscurity' were less bound by the standards laid down in academe, as expressed in the Dublin Exhibition for example, and were outside the strictures of fashion and the marketplace in portraying the reality of workaday rural landscapes. They were probably rather mediocre artists as well, however, and their very obscurity makes them inaccessible.

One important but limited source, which departs from the realms of fine art, is the work of mapmakers and cartographers. Undoubtedly from the viewpoint of changing rural landscapes, their maps are often superb sources, and the work of John Rocque, and his pupil Bernard Scalé and others less distinguished, comes close to representing 'artistic' portraits of the landscape — showing houses, hedges, and often the contents of the fields.[61] In many instances they are supplemented by little landscape vignettes of houses, mills or bleaching greens.

Throughout this essay, it has been necessary to constantly refer to written sources as a way of throwing light on the shadows and silences of the painted record of the eighteenth and early nineteenth-century landscapes. Isaac Weld was well aware of the strengths and weaknesses of the artist's efforts, and in his book on Kerry in 1812 he had his illustrations accompanied by long commentaries for, he said, 'as language, unaided by the pencil, is insufficient to convey distinct ideas of visible objects; so the productions of art, unaccompanied by a detailed verbal explanation, can communicate little knowledge of a place, beyond what may be collected from the mere glance of the eye.'[62]

3

W H Crawford

PROVINCIAL TOWN LIFE IN THE EARLY NINETEENTH CENTURY: AN ARTIST'S IMPRESSIONS

For the study of everyday life in the early decades of the nineteenth century in Ireland, we have to rely mainly on the engravings that appear in contemporary travel literature, and on the few drawings and sketchbooks that have survived. Their rarity should encourage us to analyse them from a wide range of perspectives in order to yield the maximum of information. We also have to relate the illustrations to the testimony that contemporaries have left us about their world, whether in travel literature, in novels, or even more fruitfully in the evidence collected for the voluminous government reports. So far, little attention has been paid to the detail in the illustrations of artefacts that have survived: the properties and peculiarities of raw material, construction and finish can be very revealing to the trained eye.

THE WATERFORD COLLECTION OF WATERCOLOURS

A small volume of watercolours relating to County Waterford, which has found a home in the Ulster Folk and Transport Museum at Cultra near Belfast, provides an ideal subject for such a study. The volume is leather-bound, with the remains of a brass clasp, and measures 15.7 cm by 9.75 cm. It has been rebound, and several of the original pages are missing: the first page in it is numbered 7. Of the surviving eighty-two leaves, twenty are blank, but the remainder have a watercolour on at least one side of the leaf, all of them in a finished state. The confidence with which they were finished indicates a high level of consistency and skill in this medium and suggests that they were painted from sketches made on location. The volume opens with a sequence of fifty-one paintings of individuals or groups of individuals. The location of each watercolour is indicated in the bottom left-hand corner, so that the first illustration bears the word 'England' and is followed by another seven with the abbreviation 'Eng'; in a similar fashion the next twenty-two sketches are shown to relate to Waterford, another nineteen to Dungarvan in County Waterford, and a final pair to Dublin. After a space of seventeen blank leaves, there follows a group of ten landscape paintings, four in colour and the remainder in monochrome. Five of the monochrome landscapes make up a panorama.[1] On their own, on a leaf pasted inside the front cover, are the words 'Maria and Louisa Loscombe' written in ink by what seems to be a contemporary hand, but there is no other indication of the identity of the artist. One of the landscape sketches bears the inscription 'Mrs Hobbs at Newrath House — one mil [sic] Waterford 1824': this is the only reference in the volume to a date of inception. Because it appears near the end of the volume, it probably dates its completion quite precisely.

If the paintings were made in the early 1820s, they are especially interesting for the borough of Dungarvan, because it was enjoying probably the most prosperous decade in its history. Between the years 1802 and 1818 the Duke of Devonshire, who had a small but significant interest in the town, invested £70,000 in its development. Of this, £55,000 was spent on building the bridge featured in three of the landscapes, as well as a substantial causeway 320 metres long, crossing the estuary of the River Colligan to link the suburb of Abbeyside with the duke's part of the town.[2] In contrast with the decayed condition of Abbeyside were the modern new houses around Devonshire Square, where the market was held, and the handsome street running to the bridge.[3] The population of the town increased to more than five thousand by 1821.[4] The boost that the duke's investment gave to the town was supplemented during the 1820s by the success of the fisheries, or at least by the bounties granted by the Irish Fishery Commissioners in their bid to create a national fishery and to modernise the industry so that it could look for new markets in Europe and the colonies as well as Britain (Illus 3.1). An appendix to the fisheries report of 1823 remarked:

> Previous to the year 1820, the fishing boats of Dungarvan ... had no inducement to catch fish beyond the limited quantity required for the consumption of the town... Salt importers and manufacturers are now settled there and a certain market established for the purchase of any quantity of fish.[5]

Andrew Carbery of Dungarvan, who was one of these salt manufacturers, testified to the commissioners that the success of the white fishery had brought great wealth into the town. Unfortunately, the withdrawal of the bounties in 1830 (after more than £160,000 had been spent throughout Ireland in the 1820s)[6] not only proved that they had failed to bring permanent improvements to the industry as a whole, but even had unforeseen repercussions on the prosperity of Dungarvan.

> At Abbeyside, which is a portion of the town of Dungarvan, on the east side of the bridge, most of the fishermen occupy small allotments of land, and are comparatively thriving, prosperous and industrious. Their boats [are] generally well found, and themselves and families well clothed. They rarely ever want food, as the application of their otherwise unoccupied time to the portions of land which they hold, generally gives them an abundance, and the best moral effects are produced by constant employment, and the want of time to go to the public house. On the western side, the fishermen have comfortable houses built for them by the Duke of Devonshire, and are subject to only a

nominal rent, but they are huddled up into a dense community, and have no land, nor can they obtain it for either love or money. They are therefore solely dependent on the market for food, always unemployed when not at sea, liable to idle improvident and intemperate habits, often starving, and rarely above want. The materials of their boats [are] bad, and as well as their clothes and bed clothes often in pawn.[7]

Dungarvan also suffered

great inconvenience from a scarcity of fresh water, the only supply to the public being from one well outside the town. Formerly there was an abundant supply from a stream called the Finisk; and we find that a sum of £800 was granted by the act of 29 Geo II, c 1, and a further sum of £500 by the act of 1 Geo III, c 1, for making and completing an aqueduct from that river to the town of Dungarvan. The work was completed, but the property in the aqueduct not having been vested in trustees, and the soil over which it ran not being at all transferred, some proprietor stopped it up about 40 or 50 years ago, and in that situation it remains to the present time.[8]

Among the Dungarvan paintings is one of four women and a boy engaged in obtaining water from a quite elaborate town pump (Illus 3.2).

3.1 Dungarvan, County Waterford: the bridge and estuary with beached fishing vessels, probably c1820. Artist unknown. The figures on the left are apparently caulking timbers with tar. Ulster Folk and Transport Museum

3.2 A group of women (and one child) drawing water from the town pump. Note the distinctive buckets (probably of oak staves bound with copper or brass) and the handsome pottery jugs; also the woman balancing a laden bucket on her head.

Ulster Folk and Transport Museum

The city of Waterford, with a population of just over twenty-eight thousand, impressed visitors with its broad mile-long quay along the River Suir, the number and variety of its public buildings, the scale of its food-processing industries, and the improvements to its port. Waterford was the major port in south-east Ireland, serving a wide region from Kilkenny and Carlow to Clonmel, and exporting, mainly to Liverpool and Bristol, great quantities of flour and all sorts of grain, as well as livestock and many thousands of barrels of bacon, lard, and butter.[9] In 1815 a Chamber of Commerce was incorporated by Act of Parliament, which soon secured the creation of a board of Harbour Commissioners to undertake the improvement of the port and the removal of dangers to navigation. As a result of their activities, Waterford was able to benefit from the development of steam navigation.[10]

If the artist had been commissioned to portray the commercial life of Waterford and Dungarvan, he would have concentrated in Waterford on the slaughter houses for the pig trade (just as John Rocque had done to illustrate his map of Cork in 1773)[11] or the great grain and butter markets. Waterford's exports for the year 1823 included 3032 tierces and 14,202 barrels of pork, 357,232 flitches of bacon, 112,450 cwt of butter, 14,933 cwt of lard, 379,533 barrels of corn and 256,844 cwt of flour.[12] Yet even a brief examination of this volume of paintings reveals that the artist was more interested in the people attending the open-air retail markets both there and in Dungarvan, where the fisher folk also attracted his attention. He did not make any attempt to locate them against an architectural background, but concentrated instead on depicting colourful and interesting characters, as well as groups engaged in selling or in conversation: the landscapes and scenes were added only towards the close of the volume. Although the artist demonstrated his competence in portraying such scenes, his real pleasure is reflected in the people, and his sense of humour is evident throughout.

MARKETS AND FAIRS

In Waterford the public markets were 'situated in the higher and older parts of the city' where they formed 'the centre of no inconsiderable a scene of retail trade.' In Dungarvan they were held in the new market square. It is no surprise that the majority of the stall-holders were women, for that had been a regular feature of such retail markets for centuries: they may even have controlled the market, or at least sections of it.[13] The artist depicts several of them as veterans presiding over their 'stands', and they are easily distinguished from the country-women bringing commodities to sell in the market, such as poultry, apples, honey, milk and buttermilk. The charges for customs, tolls and duties due on these commodities had to be displayed on prominent tollboards in the market-places, and schedules of them lodged with the local clerks of the peace under an act of 1818 (57 Geo III, c 107 and 108). In 1830 the following list was published for Dungarvan, but the Duke of Devonshire suspended the charges in the same year.[14]

3.3 A woman selling apples in Dungarvan's market square, protected by a wooden shelter; note the woven creels (shallow baskets). She is wearing a blue check scarf and apron, and a dark blue cloak (without armholes). She passes her time by knitting. The barefoot girl may be her daughter or younger sister.
Ulster Folk and Transport Museum

Barrel or bag of wheat	2d	Car load of straw	1d
Barrel or bag of barley or oats	1d	Car load of woodenware	3d
Bag of flour or oatmeal	2d	Car load of hoops	3d
Bag or load of 2 Kishes potatoes	½d	Car load of staves	3d
Cow	3d	Car load of cheese	2d
Sheep or lamb	1d	Car load of furze	½d
Pig	1d	Car load of turkeys or geese	1d
Calf	1d	Every load of tinware	2d
Hogshead of cider	3d	Every load felt hats	2d
Kish of apples	3d	Every piece of frieze, cloth or flannel	2d
Half Kish of apples or other fruit	1½d	Every hive of honey	1d
Kish or car load of roots	1d	Every firkin of butter 112 lbs or more	2d
Every cow or bullock hide	1d	Every crock of salt butter	1d
Every dozen of calf skins	3d	Every basket of fresh butter not less than 6 lbs	1d

3.4 Women going to market, showing the various ways of carrying a load. The loose cloak was both useful and versatile.

Ulster Folk and Transport Museum

The tolls and customs in Waterford were abolished by the corporation in 1813, except for those upon butter, hides and tallow, and the tolls upon both hides and tallow were relinquished soon afterwards. A charge of $4\frac{1}{2}$d continued to be made on every firkin of butter: 2d for weighing, 1d for tasting, and $1\frac{1}{2}$d for custom that was paid to the corporation.[15]

A common charge in other markets and fairs was for a stand or standing in the market. Although charges for a 'flat stall' were much less than for a 'covered stall', it should not be assumed that they were provided by the organisers. Because no such facilities were available for the traders, they constructed their own makeshift stalls from benches and chairs, and sold their stock out of baskets and barrels. While some of the traders brought with them 'covered standings' constructed of wood (Illus 3.3), the majority relied on their great hooded cloaks or frieze coats to protect them from the weather (Illus 3.4). As late as the 1850s, a Waterford witness told the commissioners inquiring into the state of markets and fairs in Ireland:

> …there is a great want of proper accommodation for the smaller traders who sell fruit, vegetables, and various articles of the kind in the streets. These poor people are exposed to all the vicissitudes of the weather and suffer very much in consequence of the deficiency of market accommodation.[16]

FOOD AND PROVISIONS

Although the principal food of the majority of the people was still potatoes, sales of wheaten bread were becoming more significant in these towns. Of Waterford, Henry Inglis reported in 1834: 'The wife of almost every small farmer carries a wheaten loaf back with her from market; and bread of a second quality is cheap — the large export of the fine qualities leaving the inferior qualities for home consumption' (Illus 3.5).[17] This raised bread was leavened with

IRELAND: ART INTO HISTORY

barm (for baker's yeast did not become commercial until after the 1870s), in contrast to the unleavened cakes or the soda farls baked on the griddles by the farmers' wives. It was the towns that inherited the new tastes in bread. Joshua Strangman of Waterford, in evidence to the commissioners inquiring into the condition of the poorer classes in 1836, hazarded the opinion that the switch to wheaten bread had occurred during a failure of the potato crop about 1830 and was due to the 'large importation of Indian corn which, at the time, was eagerly used by the working classes'.[18] The fundamental flaw in this explanation, however, is exposed by evidence submitted to the same commission by Beresford Boate, justice of the peace for Dungarvan:

> Bread is much more used as food in the town and neighbourhood than it was formerly, and its use has increased in as much greater proportion that the population: [whereas] 35 years ago there were only two bakers in the town of Dungarvan, there are now nearly 50, and some of them sell a great quantity. The tradesmen and artisans of the town generally eat bread, at least at one meal in the day...Small farmers, as well as labourers, eat potatoes because they cannot afford to eat bread. Potatoes can be raised cheaper than any other food...[19]

This evidence indicates that the use of baker's bread for food had been increasing for some considerable time, but it was still mainly confined to the townspeople, and even then for only one meal in the day. For the small farmers, wheaten bread was a treat and something of a luxury, according to Inglis. It was both the availability and the cheapness of the bread that encouraged its increase in the towns, and it was the farmers' wives on their journeys to market who brought the new taste into the countryside. Its penetration was limited by the lack of rural cash. The poorer classes in the countryside relied on the potatoes they grew in their gardens and on the milk and buttermilk they could procure from the farmers. Their welfare depended on a recognition by the rural community of their importance as a pool of cheap labour. The urban poor in comparison were not blessed with such security, but they were

3.6 There would seem to be at least two varieties of fish available at this market. The women are well wrapped against the weather, with headscarves and hooded cloaks.

Ulster Folk and Transport Museum

able to supplement their meagre diet from the surplus created by the food-processing industries and the foodstuffs that remained unsold. 'In the winter season, owing to the large numbers of hogs slaughtered here [Waterford], pork offal can be purchased at very low rates; and not unfrequently fish, such as hake, herrings, sprats etc, are selling at prices sufficiently low within their reach.'[20] According to Pigot's 1824 Directory, Dungarvan 'supplies a great part of the interior of Munster with fresh fish and is a remarkably cheap town'.

Evidence given to the Fishery Commissioners in 1836 by several local fishermen asserted that the supply of fresh fish in the County Waterford ports had never exceeded public demand, with the result that considerable quantities of Scottish herrings and fish from Newfoundland were sold regularly in local markets (Illus 3.6).[21] This is surprising when it is realised that the fishing fleets of the county in 1836 were reckoned to comprise 419 boats worked by 2156 men, while County Cork had 2631 boats with 13,738 men.[22] Also, in 1836 the fishing industry was declining after doubling its manpower during the decade of the bounties from 1819 to 1830.[23] A local fisherman explained the major problem of the industry: 'It is either a feast or a famine, and when a large quantity is taken, the price is so low in consequence of there being no regular curers, that the fishermen have not the fair benefit of it.'[24] In other words, they could not obtain a steady income from their work. This was the problem that the Irish Fishery

IRELAND: ART INTO HISTORY

Commissioners had tried to solve in the 1820s by providing bounties that would subsidise the development of curing enterprises and encourage the construction and operation of larger boats to exploit the deep sea fisheries. They were convinced that both local and overseas markets would be able to take all the fish they could catch and cure. About the turn of the century, the Nymph Bank Company had been formed in Waterford to exploit the fishing ground that lay just offshore, but it failed within a year.[25] The bounties proved equally ineffectual:

> Under the operation of this system, a great increase in the activity of the trade was experienced, much capital was drawn to it, and large sums were circulated among fishermen, curers, etc. At the end of ten years, when the bounties were discontinued, the trade began to fall back into languor and exhaustion; little or no new capital had been created by their assistance, and vested in the fisheries; accordingly many of the boats which had been employed under their stimulation, were immediately withdrawn from the trade, and suffered to rot on the beach, while the men sought other employment or sunk into mendicancy, etc.[26]

The probable reason for the failure of the bounties was given by one of the coastguard officers in 1836: 'The demand for the fresh market is so great, that none are cured, or sold for curing.'[27] It is possible that if a significant bounty had been given for exports of salted fish to the Continent, the entrepreneurs in the curing industry would have obtained a regular supply

3.7 A quayside scene showing a small rowing-boat to the right, and on the left one of the half-decked sailing vessels promoted by the Fishery Commissioners. The cart with its spoked wheels is drawn by a donkey wearing blinkers.
Ulster Folk and Transport Museum

of fish for curing, and this would have increased the local price for fish, thus encouraging fishermen to go to sea more often. With all Waterford's experience of curing fish in Newfoundland, a profitable industry should have developed. Several of the paintings illustrate the curing process and the sale of cured fish. Another illustrates a group of 'jolters' or carriers with a donkey-cart loaded with two kishes (large baskets) of fish for sale in the interior of the county: in the background is one of the half-decked vessels that the commissioners were promoting, and a rowing-boat manned by four men, of the type that was used by most of the fishermen (Illus 3.7). Another illustration of Waterford depicts a market-woman selling a lobster to a well-dressed gentleman (Illus 3.8). Lobsters and crabs were captured by means of wickerwork lobster pots, and sold throughout the county by the jolters. Much of the shellfish was used locally for bait.[28]

CRAFT PRODUCTS

Both the provision trade and the fisheries generated a host of other trades, such as tanners and curriers, tallow chandlers and soapboilers, rope and sail-makers, ships chandlers, shipbuilders, metalworkers, coopers and turners and basket-makers. It is difficult to overestimate the importance of these crafts in servicing the local economy. The most ubiquitous of their products illustrated in the paintings are baskets of many shapes and sizes. As wicker baskets were designed and constructed to suit their contents, they provided one of the strongest, lightest, sturdiest and cheapest means of transporting a great variety of commodities. Although Pigot's 1824 Directory lists only four basket-makers for Waterford, there is no doubt that many other baskets were made locally throughout the region. Among the Dungarvan paintings is one of a man weaving a large round basket (Illus 3.9). He is kneeling on his right knee (having first untied his breeches at the knee and rolled down his right stocking) and working in exactly the

IRELAND: ART INTO HISTORY

3.9 This method of weaving is still in use today. The upright sally rods are pushed into the earth to provide stability; the base of the basket is woven last. Barefoot children were the norm at this time.

Ulster Folk and Transport Museum

same fashion as one Joseph Hogan when photographed making the creel in David Shaw-Smith's book *Ireland's Traditional Crafts* (1984).[29] A similar creel, being carried by a rope over the shoulder, is pictured in a Dungarvan scene. Two larger baskets loaded with turf or vegetables and carried on the backs of women with the aid of a headband around the forehead, are shown in other illustrations. These baskets were not as large as the 'kish', two of which fitted into the body of a wheel car: they are filled with fish in the picture of the jolters on the quay. Most of the other baskets in the paintings are about seventy-five centimetres in diameter, from fifteen to thirty centimetres deep, and with or without wicker handles. The shallower baskets filled with fish or vegetables might be carried on the head through the streets, but the deeper baskets would have been too clumsy to carry, and too heavy if filled with apples or potatoes (Illus 3.10). Of especial interest among the illustrations are those of lip-work — shallow baskets made from bundles of rye straw sewn in coils with strips of bramble. Because of their close texture they proved to be ideal cheap containers for substances such as salt. A bee-skep made of the same material could be turned upside down to display its honeycombs for sale.

Far less frequent than baskets in the watercolours are the products of the coopers, who made tubs, barrels, casks and the like, and yet they must have been the most numerous of all the craftworkers because their products were in such great and constant demand. Eleven are named for Dungarvan and six for Waterford in Pigot's 1824 Directory, but these figures take no account of the number of employees in their establishments. If the artist had been interested in the provision trade, the pictures would have contained plenty of barrels of butter, pork or fish, all made by the 'dry coopers'. They used mainly beech for butter firkins, or sycamore and deal with hoops of split hazel or sally, but for long voyages barrels were hooped with iron. The 'wet coopers', who specialised in making the best-quality barrels to contain beer, spirits and liquids, used American or Canadian oak bound with iron hoops.[30] Almost all this timber

3.10 Two market vendors; the woman on the left (who seems to be calling out her wares) is the first to appear in these sketches without a cloak. Note again the variety of baskets.

Ulster Folk and Transport Museum

was imported, and some would have been reused: this accounts for the appearance in Pigot's 1824 Directory of a dealer in hoops and staves in Waterford. In the volume of paintings under discussion, only four illustrations contain straight-staved vessels, all of which could have been made by a 'white cooper', or even a skilled village carpenter. Those straight-staved vessels were churns, firkins, piggins and noggins for dairying. For domestic use, cheap washtubs were made from cut-down barrels that had contained imported goods.

TRANSPORT

The transport of barrels and other heavy goods from Waterford or Dungarvan 'to any parts of the kingdom at the shortest notice' was operated by car men listed in Pigot's 1824 Directory, although there were plenty of other car men available for local work. Six paintings in the volume illustrate local wheeled transport and enable us to compare it with two illustrations depicting market carts in England. Whereas the English market carts have large spoked wheels and considerable boxed bodies, all the Irish vehicles have small wheels and the minimum of superstructure. Although all the Irish wheels are similar in size, they are constructed in two completely different styles. Three of the paintings illustrate the well-known traditional solid wooden wheels (Illus 3.11), dowelled together from three pieces of wood, mortised and secured to a heavy wooden axle, and shod with an iron hoop: one of the illustrations shows a hoop nailed on to the wheel. The remaining three vehicles illustrated have spoked wheels, but at least one of them — that used by a fish jolter — has its hoops nailed to the wheels. The jolter's car also appears to have a solid axle beneath the frame of the car, but it is possible that the iron axle was attached to strengthening timber. When discussing the construction of two block-wheel cars examined in Tipperary in the early 1950s, A T Lucas noted that the floor of the car consisted of four transverse boards mortised into the

3.11 This woman is enjoying a smoke from her long-stemmed pipe as she brings her milk to market. The milk churn must be placed on a transverse plank. The cartwheels are of the solid type.

Ulster Folk and Transport Museum

3.12 An 'outside car' with the driver perched above the passengers, and their baggage precariously piled behind. Bianconi's passenger service, extended from Clonmel to Waterford in 1818, used vehicles like these in the early days. The pony's trot is correctly observed.

Ulster Folk and Transport Museum

shafts, and that three timbers or riders were bolted on top of the shafts to hold them together and support two side rails and a back rail, forming an elementary body:[31] these side rails are visible in four of the paintings. In the illustration of the jolter's car, we see that 'the spaces between the back rider and the back rail and between the inner side rails and the shafts are filled by widely spaced turned rods to give an elementary back and sides to the vehicle'. In three of the paintings, large baskets or 'kishes' are wedged into the body of the car, but two others have a floor built over the rails: on one, three people are sitting on straw, while on the other, at least five sacks (probably of potatoes) are being transported. The driver of the car carrying the people is seated on the rump of his horse with his feet on one of the shafts: while this driving position gave him better control of the horse, it required considerable agility.

One of the cars pictured differs fundamentally from the others. It is the 'outside car', with the driver perched above the passengers and their luggage piled behind him (Illus 3.12). The line of the shafts indicates that large springs were fitted between the axle and the body of the vehicle for the comfort of the passengers.[32] This traditional type of passenger conveyance was adopted by Charles Bianconi when he set up his passenger service between Clonmel and Cahir in County Tipperary in 1815 using military horses made redundant by the end of the Napoleonic wars. He extended to Waterford in 1818 and opened services from Waterford to Dungarvan and Dungarvan to Lismore, County Kerry. It was in 1825 that he began to build larger and heavier four-horse 'long cars' to his own design in special premises at Clonmel. The illustration of a one-horse car drawn by Michael Angelo Hayes for the biography of Bianconi by his daughter, Mrs Morgan John [Mary Anne] O'Connell, indicates that changes were made to this design: the precarious condition of the luggage in our illustration shows why the luggage-well had to be deepened.[33]

It was not only passenger vehicles that were revolutionised in these years. As a witness informed the Poor Commissioners in 1836 about Dungarvan district:

> The improvement which has taken place in roads has led to the use of improved carts; there is hardly one of the old block-wheel cars to be seen. The improvements have rendered it possible to convey a greater quantity with a single horse than formerly. The common carriers now take loads of from 18 to 25 cwt; formerly from 5 to 8 cwt was a full load.[34]

The witness was referring to the Scotch carts that had become more common in Ulster since the turn of the century. Their larger spoked wheels and boxed bodies made them a more efficient form of transport on the public roads, but they would not have supplanted the car in the economy of the poorer classes.

DRESS AND CLOTHING

While the illustrations under discussion interpret vehicles that were to become outmoded within a decade or so, they also clarify details about styles of everyday dress that were undergoing considerable changes (Illus 3.13). Several local people commented on these changes, but again it was Joshua Strangman, the Quaker merchant from Waterford, who endeavoured to explain their nature to the Poor Commissioners in 1836:

> With regard to clothing I think that within the last fifteen years a decided and striking improvement is apparent in both sexes, but especially among females. This arises, I consider, in great measure

3.13 Another market scene, with a shoemaker doing repairs on the spot (note the hobnails), as an old woman slumbers over her basket of food, huddled in her cloak.
Ulster Folk and Transport Museum

from the reduced price of manufactured goods, and the universal use of cotton. Formerly the females of this district were attired in garments of a particular fabric, a sort of thick woollen stuff manufactured in this city; its texture was exceedingly strong, and a gown or other article made from it would last for several years; ... the present low price of calicoes has, however, completely superseded the use of this fabric, and the manufacture of it, which about thirty years since gave employment to some hundreds of weavers and woolcombers, has now altogether ceased ...[35]

Strangman admitted that the destruction of the native woollen industry had caused great privation, but argued that both the cheapness of cotton gowns and their washability benefited many women and provided work for dressmakers, as more women were able to afford more gowns. This argument overlooks the fact that the introduction of cheap cotton goods was not responsible for the destruction of the local woollen industry, since these textiles were used to manufacture different types of clothes. The local woollen industry failed in the mid 1820s because its primitive methods and organisation could not match the lower prices of comparable woollens from Yorkshire: many other traditional woollen centres throughout the British Isles suffered the same fate as Waterford. The result was that 'by 1838 the Irish woollen textile industry, which in the late eighteenth century still supplied by far the greater part of Irish consumption, supplied only about 14 per cent of Irish needs'.[36]

In these circumstances it should not be surprising to discover that the majority of the women depicted in these paintings of the early 1820s appear to be dressed in the traditional heavy woollen materials produced in Waterford.[37] They were, after all, representative of the lower classes (or at least the more enterprising section of them), and their outdoor occupation compelled them to protect themselves against the weather. Their major defence was the hooded cloak that covered its owner from head to foot, or at least knee. In the paintings relating to Waterford and Dungarvan, as many as forty-one cloaks are illustrated. None are red,

3.14 A group of spademen waiting to be hired, probably wandering labourers who came to County Waterford from Cork or Kerry. Their light spades or 'loys' were adequate for easily worked soils.

Ulster Folk and Transport Museum

3.15 A festive group dancing to the music of the 'uileann' or union pipes. The woman's dress is similar to that of the market women; the dancing man wears trousers and a short jacket, while the piper dons a pair of breeches.

Ulster Folk and Transport Museum

twenty-seven are dark blue, nine black, three grey and two light blue. None appears to have either vertical slits for arm-holes, or even collars. In general the hoods are so capacious as to be cumbersome, but they could be gathered around the face by pulling a drawstring let into the front hem. These hems were sometimes bound with a ribbon in a contrasting colour. Although Joshua Strangman condemned the cloak 'as a cover under which the slattern may hide her untidiness', the artist proved much more complimentary to the ladies. Very few of them appear without their heads covered, but the white indoor cap is rare. Printed kerchiefs of cotton were cheap and attractive, and so they were often worn wrapped around the head, enabling the wearer to let down her hood. Coloured neckerchiefs were also popular. Most surprising is the proportion of women wearing shoes. In the Waterford illustrations, twenty-six women are wearing shoes, while only one is barefoot, wearing a patched cloak and carrying a large basket on her back. In Dungarvan, in contrast, fourteen women are shod and thirteen barefoot. This may reflect another significant difference between town and country. In 1824 a clergyman had commented: 'It is in the recollection of persons still living, that the dress of farmers who brought their goods to a market at Waterford, formerly consisted of a loose greatcoat tied around the body with a band of hay, without shoes or stockings, shirt, or hat.'[38] This observation is supported to some extent by a witness to the Poor Commissioners in 1836 relating to the Dungarvan district:

> It is said that on Sundays the peasantry are all well clothed, but their working clothes are indifferent. There is a great improvement, generally speaking, in their clothing, but there is room for much more. They manufacture at home the flannels for the gowns and petticoats, and the lining of men's clothes. They also make their own stockings; but, for the most part, purchase the materials of which the other parts of their dress are made. Women generally make all their own clothes except their gowns. The use of shoes and stockings is increasing; thirty years ago shoes and stockings were not worn by one-third of the labouring class; now a large majority have them.[39]

It could be argued that cities like Waterford imposed improving standards of civility and generated the cash to pay for it. Developing marketing and transport facilities for the sale of agricultural produce such as poultry, eggs and honey, along with cattle, pigs and crops, enabled country people to sample new consumer goods, as well as tobacco and alcohol.

It would be difficult to exhaust discussion of the many aspects of this society featured in these illustrations. The spectacle of cattle dealers in greatcoats standing about in a fair, or spademen waiting to be hired (Illus 3.14), the liveliness of a pair of dancers to the music of chamber pipes (Illus 3.15), the raggedness of a pair of labourers mixing mortar in contrast to the well-turned-out gentlemen wheeling a 'provision car' through Waterford, the sight of two women washing clothes in a stream, and a well-dressed girl riding pig-a-back as two gallants splash their way over a ford, are all portrayed in lively fashion. These images are shared with us by an artist with a sense of humour as well as concern. He deserves recognition and appreciation. His work bears a striking resemblance to the sketches of people in Youghal in 1831 made by a contemporary from County Waterford, Sampson Towgood Roche, who is considered to be one of the finest Irish miniaturists.[40]

4

Marie Bourke

RURAL LIFE IN PRE-FAMINE CONNACHT: A VISUAL DOCUMENT

W hile the broad outlines of social life in the nineteenth century are well known to both historians and art historians, the details of the standard of living and the physical appearance of the country are only gradually coming to light. This is due to problems with sources and interpretation of the material. While the parliamentary commissions of the nineteenth century collected vast amounts of information on issues that they regarded as most important, especially the ownership and occupation of land, many other aspects of society were neglected. To remedy this problem, both historians and art historians have turned to other source material, such as lists of the contents of houses and the physical remains of the past. By the standards of European society, pre-Famine Connacht was poor but not poverty-stricken. During the late eighteenth century there was a vigorous subsistence economy in Connemara, producing young cattle, oatmeal, stockings (knitted), fish, kelp and poitín (home-distilled whiskey). People gathered in settlements (a village or 'baile') and lived in houses made from local materials — stones for walls, clay for floors, 'wreck' timber for rafters, and oats or bent grass for thatch. Turf provided fuel, and the main food was the potato, which flourished in the wet acidic west of Ireland soil, fertilised by manure made from seaweed.[1] This provided a perfectly adequate existence, or so Henry Blake thought when he wrote: 'If they have turf and potatoes enough, they reckon themselves provided for; if a few herrings, a little oatmeal and above all, the milk of a cow can be added, they are rich, they can enjoy themselves and dance with a light heart.'[2] With time, the situation changed, the population increased (between

Opposite

4.1 *Self Portrait*, Frederic William Burton (1816–1900)

An intense and introspective self-portrait, skillfully drawn. Burton had studied drawing at the Dublin Society Schools, under Robert West and Henry Brocas.

National Gallery of Ireland (no 2400)

1600 and 1840 the population of Ireland soared from one million to eight and a half million), and there was a greater dependency solely on the potato crop. With foresight Thomas Malthus, commenting on the increased use of the potato in his *Essay on the Principle of Population* (1798), wrote 'that the extended use of potatoes has allowed of a very rapid increase of it [the population of Ireland] during the last century'.[3]

Connemara was facing a famine situation by 1822 due to a total reliance on the potato and because the oats crop was being sent abroad to be marketed. By 1841 the population density over stretches of Connemara was 500 per square mile, with the major portion living on the poorest soil along the coast, where a living could be made from the land and the sea. Roads had been built by this time right out to Clifden, and Charles Bianconi had established his passenger coach service, which also operated in Munster and Leinster.[4] The population census of 1841 indicated that 40 per cent were living in one-roomed cabins of stone, while 37 per cent were in houses of two to four rooms.[5] Life for the ordinary person was hard, but hospitality was widespread, particularly in the west, where traditional music, singing, dancing and story-telling were much in evidence. In their book entitled *Ireland: Its Scenery and Character*, written between 1841 and 1843, Mr and Mrs S C Hall found Galway to be a romantic city and observed that 'every peasant girl might serve as a model for a sculptor'.[6]

A society like this produces little in the way of written records, and we have to depend on the comments of outsiders, such as travellers, for descriptions of the social life and for an understanding of how contemporary society in western Ireland worked. These travellers came from a wide variety of backgrounds: there were many from England and Scotland, attracted by the romantic landscape then much in vogue; there were continental visitors, such as the French diplomat Conquebert de Montbert who toured Connacht in 1791, and the Chevalier de Latocnaye who wrote *Rambles in Ireland* in 1797. Government officials from Dublin and London visited and were concerned with the recording of social evils of the countryside. The ways in which these visitors recorded their impressions of the region were diverse. Most common was the published travel account, such as that by Mr and Mrs S C Hall, but others chose to record the landscape and social life of Connacht in paintings, drawings and watercolours. One such visitor was Frederic William Burton.

FREDERIC WILLIAM BURTON

Burton was born on 18 April 1816 in Corofin, County Clare (Illus 4.1). His mother was a Mallet, of the Dublin engineering family, and through her he was related both to Sarah Purser (1848–1923), the portrait painter and founder of An Túr Gloine (the stained glass studio), and William Osborne (1823–1901), the well-known animal painter.[7] The Burtons settled in County Clare in the seventeenth century, becoming landowners, and two centuries later the family was to be found living at Clifden House, Corofin.[8] Frederic's father was an amateur painter who exhibited and became a member of 'The Society of Artists in the City of Dublin'. The Burtons had five children: a daughter who died in infancy and four sons. The family moved to Dublin for their children's education, and in 1826 Frederic enrolled at the Dublin Society Schools, studying under Henry Brocas and Robert Lucius West. Brocas was a noted landscape painter, while West taught figure drawing. The young Burton received a well-rounded instruction in drawing, pastel and watercolour painting. At the age of sixteen he began exhibiting at the Royal Hibernian Academy, where his first work *Abraham on his Journey to Sacrifice Isaac* was well received.[9]

Burton's early career was mainly as a painter of portraits in watercolour and miniature. He was greatly influenced by the two miniature painters, John Comerford (*c* 1770–1832) and Samuel Lover (1797–1868).[10] Lover was a versatile character, being a writer of songs, novels and plays in addition to being a painter, and he and Burton became firm friends. The bishop of Killaloe recognised at an early age that Burton was determined on an artistic career, and he said of his young cousin that he thought he 'would turn out a remarkable man'.[11]

Burton was friendly with George Petrie, who reputedly had spotted the artist sketching in a Dublin gallery, and the two struck up a lifelong friendship.[12] Petrie (1790–1886) was an antiquary, writer, musician, and one of the finest topographical artists of the nineteenth century.[13] He guided and directed Burton by bringing him on sketching trips around the west coast of Ireland. He proved to be an ideal teacher, and undoubtedly for Burton the best fruits of these travels were the pictures he painted between 1838 and 1841, culminating in *The Aran Fisherman's Drowned Child*. Burton served on the Council of the Royal Irish Academy with Petrie, and was also one of the founders of the Irish Archaeological Society. While Petrie had an unerring eye for view painting, W G Strickland in his *Dictionary of Irish Artists* acknowledged how 'even in his earlier drawings, Burton showed a perception and sense of colour much beyond Petrie's limited range'.[14]

Lady Gregory, founder of the Abbey Theatre, used to tease Burton about his companions: 'Ferguson, Stokes, Petrie had been his dear friends and companions but Davis was dearest of all.'[15] Thomas Osborne Davis (1818–45),[16] together with Charles Gavan Duffy and John Blake Dillon, was one of the founders of the Young Ireland movement. The nationalism that they preached reflected ideals shared by young Romantic intellectuals in Europe at the time. They founded a newspaper called *The Nation* in 1842, seeing their task as creating a 'national spirit' and to be the voice of national self-respect.[17] Davis was a likeable and intelligent man who wanted to create a body of nationalistic art. When he saw Burton's Irish subject pictures, particularly *The Aran Fisherman's Drowned Child*, he tried to enlist his help by appealing to him through the columns of *The Nation* to 'procure for Ireland a recognised Irish Art'. Burton (a unionist) was not interested, and was politically opposed to Young Irelander ideals. He was, however, a close friend of Davis, and tried to explain to him: 'You should give Ireland first a decided national school of poetry — that is song — and the other phases will soon show themselves.' He sympathised with Davis and told him: 'Free spiritual, high-aiming art cannot be forced.'[18] In 1843, out of personal friendship, he designed the title page for the newspaper's collection of patriotic verses, entitled *The Spirit of the Nation*, published in 1845 (Illus 4.2). While Burton, as it emerged, correctly felt that painting would have to be inspired by something like a literary movement, his early works do reflect Davis's ideals. Pictures like *The Blind Girl at the Holy Well*, *Paddy Conneely, the Galway Piper* and *The Aran Fisherman's Drowned Child* can be seen to reflect the mood of the period: they are part of a search for a 'national identity'. They reflect an interest in antiquity and the past, and treat contemporary Irish subjects in a sensitive and objective manner. These works form part of the background to the period known as the Celtic Revival.

Burton completed a number of pictures between 1838 and 1841, representing ordinary scenes of contemporary life in the west of Ireland, of which *The Aran Fisherman's Drowned Child*

4.2 Frontispiece design for *The Spirit of the Nation*, Frederic William Burton (1816–1900), engraved by Carolyn Millard and published 1845.

Burton's friendship with Thomas Davis led him to design the frontispiece for a collection of patriotic verses by the writers of the *Nation* newspaper: perhaps the most influential collection of its kind ever published in Ireland.

is the most important. Based at Oughterard, Connemara, in 1839, Petrie wrote: 'The whole of this ancient territory of West Connaught is, as yet, the region of romance ... Burton, the artist, who is one of our party, is almost made with delight.'[19] *The Blind Girl at the Holy Well* (engraving, British Museum) was exhibited at the RHA in 1840, and is one of Burton's early 'western' pictures. He was in Connemara again in 1840 trying to do some drawing: 'I made a sort of wretched sketch.'[20] It proved to be a productive trip, and in 1841 the following three pictures were included among the eight works he exhibited at the Royal Hibernian Academy: *A Connaught Toilette* — Connemara girls on their way to market; *Paddy Conneely, the Galway Piper* — a sketch from nature; and *The Aran Fisherman's Drowned Child* — (unfinished) watercolour.

No reproduction of *A Connaught Toilette* survives, as both it and *The Blind Girl* were destroyed in a fire in London.[21] *Paddy Conneely, the Galway Piper* was painted for Petrie when Burton was in Connemara in 1840 (Illus 4.3). It became a popular print when in October of that year it was engraved for the *Irish Penny Journal*, in which, Petrie observed, 'Our Irish readers ... are presented with the genuine portrait of a piper'.[22] A watercolour entitled *A Connemara Peasant Girl* (National Gallery of Ireland), which is undated and unsigned, may be part of his work of this period. The young lady who coyly smiles at us may have been the young girl from Maam in Connemara to whom Burton referred during his last illness.[23]

THE ARAN FISHERMAN'S DROWNED CHILD

Of these records of life in Connacht in the early nineteenth century, none seems to provide such a detailed record of social life and the social fabric as *The Aran Fisherman's Drowned Child*, which is a watercolour on paper, is signed 'Frederic W Burton invt. 1841', and was exhibited that year at the RHA. It received wide acclaim when exhibited at the Royal Academy[24] in 1842; that same year William Thackeray, the celebrated English novelist, wrote: 'The drawings and reputation of Mr Burton are well known in England: his pictures were the most admired in the Collection.'[25] The Royal Irish Art Union had the picture engraved in 1843, when the honorary secretary Frederic Bacon reported that they had secured 'The highly acclaimed work of Mr Burton and the print went on to become one of the most popular ever produced by the Union'.[26]

For a description of *The Aran Fisherman's Drowned Child* we turn to the *Dublin Review* of 1888:

> We are shown the interior of a Galway fisherman's cottage, filled by the crowd of peasants who have hurried in on hearing the calamity that has fallen on the house. The dead child lies across the mother's lap, who, bending over it with passionate gesture, pushes back the hair from its pallid brow as she searches its face for some sign of life, every nerve of her body strained, her bare feet seeming to clasp the clay floor of the cabin, in the tension of her agonised frame. Still as a marble statue, stands the unhappy father, looking out from the picture, too deeply moved for sound or movement, yet with that in his face that tells of the wrench his heart endures.

The subject of death is an emotional one, and the picture centres around the tragedy that has afflicted these seafaring people. The mother, the fisherman and the drowned child provide the focal point of the picture, and they are surrounded by friends and neighbours who have come to sympathise and mourn.

It was during his twenty-fifth year that Burton painted *The Aran Fisherman's Drowned Child*. It was a difficult task for a young artist, and it is notable that when Sir William Stokes visited the

4.3 *Paddy Conneely, the Galway Piper*, Frederic William Burton (1816–1900), Pencil and watercolour on paper

This effective portrayal of a musician playing the Irish 'uileann' (elbow) pipes was painted for the antiquary George Petrie during a tour of Connemara in 1840.

National Gallery of Ireland (no 6036)

Aran Islands sixteen years later, he commented: 'It would have required a Rembrandt to paint the scene.'[27] Burton reputedly made fifty preliminary sketches for the picture. Executed in pencil, chalk, pen and ink, few of these drawings survive. Those that do, such as the sketches illustrated here (Illus 4.4, 4.5, 4.6), show his skill at observing people in a variety of everyday poses. He experimented with the composition; one early study illustrated the mother throwing her head back as if she was 'going mad', while in another sketch he caught the mother in a faint, being attended to by the assembled women.

An unsigned and undated preliminary watercolour (Illus 4.7), shows that Burton had made his mind up about the final composition and that the main object was to concentrate the attention on the grief of the parents. This preliminary sketch reveals the artist painting in a much freer and bolder manner than his customary style. His technique was to apply overlapping layers of paint in fine and delicate brushstrokes until the watercolour acquired the depth of colour and tone that he required.

Burton more than likely used somewhere familiar to him, such as the Claddagh area of Galway or a coastal village in Connemara, and not the Aran Islands, as a setting for the picture. The Claddagh, located on the western side of the Corrib River, originally consisted of a colony of fishermen who were superstitious, elected their own leaders and claimed sole fishing rights to Galway Bay.[28] A distinct community, its members were comfortably dressed, industrious and tidy, and they had larger and better furnished thatched cottages than most Galway dwellings. Details like the old man's costume, the patterned shawl, the fishing nets, the terrier, the dress and physical appearance of the fisherman, suggest a mainland origin for

4.4, 4.5, 4.6 Preliminary sketches for *The Aran Fisherman's Drowned Child*, Frederic William Burton (1816–1900), Pencil and chalk on paper

Burton reputedly made fifty sketches in preparation for this picture. These three show him working on the central figures, the bereaved parents: note the father's downcast gaze in Illus 4.6 (in the finished picture, he looks to the viewer).

National Gallery of Ireland and the Clare Heritage Centre, Corofin

4.7 Preliminary watercolour sketch for *The Aran Fisherman's Drowned Child* , Frederic William Burton (1816–1900)

A rapidly painted sketch showing that the main elements of the composition have been settled, apart from the seated woman added later to the right foreground. Note how the father looks resolutely away from the dead child, to which all other eyes are turned, as though unable to face the sight.

National Gallery of Ireland (no 19,353)

the picture. The people are neatly dressed and the dwelling is clean and spacious in the Claddagh tradition, with fishing nets hanging from the rafters. The masts of the boats seen through the doorway include those of the Galway Hookers, commonly used by the Claddagh fishermen, and the position of the masts indicates a busy pier nearby, such as that found in the Claddagh.[29] All these factors combine to reinforce the idea that the scene is not taking place on the Aran Islands, but in Galway.

There is no doubt that Burton's gift as a painter of genre pictures was acknowledged and that *The Aran Fisherman's Drowned Child* brought him public recognition. Stewart Blacker, a contemporary writer, summed up his achievements in 1845 when he wrote: 'I only trust he will … continue to teach us to feel the poetry of everyday life, and to view Irish scenery and Irish character not as it is usually represented in caricature, but through the refined and intellectual medium with which he has so gracefully invested it.'[30]

On the surface, therefore, *The Aran Fisherman's Drowned Child* would seem to provide an important source for the understanding of social life in pre-Famine Connacht. However, as with written travellers' accounts, such works of art frequently reflect the particular bias of the author and are certainly not neutral. One problem for the historian who wants to use images to recreate the past, and for the art historian who wants to understand the social context of the work, is to decipher the artist's perception of the scene being recorded and the reality of that scene. In this case it involves an understanding of the conventions within which Burton was operating and how they affected his treatment of the subject.

The influence of contemporary painters and also of the Old Masters is to be found in *The Aran Fisherman's Drowned Child*. The picture is a romantic image and illustrates Burton's preoccupation

4.8 *A Scene from Gil Blas* 1839, Daniel Maclise (1806–1870), Oil on panel

Burton's composition for the *Aran Fisherman* picture may have been influenced by the placing of the figures in this theatrical scene by his fellow Irishman, Maclise, painted two years earlier in 1839.

National Gallery of Ireland (no 1927)

4.9 *The Massacre of the Innocents* (detail from engraving), Marcantonio Raimondi (after Raphael)

Burton may have drawn on Raphael for the position of the mother bending over her dead child; the similarity is more marked in the preliminary watercolour, where (as here) the mother's face is fully obscured.

with community life, such as that in the west of Ireland. This would have been in keeping with the aspirations of Victorian artists, who looked to the Middle Ages for their models and who painted mainly literary and historical subjects in a dramatic and sentimental manner. Burton's picture would have formed part of a broad Romantic movement which was sweeping Europe in the nineteenth century.

The young artist was familiar with the Old Masters, and it appears that Raphael (1483–1520), one of the main painters of the Italian High Renaissance, made a special impression on him. There are striking similarities between the construction of the cartoon *St Paul at Athens* (Victoria and Albert Museum, London) by Raphael and *The Aran Fisherman's Drowned Child*.[31] It is likely that Burton was also influenced in the layout and design by a picture entitled *A Scene from Gil Blas* (Illus 4.8) painted in 1839 by his fellow countryman Daniel Maclise (1806–70).[32]

Burton turns to Raphael again for inspiration when two motifs appear transcribed from Renaissance models. The 'mother and child' group seems to have been taken from *The Massacre of the Innocents* (Illus 4.9), engraved by Raimondi after Raphael.[33] An added feature is the young girl, to one side of the mother and child, who bears close resemblance to the kneeling figure of the Virgin Mary in Raphael's picture *The Mond Crucifix* (National Gallery, London). Petrie, in a letter to Burton dated 1839, described the Connemara dress: 'The costumes of the women, so exquisitely beautiful and simple — exactly as if they stepped out of a picture by Raphael or Murillo.'[34]

Connemara and the Aran Islands were rich in classically popular colour, a fact that Petrie commented on after a visit to the Aran Islands in 1821–2: 'The colouring of the dresses of

the peasantry was such as the painters of the Roman School have always loved.'[35] It is not surprising, therefore, to find the influence of another Renaissance master, Michelangelo (1577–1640), in the figure of the old man, inspired by one of the lunettes in the Sistine Chapel. The keening woman is clearly influenced by classical painting. She is a familiar figure in picture subjects, such as *The Massacre of the Innocents*, *The Rape of the Sabine Women* or even *The Horrors of War*, of which Burton made a copy (National Gallery of Ireland) after the original by Rubens in the Pitti Palace, Florence.

The Aran Fisherman's Drowned Child is a 'genre' painting, in that it illustrates a scene from ordinary life. The nineteenth-century fashion for subject and genre painting was inspired chiefly by seventeenth-century Flemish and Dutch prototypes. This type of picture was popularised through the works of British artists such as Wilkie[36] and Landseer, and the Irish painters Mulready[37] and Maclise. Landseer, who was renowned for his realistic portrayal of animals and was a great favourite of Queen Victoria, was commissioned by her in 1838 to paint *Macaw, Lovebirds, Terrier and Spaniel Puppies* (Royal Collection).[38] The terrier in this work is very similar to the dog in Burton's picture. Landseer exhibited his work at the Royal Academy in 1840, the same year that Maclise exhibited *A Scene from Gil Blas*, and there is every possibility that Burton saw the pictures while visiting London.

By understanding the artistic influences at work on Burton, we are able to see more clearly the strengths and weaknesses of his work of art as evidence for the social conditions in which it was produced. The details in the watercolour become as important as the composition in helping to understand pre-Famine Connacht. We can observe Burton's accurate eye at work, and by making comparisons with the available documentary and oral evidence, we can use this material as a way of understanding the social fabric in nineteenth-century Connacht. This is particularly relevant when dealing with costume, traditions and customs, folklore and folklife, all of which were central to the environment in which the watercolour was produced, yet about which traditional historical sources are often very unsatisfactory.

COSTUMES

The Aran Fisherman's Drowned Child illustrates Burton's interest in costumes, the majority of which have been observed with an accurate eye (Illus 4.10). One notices that the costumes of the people are shabby when compared to their well-fed appearance.[39] These costumes were worn throughout the nineteenth century, were uninfluenced by fashion, and depended on the availability of local resources and fabric. The Aran islanders tended to wear more clothing of a heavier kind than the people of the mainland, while in this picture the people represented appear to reflect a comfortable class of society, such as in the Claddagh area of Galway. The old Claddagh was a separate village until the late 1880s, when it was incorporated into the town of Galway, itself the provincial capital. The Claddagh boasted the largest fishing fleet in Ireland.

Along the west coast of Ireland, women's clothes were predominantly of a red hue, according to Hely Dutton in 1824, and Burton appears to relish this fact in *The Aran Fisherman's Drowned Child*, where he gives them the full strength of red pigment using fine overlapping brushstrokes. Petrie also wrote about colour in his Journal in 1821: 'The deep red and blue tints of the female costumes were relieved by the azure dresses of the men.'[40] The poses of the women seem quite natural considering the tragic circumstances, as the critic of the *University Magazine* noted in September 1842: 'The homely and touching native expressions of the characters are strikingly preserved.'

Countrywomen in the nineteenth century generally wore a skirt and blouse or bodice.[41] The skirt or petticoat was made of flannel, in red, black or dark blue, and also of 'drugget', which was a mixture of wool and linen. It often contained four to five metres of material, had insets of calico at the waist and was worn calf-length. The skirt was worn over a linen shift, and on top was a high-necked buttoned bodice called the *corpán*. In *The Aran Fisherman's Drowned Child*, women can be seen wearing hooded cloaks. These were made of broadcloth by a travelling tailor, were valued possessions and lasted a lifetime. The Halls commented favourably on them in 1824: 'the material falls well and folds well.' The red and blue cloaks seen in the picture were expensive items, which tended to be handed down from one generation to another. Large shawls gradually replaced cloaks.[42] The shoulder shawl was crossed over the front and tucked into the waistband. The women in the picture wear plain and patterned shawls in addition to small headscarves tied under the chin. Plain and striped aprons can be seen on several of the women, tucked up at the waist and exposing the petticoat. Girls and young women wore their hair loose or tied back, but as can be seen in the picture, as soon as they began to wear skirts and bodices, they pinned their hair up in a bun.

Burton created the Aran fisherman himself, the most important figure in the picture, and drew attention to him by his exaggerated stance, the anguished expression on his face and his clenched hands. He is a romantic figure, emphasised by his dramatic pose, his colourful costume and his grief, which distances him from his family and the mourners. According to an 1824 survey of the County of Galway: 'On the Coast of Connemara the men very generally dressed in blue jackets and trousers.'[43] While Burton may have taken liberties with the fisherman's outfit, combining traditional garments with more decorative items of apparel such as the red cravat and the jacket, there was a custom of borrowing parts of a costume for mourning or special occasions.[44] The blue jacket with its brass or silver buttons is similar to a sailor's costume, while it is also local to Connemara and the Claddagh area of Galway, where the men were renowned for their seafaring abilities. Although this might seem to conflict with the title of the picture, our subject does not have the long oval-shaped face of the Aran islanders, nor does he have their 'lean, stocky and athletic' build.[45] His outfit is topped with a tall hat known as 'The Caroline', which was worn throughout Ireland and differed from the wide-brimmed felt hat worn by the islanders.

Traditionally, the Aran islander wore next to his skin a *léine ghlas*, a blue flannel inner shirt, and on top a *bascóta*, a sleeved waistcoat of white flannel. Flannel was cheap and was 'woven by a weaver in Kilronan'.[46] The *bheist* or waistcoat, the outer garment, was worn at about eighteen years of age, and consisted of grey or brown in front and blue frieze on the back. The wide loose trousers of blue frieze was worn with pampooties and a white *báinín* jacket.[47] 'Pampooties' were heelless single-piece shoes made from raw cowhide.[48] Simple to make, the 'pampootie' was functional and cheap and lasted about a month. The shoe was laced over the toe, around the heel, and tied about the instep with fishing line. They were normally soaked overnight in water to keep them supple. A person wearing 'pampooties' was characterised by a dignified bearing that came from walking on the toes and not on the heels like city folk.

Shoes of this kind dated back to Early Christian times, when they were commonly worn in Ireland.

Children were dressed in a similar style to their mothers until about the age of twelve years. The custom of dressing young boys as girls survived throughout much of the nineteenth century.[49] Tradition tells us this was done to deceive the 'good people' — the fairies — as to the sex of the child. Having unattractive offspring, the fairies were reputed to steal young children, especially boys, and replace them with one of their own changelings.[50] There was a high infant mortality rate in Ireland in the nineteenth century. Many infants died very young and were buried in unconsecrated ground. In the picture, the small barefooted child clinging to the grandfather wears a cotton sleeveless petticoat, while the dead child wears a white flannel frock known as the *cóta cabhlach*.[51]

The grandfather, who is seated to one side of the picture, thoughtfully puts a protective arm around the young child. He wears an overcoat derived from an eighteenth-century riding coat. Known as the 'swallowtail', it was commonly worn by farmers in the early nineteenth century. In the picture it is worn with knee breeches and pampooties, although it might have been more customary to wear shoes called 'brogues'. Brogues were the everyday footwear of the common people, as distinct from the more modern 'shoe'. Shoes cost more than brogues and were worn on special occasions. Knitting, which can be seen on the floor, was not introduced to Ireland until the seventeenth century. The mother was probably knitting either grey socks or stockings called *máirtíní* or *lóipíní*, which provided a small income for women. *Máirtíní* [52] were knee-length soleless stockings; one part covered the heel and the other part had a loop which wound around the middle toe. They were worn by women and boys to protect the shins from cracking, caused by wet work outside or exposure to the fire indoors.

In the background of the picture, a young man discusses the recent tragedy with two women. On his head he wears a blue hat with a chequered headband, similar to the 'Tam o' Shanter' they made on the Aran Islands. He could be a sailor from a Galway Hooker, the masts of which can be seen through the doorway. The Galway Hooker [53] was the most commonly used sailing craft in Connemara in the nineteenth century and it dated to about 1800. It was a strong, sturdy boat, with a single mast on which traditionally a cross was marked. The boat had dark sails and was a familiar sight plying between Aran and Galway, carrying livestock and turf from Connemara.

TRADITIONS AND CUSTOMS

The costumes appear to indicate a mixed background to the couple in the picture. While it is possible to surmise that a marriage had been arranged between a woman from the mainland and an Aran fisherman, there was considerable antipathy between mainland people and the islanders, and such an engagement would certainly have been very uncommon.[54] 'Marriages' did not necessarily come about from love, but tended to be arranged for convenience. Matchmaking was a serious business and hard bargains were driven before consent was given, although one seldom heard of unhappy unions.[55]

Death, resulting from hunger, fever or disease was particularly common among poor people, where the standard of living was very low. Because death occurred so frequently, it became an accepted part of the way of life, acquiring many traditions and rituals.[56]

4.10 *The Aran Fisherman's Drowned Child* 1841, Frederic William Burton (1816–1900), Watercolour on paper Burton's finished picture was an immediate success, though some of the details — the old man's costume, the patterned shawl, the fishing nets, the terrier — suggest it may have been based on observations in the Claddagh district of Galway rather than on the Aran Islands.

National Gallery of Ireland (no 6048)

IRELAND: ART INTO HISTORY

Unforeseen or sudden death in the young was judged unnatural and was attributed to the fairies. A drowning was considered an unnatural death, and in parts of Ireland it was customary not to bring the body of a drowned child into the house but to 'wake' it elsewhere.[57] People were superstitious about drownings, and in many areas it was thought that the body should not be recovered as the 'sea had claimed its own'. If the child was baptised, the wake would begin immediately and last two days and nights. An unbaptised child would be buried in unconsecrated ground — *cillíní* — such as a field or a fairy fort.

In *The Aran Fisherman's Drowned Child*, the distracted mother clings to her child while an elderly woman leans over as if to take the infant from her so that the wake can begin. The child appears to be about three or four years old, and it is not clear if it is a boy or a girl. Already the keening is in evidence, begun by a woman who raises her arms in a gesture of sorrow and begins the low-toned lamentation known as *caoineadh* for the dead child.[58] The tradition of keening was not performed for everyone; it was generally done for people from the community and of some standing. It was customary to hire a professional keener to wail and cry over the dead. The usual number of keeners was four. In *The Aran Fisherman's Drowned Child*, one woman has begun the lamentation, while the three women entering the doorway, all of whom are wearing similar cloaks, are probably going to assist. One would stay near the head, one would remain at the feet, one took care of the candles, and the other would stand at one side of the corpse.[59] The *bean caointe*, the keening woman, would cry over the corpse, composing improvised verse praising the dead child and expressing grief at its demise. This ritual was seen as a symbol of the voyage of the deceased to an afterlife consisting of a mixture of Christian and ancient Celtic/fairy worlds. Due to the unnatural death, the activities of the 'borekeen' or *cleasaí*, the male jester who would organise the wake games, were severely curtailed. Merry lively wakes were normal throughout Ireland when death was expected. Fairy abduction was a traditional way of reconciling accidental or unexpected death, and the merrymaking activities of the borekeen would reaffirm life and restore social order.[60] The games at the wake and the keening are descended from the same ultimate source as the *cliche caointeach* — game of lamentation — which took place when a great warrior died in Ireland.

FOLKLORE AND FOLKLIFE

The scene in the picture appears to be taking place in a one-roomed dwelling of the type used by 40 per cent of the Irish population at that time. The roof would have been thatched with rye straw, and on the inside many kinds of fish and fishing nets can be seen hanging from the rafters. The fishing nets were made from cotton, imported from Spain, while the thick cord holding the cork floats was grass rope.[61] The nets were used for drift-net fishing, carried out by night from currachs. The mackerel or herring caught in the summer were for winter use and were cured by being put in a barrel of salt and water and hung out to dry and smoke.[62] Salted fish was in great demand in the nineteenth century as a supplement to the potato diet. If this was an Aran Island dwelling, one would have expected to see long fishing line, used by the islanders to catch fish such as ling, sole or pollock.

The kitchen was the core of the Irish home, where traditionally a fire was kept burning as a sign of hospitality and of the continuity of life. While Sir William Wilde wrote generally about an Irish kitchen 'always lighted up by a blazing turf fire', Synge's graphic description fits this kitchen: 'The walls have been toned by the turf smoke to a soft brown that blends with the grey earth colour of the floor.'[63] The furniture was simple and basic, and consisted of fireside stools, forms and benches. The grandfather sits on a four-legged stool, while the mother is seated on what is possibly a settle-bed, which was a seat by day and converted to a bed by night.[64] The size of the kitchen seems unusually large, even for a mainland dwelling. About the fire there is a structure called a 'crane' — a horizontal beam with hooks attached to it that was used for holding kettles and cooking pots.[65] A cast-iron three-legged cooking pot called a 'skillet', which is full of potatoes, can be seen hanging from the crane. This fixture was movable and made cooking easier for the woman of the house. To one side of the hearth a woman rests herself, while over her head there appears to be a keep-hole set into the wall. Most dwellings had a keep-hole, also known as *poll an bpáirc*, into which rosary beads and small items like tobacco, tea, knitting and a pipe were put. The keep-hole in this picture seems to contain bread or salt, both of which needed a warm place to keep them dry.[66] A dark boat-shaped vessel can be seen above the keep-hole, and this is probably a primitive oil lamp called *an slige*, meaning a 'grisset' or a 'cresset'. The lamp contained fish oil, seal oil or tallow, and the rush lights burned in it provided sparse light, while the fumes escaped through the smoke hole in the roof. In the foreground of the picture behind the seated woman, a conical-shaped basket can be seen. It is a food-carrying basket of the type commonly used on the Aran Islands.[67] It is fascinating to discover from the variety of details in this painting what a simple and comfortable self-sufficient lifestyle these people led.

In the background, a St Brigid's Cross has been placed above the door, where it would prevent evil spirits entering the house.[68] The cross was notable because it was simply made from two peeled sticks or thin slips of wood which were tied together, while at the junction plaited straw or rushes were bound to hold it firmly.[69] St Brigid's Day, 1 February, was the first of four quarterly feasts of the Folk Calendar. While each festival had its own distinctive customs and beliefs, St Brigid's Day signalled the beginning of spring, when the fisherman and the farmer hoped the weather would improve. One custom associated with the holy day was the placing of a cross above the doorway — it was possible to tell the age of a house from the number of crosses in the rafters. The St Brigid's Cross protected the house from harm or fire. The cross in this picture is of a Latin type commonly found along the west coast, on the Aran Islands and in Galway.

BURTON'S LAST YEARS

Never a very productive artist, Burton completed fewer works as the years went by, and gave up painting entirely in 1874 when Gladstone appointed him director of the National Gallery in London. He threw all his energies into improving the National Gallery and enlarging its collection.[70] Under his directorship major acquisitions were made, including works by Leonardo, Raphael, Botticelli and Velázquez. Unlike Hugh Lane, Burton was a hesitant man, 'I have never in all my life been able to have the same confidence in my own judgement.'[71] He was created a Knight Bachelor in 1884,[72] and retired from the National Gallery in 1894 after twenty years' service. Assessing Burton, a critic in *The Connoisseur* wrote: 'He was a man of prepossessing personality as well as distinction of manner, and among his friends were the most distinguished representatives of science, literature and Art.'[73] He died on 16 March 1900, and was buried in Mount Jerome Cemetery, Dublin. Late in life he commented to Lady Gregory: 'It is so with me; my best joys have been connected with Ireland.'[74]

CONCLUSION

This case study demonstrates that by acquiring knowledge of the art historical context of Burton's *Aran Fisherman*, historians can begin to take from the watercolour valuable information on the social life in pre-Famine Connacht. In the same way as with written documents, biases can be accounted for and allowances made. From an art historian's perspective, examining the social context of the work provides background material missing from the painting. The interdisciplinary approach applied to the study of *The Aran Fisherman's Drowned Child* produces a rich tapestry of knowledge, allowing the fullest possible understanding of the painting and its social, economic and historical background.

Burton absorbed the folklore and customs of the people on his trips to Connemara, where he probably spent hours sketching and listening to their tales. He knew the west intimately, and although it appears that he did not visit the Aran Islands until 1857,[75] Petrie, who had been there in 1821–2, would have told him all he needed to know. On returning to his studio in Dublin, he would have begun the process of assessing his drawings prior to creating a large-scale picture. When this complex assimilation is understood in the context of the ideas Burton absorbed in Connacht, the picture can be more fully interpreted.

5

Margaret Crawford

THE GREAT IRISH FAMINE 1845–9: IMAGE VERSUS REALITY

By the nineteenth century, Britain had been largely free of the experience of widespread famine for several generations, and mental pictures had faded away. Ireland, however, experienced periodic and local subsistence crises in the early decades of the century, and was given a final reminder of the horrors of mass hunger by hosting the last Great Famine of the Old European Order in the mid 1840s. Between 1845 and 1851, Ireland lost two million of its population: one million by death and a further million by emigration. The reason for this tragedy was the failure of the staple crop, the potato, in three seasons out of four, beginning in 1845. *Phytophthora infestans*, more commonly known as potato blight, was the culprit devastating the crops. Because over three million Irish people were totally dependent on the potato as their sole source of sustenance, famine ensued, the horrors multiplying with each successive failure.

Despite the enduring importance of the Famine, it has attracted relatively little scholarly research. A pioneering study of the Irish Famine appeared in 1875 entitled *The History of the Great Irish Famine of 1847*, written by Canon John O'Rourke.[1] Almost eighty years elapsed before another major work appeared on the subject, in the form of a collection of essays edited by R D Edwards and T D Williams, entitled *The Great Famine*,[2] published in 1956. *The Great Hunger* by Cecil Woodham-Smith[3] followed in 1962. These remained the chief works on the subject for almost three decades. In recent years, however, there has been an increase in the number of books and articles published on different aspects of the crisis. *Why Ireland Starved* by J Mokyr,[4] and slimmer volumes by Mary Daly[5] and Cormac Ó Grada[6] have added to the historiography, together with numerous articles by S H Cousens, Austin Bourke, J S Donnelly Jnr, and others.[7] Despite a large corpus of pictures appearing in illustrated newspapers and weekly magazines during and after the Famine years, illustrations of the Famine have played only a minor role in these books, merely embellishing the text, serving as chapter dividers, cover pictures or frontispieces.

Today, images of famine are imprinted on our consciousness by television pictures and newspaper photographs brought to us from regions in Africa and Asia. Breathing skeletons scarcely able to walk, pot-bellied children with match-stick limbs, aged countenances on childhood bodies, convey the visual horrors of famine. In contrast to those of the present, famines of the past have left primarily written legacies, although survivors of one generation passed images of the event on to the next through oral tradition. The Great Irish Famine has been amply recorded in print. The medical profession wrote prolifically of sickness and death.[8] Poor Law records are a litany of the inability of a new institution to meet the needs of the crisis. The government, meanwhile, produced numerous large volumes documenting the crisis. The Society of Friends had a more pragmatic approach: they offered money, soup and vivid descriptions, the last of which provided an enduring record of the catastrophe.

An unusual aspect of the Great Famine, apart from its length, severity and late appearance, is the pictorial record created by several British publications; the best known are *Punch*, *The Lady's Newspaper*, *The Pictorial Times* and *The Illustrated London News*. This article concentrates on the pictures that appeared in *The Illustrated London News*[9] between 1846 and 1850, and assesses to what extent they reflected the tone and tenor of the written documentation.

THE ILLUSTRATED LONDON NEWS

The Illustrated London News was the world's first illustrated newspaper.[10] The inaugural issue was published on Saturday 14 May 1842, and thereafter it appeared weekly. From the outset the editor was 'determined to keep continually before the eye of the world a living and moving panorama of all its activities and influences.'[11] During the early years, all its illustrations were engravings. Herbert Ingram, the founder of the paper, realised that its major attraction was the illustrations. From a very early stage, therefore, the newspaper employed its own staff of engravers, and provided accommodation and facilities on the premises to carry out the work in order to 'be able to keep our wood engraving department further in advance by the retention of permanent artists ready at a moment's notice for the contingencies of every public event'.[12]

The medium used for engraving was box-wood, which had a very close grain. It was sliced across the trunk, the bark was removed, the slices were cut into rectangular pieces, and the surface was smoothed, ready for engraving. When an illustration was entirely produced on the premises, an artist first sketched the picture onto the smooth surface of a wood-block, or a number of blocks, depending on the finished size of the illustration. The engraver would then apply his skill to the wooden block and engrave the picture. On completion, the block or blocks were ready for printing. When *The Illustrated London News* was reporting an event from abroad, a number of strategies could be adopted, depending on the circumstances, in order to get some pictorial representation. If there was advance notice, a sketch artist was dispatched to the location, or a known local artist was commissioned to send sketches to London. Alternatively, an artist was given the copy of an existing print illustrating the location, and by a combination of research and artistic licence an appropriate picture was produced.

During the five-year period between 1846 and 1850, over forty pictures appeared in *The Illustrated London News* relating to the Great Irish Famine, the majority showing scenes in the south, south-west and west of Ireland. The work of one Irish artist, James Mahony, and two English engravers, Ebenezer Landells and F G Smyth, can be identified. Two other names — Fitzpatrick and H Smith — occur on two pictures, but both have proved more elusive to track down.

James Mahony (1810–79) was a watercolour artist from Cork. By 1847 he had acquired a reputation as a watercolourist, exhibiting work in the Royal Hibernian Academy periodically between 1843 and 1859.[13] During the mid 1840s Mahony was retained by *The Illustrated London News* as their artist of Irish events. He sketched the grounding of the steamship *Great Britain* at Dundrum Bay, County Down, in 1846, and provided illustrations of Daniel O'Connell's funeral in 1847. For a time he lived and worked in Dublin, where he produced some of his best-known works. One watercolour in particular — *Dublin from the Spire of St George's Hardwick Place* (National Gallery of Ireland) — is familiar to historians of nineteenth-century Ireland, and a portion of it appears on the jacket of *Irish Historical Statistics* edited by W E Vaughan and A J Fitzpatrick. Mahony left Ireland in 1859 and settled in London, where he spent the rest of his life. There his work was exhibited at the Royal Academy and the New Watercolour Society during the 1860s and 1870s. He also became well known for his magazine and book illustrations, his pictures appearing in numerous periodicals and novels. Three of Charles Dickens' books were illustrated by him in the 'Household Edition'.

It is not surprising, therefore, that *The Illustrated London News* should have commissioned Mahony to do a special series of Famine illustrations at a time when local newspapers from his home territory were reporting great distress. These drawings appeared in 1847 and accompanied a two-part article entitled 'Sketches in the west of Ireland'.[14] The first part included seven illustrations from the Skibbereen and Clonakilty districts of County Cork. The second part contained a further five sketches from the same locality, and appeared in the next issue. Two years later, in 1849–50, a long-running series of seven articles entitled 'Condition of Ireland: Illustrations of the New Poor Law' was published, four of which were accompanied by illustrations. The artist referred to as 'our own artist', although unnamed, was probably Mahony.

Ebenezer Landells (1808–60) had a well-established reputation as a wood engraver by the time *The Illustrated London News* was launched, and a large staff of assistants and pupils worked for him. Herbert Ingram frequently commissioned Landells for special assignments, and his name appeared on many of the paper's engravings during the 1840s and 1850s, although he was not necessarily the engraver. According to the custom of the day, Landells' name was put on blocks that were engraved under his direction, as well as on his own work. Of the Irish Famine collection of illustrations, two bore Landells' name.

Several famine sketches carry the name of Smyth. This was F G Smyth, and he too was an engraver.[15] His name appeared on many engravings published in the paper throughout the 1840s and 1850s. The subjects of his pictures were very diverse, and the locations worldwide. A clue that Smyth was not a travelling artist but a resident engraver is revealed in a sketch illustrating an article about India. The Indian story stated that the artist of the illustration was a traveller, G T Vigne Esq, yet the published illustration bears the name of Smyth.[16] He is also named in a National Gallery of Ireland catalogue as an engraver; the work to which his signature is attached is an engraving of Dublin dated 1846, and the National Gallery cites *The Illustrated London News* as the source.[17]

Of Fitzpatrick and H Smith we have no definite information. Only one illustration bears Fitzpatrick's name. The names of artists and engravers, however, did not always appear on published pictures, and so Fitzpatrick may well have been responsible for other illustrations. A noteworthy feature of the Fitzpatrick picture is that it was also signed by the engraver Landells. This suggests either that Fitzpatrick was the artist of the original sketch, or alternatively, that he was an engraver working under Landells' direction. Of the two possibilities, the former is the more likely. If Fitzpatrick is to be identified as an Irish artist, then the most likely candidate was Edmond Fitzpatrick, who worked from the 1840s through to the 1860s and was particularly noted for his peasant scenes. Like Mahony, he too went to London and worked for illustrated London magazines.[18]

H Smith was identified as an artist from Cork. We know nothing of him other than his name and place of residence, which appears as a caption at the bottom of one illustration, *Funeral at Skibbereen* (Illus 5.9).

PICTURES AND COMMENTARY

The first picture in *The Illustrated London News* on the theme of the Great Famine appeared in 1846 and depicted the government's sale of Indian meal in Cork. The original sketch by James Mahony was dispatched to London, and an engraving of it was made. Some months later, a pair of sketches appeared showing two locations where food riots had taken place. In the following year, 1847, a total of nineteen illustrations was published. In 1848 only two illustrations of the Great Famine were produced, though the paper returned to this subject in 1849 with the lengthy seven-part series on the operation of the new Poor Law. Five of the seven parts were illustrated with a total of eighteen pictures.

Viewing the entire collection as a whole, the pictures fall into three broad categories: misery, mortality, and scenic views. Dealing with the last group first, these were pleasant views of places where distress was being experienced. Among the early Famine pictures to appear in *The Illustrated London News* relating to food shortages in Ireland were a pair of pleasing views of Dungarvan, County Waterford, and Youghal, County Cork (Illus 5.1). They were signed by Smyth, and were probably engraved either by him or under his instruction. The artist is unnamed and is referred to only as 'our artist'. However, since Mahony was previously mentioned as the paper's artist for other Irish events, it is likely that the drawings were his work. Furthermore, we know the sketches were done on location, for the paper reported that while sketching, the artist was approached by the local population who left him in no doubt about the hunger and misery currently being suffered:

> Annexed is a pair of melancholy sketches of the localities of the late food riots in the south of Ireland — Youghal and Dungarvan; the afflicting details of which have been duly reported in our Journal. The Artist has refrained from heightening the picturesqueness of these scenes; but they are stern and striking realities of the sufferings of the people, and must bespeak the sympathy of every well-regulated mind.

THE MALL AND MALL-HOUSE, YOUGHAL, A SCENE OF THE LATE FOOD RIOTS.

Youghal was the grand centre of the late Food Riots and turn-outs for wages. Our Artist was received somewhat roughly whilst he was sketching in the street, because he would not promise the mothers that their children, then working on the part of Government, should have an increase of wages over five or sixpence, which was insufficient to support them with Indian meal at 1s 8d per stone.

The distress, both in Youghal and Dungarvan, is truly appalling in the streets; for without entering the houses, the miserable spectacle of haggard looks, crouching attitudes, sunken eyes, and colourless lips and cheeks, unmistakably bespeaks the suffering of the people.[19]

If these illustrations were supposed to conjure an atmosphere of want and distress, they failed. Although the paper described the sketches as 'melancholy', and the artist felt that he had 'refrained from heightening the picturesqueness of these scenes', his sketches did not capture the 'stern and striking realities of the suffering of the people'. Nor did they convey 'the miserable spectacle of haggard looks, crouching attitudes, sunken eyes, and colourless lips and cheeks'[20] that the reporter asserted.

Further pleasant pictures followed. Whether it was felt that there was only a certain level of tolerance among the British readership to doleful illustrations is difficult to gauge, but one comment sheds a glimmer of light on this point. The artist of the series of drawings depicting the miserable conditions in the west of Ireland in 1849 included among his illustrations a pleasing scene of cattle being driven to market, with the comment 'I send you herewith a Sketch of Driving [cattle] for Rent. It may serve to vary a little the miseries I have to portray'.[21]

Alert to newspaper reports of the increasing seriousness of the food crisis, *The Illustrated London News* carried an article in January of 1847 entitled 'Famine and starvation in the county of Cork'. A large portion of this piece was a reproduction of text from the *Cork Examiner*, and

5.1 *The Mall and Mall-House, Youghal, a Scene of the Late Food Riots*
The caption refers to 'the late food riots' in Youghal, but the artist chooses here to show a pleasant scene, almost tranquil, with no obvious sign of hunger or distress.
From *The Illustrated London News*, ix, 1846

THE CORK SOCIETY OF FRIEND'S SOUP HOUSE.

the picture published was of the Cork Society of Friends' soup kitchen (Illus 5.2).[22] As the Famine worsened, the pace of private philanthropic activity increased during 1846, and the Society of Friends was at the forefront of this work. Indeed the contribution of the Society of Friends cannot be overstated, both in the tangible aid it provided to the starving and in its major contributions to the historical record of events. These were published in the *Transactions of the Central Relief Committee of the Society of Friends during the Famine in Ireland in 1846 and 1847*.[23] The *Transactions* contain detailed reports of the crisis during the years 1846 and 1847, and provide the historian with a good contemporary source against which to set the illustrations of *The Illustrated London News*.

As Irish provincial newspapers continued to report the unmitigated sufferings of the starving population, *The Illustrated London News* was prompted to examine the crisis in more detail:

> with the object of ascertaining the accuracy of the frightful statements and of placing them in unexaggerated fidelity ... We have commissioned our Artist, Mr James Mahony of Cork to visit the seat of extreme suffering, viz Skibbereen and its vicinity; and we now submit to our readers the graphic results of his journey, accompanied by such descriptive notes as he was enabled to collect whilst sketching the fearful incidents and desolate localities; premising merely, that our Artist must already have been somewhat familiar with such scenes of suffering in his own locality [Cork], so that he cannot be supposed to have taken an *extreme* view of the greater misery at Skibbereen.[24]

On this occasion Mahony acted both as artist and correspondent.

In all, *The Illustrated London News* published seven pictures to accompany Mahony's article. The most harrowing was of a woman with a small child in her arms begging in Clonakilty (Illus 5.3). The pained grimace of her countenance and outstretched hand for alms conveyed her need for food. Perhaps the best-known famine illustration is that of the *Boy and Girl at Cahera* (Illus 5.4). The atmosphere of the picture is of misery and despair as the two children scour a barren field in search of a potato or two that may have evaded blight and escaped the eye of previous scavengers. The expression on the boy's face is pained and his stance is of one starved of both food and heat. His clothes, and those of the girl, are ragged. The girl's hair is spiky and scant, a sign of severe starvation. On the other hand, the limbs of both children appear sturdy, contrary to what one would expect in prolonged famine conditions. Two years later, a similar picture by an unnamed artist was published, entitled *Searching for Potatoes* (Illus 5.5). Once again the figures cannot be described as appearing severely malnourished in anatomical terms. On the contrary, the limbs appear strong and muscular. The one notable symbol of distress is the ragged condition of their clothing. It is the short commentary accompanying the illustration, rather than the picture itself, that provides the more powerful image:

> *Searching for potatoes* is one of the occupations of those who cannot obtain out-door relief. It is gleaning in a potato-field — and how few are left after the potatoes are dug, must be known to everyone

5.3 *Woman Begging at Clonakilty*
The artist makes some effort to show distress: the woman's eye seems swollen, her cloak is torn, her baby is a tiny bundle, but she herself is not notably emaciated.
From *The Illustrated London News*, x, 1847

5.4 *Boy and Girl at Cahera*
The children gleaning stray potatoes in the empty fields are shown in rags to indicate their misery, with harrowed expressions: but they are surprisingly well-muscled given that it is the third year of the Famine.
From *The Illustrated London News*, x, 1847

WOMAN BEGGING AT CLONAKILTY.

BOY AND GIRL AT CAHERA.

5.5 *Searching for Potatoes*

But for the haggard faces in the background, this could be an everyday farming scene: the foreground figures show no real evidence of their supposed misery.

From *The Illustrated London News*, xv, 1849

5.6 *Bridget O'Donnell and her Children*

This pathetic group is one of the few in these illustrations showing clear signs of emaciation, and the desperation of the mother's expression is well rendered.

From *The Illustrated London News*, xv, 1849

who has ever seen the field cleared. What the people were digging and hunting for, like dogs after truffles, I could not imagine till I went into the field [where] I found them patiently turning over the whole ground in the hope of finding a few potatoes.[25]

Another illustration depicting famine victims shows *Bridget O'Donnell and her Children* (Illus 5.6), and again most of its poignancy comes from the facial expressions and raggedness of the clothing. The limbs of the mother appear particularly sturdy, although the child on the left has thin legs, one of which has texturing that could represent shadow or an open sore, the latter being a common feature among the severely malnourished.

IMAGE AND REALITY

Given that British readers viewing these illustrations were generally unfamiliar with the human features of famine, their 'uninformed eye' possibly failed to recognise the divergence of image from reality. Indeed a precise representation of famine was less important than the overall atmosphere of misery that the engravings were seeking to portray. For the 'informed eye',

IRELAND: ART INTO HISTORY

however, two questions arise. Were famine conditions in Ireland less severe than the written commentaries of the day asserted? Or, were the artists less than faithful to reality, and if so why?

At this point the historian must turn to the written word. The writings of the medical profession offer a major contribution. A medical doctor, Daniel Donovan, working in the Skibbereen district, sent to the *Dublin Medical Press* his observations of the effects of intense hunger on the starving population in his locality:

> I have made particular inquiry from those who have suffered from starvation relative to the sensations experienced from long fasting; they described pain of hunger as at first very acute, ... [which] subsided, and was succeeded by a feeling of weakness and sinking ... with insatiable thirst, for cold water particularly, and a distressing feeling of coldness... In a short time the face and limbs become frightfully emaciated; [and] the eyes acquire a most peculiar stare.[26]

Such reports were not confined to the south-west. From the east of the country, Dr Lalor, physician to the Union Fever Hospital and Workhouse of Kilkenny, published the following observations:

> Many cases, admitted for the first time to our fever wards as cases of fever, were really of such a nature as not to admit of any correct classification: they were often persons totally broken in constitution by long continued privations and hardships, and in the last stages of emaciation and exhaustion.[27]

Comments about the appalling physical condition of the labouring classes were not confined to the medical profession. William Bennett of the Society of Friends was acutely moved by the scenes he found in the west of Ireland:

> My hand trembles while I write. The scenes of human misery and degradation we witnessed still haunt my imagination, with the vividness and power of some horrid and tyrannous delusion... We entered a cabin. Stretched in one dark corner... were three children huddled together, lying there because they were too weak to rise, pale and ghastly, their little limbs... perfectly emaciated, eyes sunk, voice gone, and evidently in the last stages of actual starvation. On some straw, ... was a shrivelled old woman, imploring us to give her something, — baring her limbs partly, to show how the skin hung loose from the bones.[28]

The clergy also were very prominent in the hopeless task of trying to alleviate the suffering of the starving population. The Rev Thomas Armstrong ministering in Ballina, County Mayo, witnessed in 1846:

> a vast number of impotent folk, whose gaunt and wasted frames and ghastly, emaciated faces were too evident signs of the sufferings they had endured. The little boys and girls presented a hideous sight. In many instances, their heads had become bald and their faces wrinkled like old men and women of seventy or eighty years of age.[29]

Many of the starving found themselves not only without food, but also without habitation. In the pre-Christmas edition of 1848, *The Illustrated London News* published a scathing article condemning those Irish landlords who were using the current crisis to unpeople their property. The two illustrations that accompanied the text were engraved either by Landells or by one of his assistants. The first depicted an ejection scene, and is one of the most exquisite engravings of the entire Famine collection (Illus 5.7). The picture contains considerable action. We see the tenant remonstrating with the bailiff seated aloft a black steed. Meanwhile, the bailiff's men are already denuding the roof of thatch, and driving away the tenant's donkey.

EJECTMENT OF IRISH TENANTRY.

5.7 *Ejectment of Irish Tenantry*

A grimly effective rendering of an eviction: the brutal bailiff, the pleading tenant, his weeping wife and children, the unfeeling onlookers and the stony-faced soldiers standing by are all convincingly presented.

From *The Illustrated London News*, xiii, 1848

Looking on are uniformed officers. Their presence was intended to ensure that the bailiff was not impeded in his duties, and to discourage civil disturbance. A second illustration shows the makeshift shelter along the ditch, into which the evicted tenant retreated. The stance of the major figure in the picture is one of utter despair.

The apparent callousness of landlords stemmed from two major problems. On the one hand they suffered a drastic reduction in their incomes as tenants defaulted on rent. On the other hand they were faced with rising taxation. Circumstances varied from district to district. Nevertheless, some landlords were particularly ruthless, justifying their action by the slogan, 'evict ... debtors or be dispossessed'.[30] Eyewitness accounts confirm instances of extreme suffering. For example, Bridget O'Donnell and her family, subjects of an illustration already referred to, were enduring not only starvation and sickness, but also homelessness. Prior to the food crisis, her husband was a tenant holding a small parcel of land, but late in 1849 the family was evicted for non-payment of rent. Bridget was left without a home. To add to her

IRELAND: ART INTO HISTORY

misfortunes she was ill with fever, as were her children, and she was expecting another child. The child was born dead, and her thirteen-year-old son died of hunger. Even some hardened administrators were sometimes shocked by the scenes they saw. Captain Arthur Kennedy, a Poor Law inspector, recounted years later how he felt at the time:

> I can tell you…that there were days in that western county [Clare] when I came back from some scene of eviction so maddened by the sights of hunger and misery I had seen in the day's work that I felt disposed to take the gun from behind my door and shoot the first landlord I met.[31]

The captain, though, stopped short of violence. Instead, as *The Illustrated London News* tells us, he sent his young daughter to dispense clothing to the poor. The child was described by the paper as 'filling the place of a saint and performing the duties of a patriot'.[32]

The pace of evictions increased during the late 1840s. Reliable figures are unavailable before 1849, but in that year the constabulary recorded the eviction of 16,686 families representing over ninety thousand people. In 1850 numbers increased to almost twenty thousand families and over one hundred thousand people.[33]

The landscape that was left after systematic clearances of small villages was one of utter desolation (Illus 5.8). The unroofed cabins presented a picture of emptiness and destruction, which made a strong impact on *The Illustrated London News* reporter who remarked that, 'no conqueror ever left more conspicuous marks of his devastation'.[34] Yet these settlements were not entirely empty. As the reporter continued:

> the sketch is not of a *deserted* village — though that was a miserable enough spectacle, for the wretched beings who once viewed it as the abode of plenty and peace still linger and hover about it …The ruthless spoiler has been at work and swept away the shelter that honest industry had prepared

5.8 *The Village of Tully*
This powerful and well-drawn scene shows the outcome of the policy of eviction and clearance of unwanted tenants: a ghost village, whose inhabitants are surplus to economic requirements.
From *The Illustrated London News*, xv, 1849

THE VILLAGE OF TULLIG.

THE FAMINE IN IRELAND.—FUNERAL AT SKIBBEREEN.—FROM A SKETCH BY MR. H. SMITH, CORK.—(SEE NEXT PAGE.)

[COUNTRY EDITION.]

5.9 *Funeral at Skibbereen*

The body of a young man is laid on a cart; a second man whips the horse into action; a third stands by with a spade; onlookers gossip and argue: this well-observed scene shows us death stripped of all dignity.

From *The Illustrated London News*, x, 1847

for suffering and toiling humanity. A conqueror would not have had time or security to do the mischief which is perpetrated in safety under guardianship of the laws… Within the Union of Kilrush in … 1849… about 16,000 persons have been unhoused out of 82,358.[35]

Where did these homeless people go? To the workhouse possibly, although as a last resort, many taking that road only when near the point of death. Others found very rudimentary shelter in hedges and ditches by digging out pits.

The spectre of death was brought very forcefully to the attention of the readership of *The Illustrated London News*, both by the written text and the illustrations. The paper spared no reader the realities of the horrifying deaths common in every community. Details of the scale and conditions of interment of corpses, described as follows in a January edition of 1847, would seem almost a preparation for an illustration in a later issue: 'In the parish of Kilmore [Skibbereen], fourteen died on Sunday; three of these were buried in coffins, eleven were buried without other covering than the rags they wore when alive.'[36] A few weeks later the paper carried a heading, 'Mortality in Skibbereen'. The short article gave graphic details of disease and high mortality. The illustration, with its caption 'Funeral at Skibbereen', was intended to shock Victorian England. The focus of attention was the cadaver of a young man being transported to his grave coffinless (Illus 5.9). Other, more conventional, funeral scenes also appeared. While many died in the workhouse, many more died along the roadsides and in ditches. *The Illustrated London News* captured the details:

IRELAND: ART INTO HISTORY

A specimen of the in-door horrors of Scull may be seen in [a] ... sketch... of a poor man named Mullins, who lay dying in a corner upon a heap of straw, ... whilst his three wretched children crouched over a few embers of turf, as if to raise the last remaining sparks of life. This poor man ... buried his wife some five days previously, and was in all probability on the eve of joining her, when he was found out by the untiring efforts of the Vicar, who, for a few short days saved him from that which no kindness could ultimately avert.[37]

Civil Registration of deaths was not introduced to Ireland until 1864, and so the precise number of those who died during the Famine years from starvation and famine-related diseases is unknown.[38] We do know, however, that the rate of mortality varied from region to region, and that more people died from disease than from starvation. In some districts, nevertheless, deaths from starvation were high. For example, Edmund Richards, in a letter written in March 1847, commented that for the barony of Erris in County Mayo, 'from the best statistics I could gather, the deaths from starvation are twenty per day'.[39] The reporter for the paper noted that:

all sympathy between the living and the dead seems completely out of the question; ... I [the reporter] certainly saw from 150 to 180 funerals of victims to the want of food, the whole number attended by not more than 50 persons; and so hardened are the men regularly employed in the removal of the dead from the workhouse, that I saw one of them with four coffins in a car, driving to the churchyard, sitting upon one of the said coffins, and smoking with much apparent enjoyment.[40]

INTERPRETING THE EVIDENCE

To return to the central question: the extent to which the pictures of *The Illustrated London News* provide us with an accurate contemporary record of the Famine crisis. It goes without saying that they were not intended to be a statistical record of the events, but did they succeed in capturing the atmosphere of despair and hopelessness? The value of the illustrations from this perspective varies considerably. Those pictures emphasising scenic beauty ignore the suffering endured during the crisis. By contrast, other illustrations which can be matched to written evidence do evince the air of desolation that enveloped the country. Many of the sketches were done 'on location', a point very carefully noted by the paper, and the personal experience that the artists had of the suffering population gave a realism to many of their sketches. In one issue of the paper, the artist assured the readership that 'the objects of which I send you Sketches are not sought after — I do not go out of my way to find them'.[41] The conditions under which one drawing — of the starving man, Mullins, breathing his last — was done, left such a deep impression that the artist described the event in detail.[42]

The power of image is most strongly illustrated in three sketches, the *Woman Begging in Clonakilty*, *Boy and Girl at Cahera*, and *Bridget O'Donnell and her Children*. The human suffering is given strength through facial expression, ragged clothing and limited detail. By contrast, in the eviction illustrations the skill, detail and intricacy of the artwork detract from the drama and despair of the episodes, and so require more careful study to reveal all the activity and emotion of the scenes. As Rabb and Brown in *Art and History* point out, 'some pictures have to work hard to convince ... while others achieve their aims with consummate ease'.[43] The fact that most of the 'Famine' pictures were accompanied by emotive text conditioned the response of readers to the visual image. Had they appeared in isolation, their impact on the viewer might have been less. Take, for example, the anatomical sturdiness of the individuals portrayed in many of the pictures. But for the accompanying text, the reader might well gain the impression that the Irish crisis was not severe, but merely a temporary problem with food supply, whereas we know from the written documentation that this was not so.

We need to ask, therefore, why was this aspect of the illustrations sanitised? In the artists' defence, such a form and style was not uncommon. One famous example demonstrates the point. In the painting of the *Wreck of the Medusa* by Jean-Louis Géricault (1819; Louvre, Paris), survivors of a shipwreck, who were marooned on a raft for well over a month, with little to drink and almost nothing to eat except each other, are displayed with beautifully proportioned muscular backs and limbs.[44] Considerable artistic licence was used here to heighten the drama. But why such a technique was also employed in the illustrations of the Great Irish Famine is more of a mystery. One explanation lies in the perception of the observer, in this case the artist. Even with photography, we should not expect exact images of famine; after all, the camera can and does distort. With visual art, the gap between reality and image is even wider, not only because of the limitations of the medium — especially important in the case of engravings — but also because of the filter of the artist's imagination. As Ernst Gombrich points out, artists tend to 'supplement from … experience what is not actually present'.[45] In the case of emaciated human figures, many artists working in the 1840s were unfamiliar with such a visual image and so failed to capture the full horrors before them: consciously or unconsciously they filtered out some of the more shocking human features of famine. It is interesting to note that L P Curtis, author of *Apes and Angels*, when studying the images of Irishmen as portrayed later in the century, observed that in illustrated magazines and weekly papers that did not contain cartoons, a certain idealising of the Irish could be detected. *The Illustrated London News* in particular, although directing their 'artists … to draw as much as possible from life rather than fantasy … [published] black-and-white illustrations [which] tended to verge on the ideal and the sentimental, especially when and where human suffering was concerned'.[46]

Hence in the Famine illustrations we are not witnessing a concerted policy to deceive or shelter the British readership from the realities of what was happening in Ireland. Rather, we are observing a phenomenon familiar to art historians, though less obvious to general historians, that of perceptual behaviour: what an artist perceives at any given time is conditioned by experience and purpose rather than by his/her mental mirror of the scene.[47] Thus attention was focused on the features that presented to the artist the strongest symbols of hunger — gaunt and haggard countenances, and ragged clothing. Such images can be convincing without being objectively realistic.[48] Sketches are subjective creations, and as a source are of a different ilk from a file of state papers, the contents of a Poor Law minute book, or a doctor's case notes. Their effectiveness depends on the way in which the message relates to the political and social context.[49]

PART TWO

IMAGES AND IDENTITY

6

Fergus O'Ferrall

DANIEL O'CONNELL, THE 'LIBERATOR', 1775–1847: CHANGING IMAGES

The visitor to Dublin, no matter how unobservant, will quickly encounter an image of Daniel O'Connell. John Henry Foley's impressive statue and monument in O'Connell Street, facing O'Connell Bridge, can hardly be avoided. The more perceptive tourist will find a portrait of O'Connell in the Council Chamber of City Hall, another in the entrance hall of the Mansion House, a bust of O'Connell in the entrance hall of Áras an Uachtaráin, an evocative symbol of O'Connell — the round tower — at his grave in Glasnevin Cemetery, and a statuette of O'Connell in Leinster House, the seat of the Irish parliament. The Irish twenty pound note, issued in 1992 and designed by Robert Ballagh, features a vigorous O'Connell set against the backdrop of Derrynane House, his home base in County Kerry; the reverse of the note shows the Four Courts, symbol of the constitutional and legal basis of O'Connell's career, and in the background an 1845 repeal pledge to establish an Irish legislature. O'Connell's image is both ubiquitous and significant in contemporary Ireland.

Daniel O'Connell's career and personality were crucial formative influences on modern Irish political consciousness. It is fitting, therefore, to encounter his image at the centre of the nation's political institutions, and at the centre of its capital city. The visual evidence concerning O'Connell enriches our understanding of the O'Connellite heritage, yet this aspect of O'Connell studies has been almost totally neglected. In this essay, a brief survey will be made of O'Connell portraiture throughout his life, and possibilities will be suggested for future research.

ORGANISING THE VISUAL EVIDENCE

O'Connell's public image was created without the help of radio, cinema, television or modern mass advertising. His career ended at the very dawn of the age of photography. Hence, unlike subsequent politicians, he had to rely solely upon frequent public appearances, political journals, pamphlets and newspapers, popular engravings and portrayals of his image in illustrated journals. Other ephemeral formats, such as ballad sheets, which often carried a rough drawing of O'Connell, placards, banners and handkerchiefs, were also important in popularising his image.[1] A great volume of visual evidence survives in relation to O'Connell. The starting point used here in assessing this evidence is the National Gallery of Ireland's *Illustrated Summary Catalogue of Prints and Sculpture*, published in 1988, and the Gallery's *Illustrated Summary Catalogue of Drawings, Watercolours and Miniatures*, published in 1983. In addition, Rosalind M Elmes' *Catalogue of Engraved Irish Portraits* (Dublin 1943) includes approximately eighty images of Daniel O'Connell. About forty representations of O'Connell in the form of painted portraits, statues, prints and numerous caricatures are recorded in the National Portrait Gallery, London.

The first step in exploring the images of O'Connell must be to categorise portrayals of him into some iconographical order so that they may be systematically studied. This has already been done with the two hundred or so caricatures of O'Connell that were produced by John Doyle (better known as HB) (1797–1868) between 1829 and 1847.[2] O'Connell was the pioneer of popular democratic politics, and perforce he was also a pioneer in the development of the concept of 'public image': he had to attempt to fix in the public mind an 'image' that would have emotional as well as memorable visual impact. The result of his efforts and those of his opponents was the creation of stereotypical images, both favourable and unfavourable, in the course of his long political struggles. This was assisted from the 1820s by the new process of reproducing lithographic prints, on which John Doyle's career rested. The technology suited the new era of popular parliamentary politics inaugurated by O'Connell's campaign for Catholic Emancipation.

The large quantity of visual evidence concerning O'Connell is impressive. The quality is a matter for judgement. The first half of the nineteenth century was not an especially distinguished period for portrait painting in Ireland. Anne Crookshank and the Knight of Glin found it difficult to select portrait painters of the early nineteenth century for their *Irish Portraits 1660–1860* 'as nearly all the painters can be described as competent but mediocre ... the sheer dullness of the average portrait was too much for us...'.[3] The main portrait painters, John Gubbins, John Comerford, Joseph Haverty, Nicholas Crowley, George Mulvany, Daniel Maclise and Stephen Catterson Smith, all portrayed O'Connell, and a review of their images of O'Connell throughout his life is one way to commence our exploration.

THE PORTRAITS

It is recorded that O'Connell as a youth read the *Dublin Magazine*, with its notices of celebrities and their portraits, and that he once observed: 'I wonder will my picture ever appear in it?' To have his portrait in the *Dublin Magazine* seemed to represent the pinnacle of ambition. Much later, when as a lawyer O'Connell was defending a client, John Magee, in 1813, he saw, as he walked the streets of Dublin, 'a magazine in a shop window containing the portrait of

6.1 'Counsellor O'Connell', as published in *Dublin Magazine*, March 1813.

This is the earliest published image of O'Connell, already a successful barrister but only at the start of his political activities. The face, still boyish, is slim when compared to later portraits.

National Gallery of Ireland (no 10,598)

IRELAND: ART INTO HISTORY

SHOOTING OF D'ESTERE.

Counsellor O'Connell, and I said to myself with a smile "Here are my boyish dreams of glory realised" '.[4]

The earliest extant image we have of O'Connell is that published in *Dublin Magazine* of March 1813 (Illus 6.1), but it is recorded that John Comerford executed a miniature of O'Connell about 1800.[5] The image of 1813 depicts O'Connell in his late thirties: it is quite unadorned, indicating a slimmer figure and less full face than later portraits. This was precisely the point in O'Connell's career when the outstanding Catholic barrister merged into the role of leader of popular agitation in Ireland. As Oliver MacDonagh has noted, during 1813: 'O'Connell began to manifest a new style, suited to a wider and more popular audience. He had already become a daily public spectacle in Dublin's streets, known to and watched with awe by multitudes.'[6] From this period O'Connell's image appeared more frequently, especially in rough sketches, such as that of O'Connell's fatal shooting of D'Esterre which occurred in February 1815 in a duel in County Kildare (Illus 6.2). O'Connell emerged from this duel as the Catholic champion and popular hero, despite his personal remorse.

The first of the portraits of O'Connell as public man was that produced by John Gubbins to O'Connell's commission in 1818 (Illus 6.3). Gubbins, a native of County Limerick, practised as a portrait painter in Limerick, Dublin and Belfast. What is significant about this portrait is that it was published in February 1823, just at the start of the Catholic Association, the last in a series of movements that sought to secure Catholic Emancipation. The portrait shows O'Connell in his early forties, and his interest in his public image at this time was evidenced by his exercise of control over the finished product. O'Connell told his wife how a Mr O'Reilly

6.4 Daniel O'Connell in 1823, as issued on 13 September 1823 by the London publisher J Robins.

Dated just seven months after Illus 6.3, we may take it that this is a more faithful image, though less flattering.

National Gallery of Ireland (no 10,600)

6.5 Daniel O'Connell, 1824, after a drawing by John Comerford (?1770–1832), published by J Molteno, London, 14 June 1825.

An attractive portrait of O'Connell the advocate, holding his proposal for a 'Catholic Rent' to support the campaign for Catholic Emancipation.

National Gallery of Ireland (no 10,065)

of 176 North King Street, Dublin, came to see him on 4 June 1822. O'Reilly had just finished his education as an engraver in London:

> He was very anxious to get a portrait of me and was delighted at my allowing him to engrave Gubbins' picture of me. He does it purely as a speculation of his own and he promises to have the engraving in about six weeks. I hope to carry you over a proof impression in August. I will have nothing under it but my simple name and surname and beneath the two lines 'Hereditary bondsman etc.' He seems to me to be a young man of talent and he showed me some good specimens of his engravings. I think *this time* we shall not be disappointed…[7]

O'Connell was obviously very interested in conveying an appropriate image. The silver cup in the portrait, presented to him by the Catholic Board, the vigour of his stance, the formal classical background, and the concern to have his much-used motto printed under the engraving, all point to this image-building interest. That O'Connell had cause for concern and indeed for disappointment is obvious if the engraving from the Gubbins' portrait is compared with that published later in 1823 in London (Illus 6.4). The latter portrait would have done little for O'Connell's public image and was presumably published to satisfy curiosity about the Irish agitator.

We next see O'Connell shaping his public image in 1825 when he had John Comerford produce his portrait in which he appears holding the Catholic Rent proposal, the key to the popular success of the Catholic Association founded in 1823 (Illus 6.5). Comerford (?1770–1832) was a very successful artist, noted for miniature and small drawings; his portrait subjects include John Keogh, the Sheares brothers and Robert Emmet. On 14 May 1825, during a stay in London for the famous negotiations concerning the possible concession of Catholic Emancipation, O'Connell wrote impatiently to his wife:

> Do you hear anything of Comerford and his picture of me?…I should have had the first artists in London pressing to do my portrait if he had not made me promise, and yet there is not the slightest symptom of his engraving, ever coming out…Darling, I wish I had time to get you a handsome miniature but what is the use of wishing…

On 28 May he wrote again:

> Comerford, the painter, is here about the engraving. It will certainly be out in a few days. The first sketch of the print did not satisfy Comerford and it was on that account he came here. I confess I think it very fine. However, it is now certain that he will very soon have it published. I believe I will give you another miniature during the winter by Comerford.[8]

The engraved print (Illus 6.5) was published by J Molteno, London, on 14 June 1825, just when O'Connell's political efforts in London had failed and he had to return to public agitation and rebuilding the New Catholic Association to achieve his aims. This Comerford print portrays an image of O'Connell that he believed was very serviceable in building his public image at a critical time in his political struggles: O'Connell, the wielder of the Catholic Rent weapon, is shown in a characteristic, if stylised, pose as the great orator. One notes O'Connell's careful attention to his visual image on his public appearance at the critical meeting in Dublin upon his return from London on 8 June 1825. He appeared in the uniform of the New Catholic Association, which he had personally designed to lend colour and vigour to his new campaign. He described it to his wife in detail: 'It will be a blue frock-coat with blue velvet collar, the king's collar, buff waistcoat and white pantaloons…There will be two gilt buttons with the Irish Crown and Harp.'[9] O'Connell also had a medal struck in honour of his work for the Catholics of Ireland, portraying, in Roman imperial fashion, his bust upon the obverse side and a half-laurel wreath with the other half shamrocks upon the reverse.

It is instructive to compare the 1825 Comerford print with a portrait of O'Connell produced by Stephen Catterson Smith the elder (1806–1872) when the artist was only nineteen years old (Illus 6.6). Catterson Smith, born in Yorkshire, became a very prolific artist:

> …most of his oil portraits of male sitters rarely rise above the level of boardroom tedium. However his drawings, often done in black chalks, and his rare female portraits, can be enchanting… He was the most fashionable portrait painter of his day in Ireland and his son carried on this tradition.[10]

Catterson Smith produced a further portrait of O'Connell in which he was perhaps more successful in capturing the politician's self-possession. This was presented free with *Carpenter's Political Letter* in 1830 (Illus 6.7). Despite Catterson Smith's failure to portray what his contemporaries most noted about O'Connell's person — his cunning look, his eye 'like a weasel' as the painter Benjamin Robert Haydon observed in 1834[11] — his unadorned image does allow us a counterbalance to the O'Connell-inspired public relations effort by Comerford in 1825. By the late 1820s O'Connell had reached an unprecedented position as the leader of public opinion in Ireland, and he had aroused intense interest in his cause in Europe and indeed worldwide. As one of the celebrated figures of the age, countless images were reproduced to satisfy public curiosity. For example, O'Connell became the central figure in 'la cause Catholique' in Germany, notably in the Prussian Rhineland where:

6.6 Daniel O'Connell in 1825, by Stephen Catterson Smith the elder (1806–72), published by J Robins, London, 1 September 1825.

A less effective portrait than Illus 6.5, curiously limp in its attitude to the viewer. One cannot imagine this languid fellow winning too many cases.

National Gallery of Ireland (no 10,981)

6.7 Daniel O'Connell in 1830, by Stephen Catterson Smith the elder (1806–72). Free insert in *Carpenter's Political Letter*, 1830.

An updated version by Catterson Smith, five years later than Illus 6.6. The face is clearly derived from Gubbins' portrait (Illus 6.8), while the stance and outer clothing are much the same as in Illus 6.6.

National Gallery of Ireland (no 10,977)

6.8 O'Connell in the year of Catholic Emancipation, 1829, by John Gubbins (*fl* 1820s), published by Thomas MacLean, 7 July 1829.

O'Connell is presented at the very height of his achievement as lawyer and statesman, in a portrait that exudes confidence, intelligence and charm. Note the discreetly placed harp emblem on his breast. The brief in his hand is unmarked: no need to remind the viewer by now of what O'Connell stood for.

National Gallery of Ireland
(no 10,975)

6.9 'The Humble Candidate': O'Connell kneeling before a Catholic bishop during the 1828 by-election campaign in Clare, published by Thomas MacLean, London, 1834.

An incisive political cartoon, emphasising O'Connell's subservience to the clergy, while his motto of self-respect lies in the dust and his liberal supporters stand by in embarrassment: but O'Connell won the election all the same.

National Gallery of Ireland
(no 11,401)

…many homes in this area had portraits of O'Connell on the wall; advertisements for his portrait appeared in the press, such as that in the (non Catholic) *Allgemeine Zeitung* of 6 October 1844 which reminded its readers that 'the best likeness that has ever been produced' of O'Connell, was on sale at all booksellers…[12]

A second Gubbins' portrait shows O'Connell in 1829 — the year of his victory, when Catholic Emancipation was achieved. This was published in July 1829 by Thomas MacLean (Illus 6.8). MacLean was the leading print publisher in London. He had begun to tap very profitably into the O'Connell phenomenon in 1828 with the famous lithograph of the Clare Election, *The Humble Candidate*, showing O'Connell on his knees in the street in Ennis before Bishop McMahon (Illus 6.9). Some of the details in this lithograph are very accurate, for example, the poster of the centre gable end is a copy of an actual poster used in the campaign.[13]

MacLean was also the publisher of the celebrated 'HB' sketches of John Doyle in the 1830s and 1840s — a quarter of which dealt with Daniel O'Connell.

O'Connell's pre-eminent place as the author of *Agitation* was recognised by Daniel Maclise (1806–70) when he included O'Connell with Richard Lalor Sheil, MP (O'Connell's key associate in the Catholic Emancipation struggle and author of *The Apostate*) in his 'A gallery of illustrious literary characters' produced for *Frazer's Magazine* in the 1830s. The O'Connell portrait (Illus 6.10) was published in 1834 and is notable because of Maclise's importance as a portraitist.

THE HISTORICAL IMAGES

By the 1830s, O'Connell was perceived as a figure of profound importance in Irish, British and European terms. Thomas Davis in his essay 'Hints for Irish historical paintings', published in the 1840s, identified at least four O'Connellite subjects for the nationalist canon of Irish history, which he hoped to see executed as historical paintings: 'O'Connell speaking in a Munster Chapel' as described in Thomas Wyse's *History of the Catholic Association*; 'The Clare Hustings — Proposal of O'Connell'; 'The Corporation Speech' and 'The First Meeting of the Catholic Association'. Davis hoped for 'good paintings':

> …the marked figures must be few, the action obvious, the costume, arms, architecture, postures, historically exact, and the manners, appearance, and rank of the characters, strictly studied and observed. The grouping and drawing require great truth and vigour.[14]

History painting concerning canonical events in history has long served an ideological purpose. Prior to O'Connell, the use of history painting was dominated in Ireland by the Protestant establishment. Constitutional nationalists were later to incorporate into their canon such work as Francis Wheatley's *Volunteers in College Green* (National Gallery of Ireland, no 125) or his representation of Henry Grattan in the old Irish House of Commons (Leeds City Art Galleries). James Barry (1741–1806), the neo-classical artist, was the leading Irish history painter of the second half of the eighteenth century, and he may be seen as the key transitional figure in making possible the later full-blown nationalist historical works of art. In the words of Pressly, Barry's biographer:

> Barry's identity as an Irish Roman Catholic provided the driving force behind his productions; his devotion to the principles of equality, justice and religious toleration gave meaning and energy to his entire career.[15]

From the liberal Catholic ideology of Barry, there was a move to the explicit creation of a nationalist art during O'Connell's era, and the key artist in this movement was Joseph Patrick Haverty (1794–1864).

Haverty was born in Galway, where he began his career as a painter. He moved to Dublin in 1815 and also worked in Limerick and London. He painted O'Connell in historical situations, approximating to the aspirations of Davis. Haverty executed a number of retrospective O'Connellite historical portraits, including many of his key associates in the Catholic Association. He also completed a drawing of O'Connell's monster meeting at Clifden in 1843, which was lithographed in 1845. A full-length portrait of O'Connell by Haverty portrays him romantically as the Gaelic chieftain in his great cloak, hound by his side, with the picturesque

6.10 O'Connell and Richard Lalor Sheil, drawn by Daniel Maclise (1806–70) ('Alfred Croquis'), published in *Frazer's Magazine,* 1834.

Sheil was an important supporter of O'Connell in the struggle for Catholic Emancipation, but had differences with him at various times. Here, in a gentler cartoon than Illus 6.9, a worried Sheil is reassured by a genial O'Connell.

National Gallery of Ireland (no 10,601)

6.11 Daniel O'Connell *c*1836 by
Joseph Patrick Haverty (1794–1864),
engraved by W Ward.

The apotheosis of O'Connell's self-
image as a Kerry chieftain, complete
with wolfhound, chained cloak and
romantic landscape. For all that, it is
less engaging than Gubbins' busi-
nesslike portrait of 1829 (Illus 6.8).

National Gallery of Ireland
(no 10,000)

landscape as background (Illus 6.11). It was published in London in 1836. This portrait now hangs in the Reform Club in London. Jeanne Sheehy has traced the change in Irish cultural life which was marked by a growing sense of national identity, linked to the Celtic past and using symbols and motifs to represent this newly cultivated nationalist sense of the Irish past: the harp, wolfhound, shamrock and round tower began to surround images of O'Connell.[16] O'Connell's political movements for freedom opened up the possibility of a new Irish cultural life, distinguished from British culture but completely anglicised in respect of taste and language.

O'Connell's wife so liked Haverty's portraits of O'Connell that, in 1836, she even suggested sending one to the Pope.[17] O'Connell shared this enthusiasm for Haverty's portrayals — he presented his key political agent, P V Fitzpatrick, with Haverty's picture of him reading the Address to the Electors of Clare to F W Conway and P V Fitzpatrick. This picture was completed in 1846 and was exhibited at the Royal Hibernian Academy in 1847.[18]

A number of Irish artists became explicitly associated with O'Connell's Repeal Association. Henry O'Neill (1798–1880), himself a member of the Association, painted a portrait of O'Connell which was not particularly successful. He was also commissioned by Thomas M Ray, O'Connell's full-time secretary of the Association, to produce a set of nineteen watercolours relating to O'Connell and the 'Traversers' in jail in 1844.[19]

As a friend of Charles Gavan Duffy and a native of County Monaghan, Henry MacManus (c1810–78) was encouraged to move from Orangeism to nationalism. MacManus painted portraits of the Young Irelanders, John Blake Dillon, William MacNevin and Thomas Davis, as well as several of O'Connell. He also helped the Young Ireland leader Charles Gavan Duffy to design the famous 'Repeal cap', which was placed on O'Connell's head by the sculptor John Hogan at Mullaghmast, County Clare, in 1843. MacManus's best-known picture, Reading 'The Nation' (National Gallery of Ireland, no 1917) reflects his conversion to the Young Ireland ideal.[20]

After his Emancipation triumph in 1829, O'Connell was the subject of many notable portraits. In 1845 Nicholas J Crowley (1819–57), an Irish portrait painter who resided in London, exhibited at the Royal Hibernian Academy a portrait of O'Connell that was painted during the 1844 imprisonment. Other well-known artists produced their 'O'Connell': Bernard Mulrenin's 1836 portrait, Robert M Hodgett's portrait of 1835, Sir David Wilkie's portrait (c1838), and the portrait by George Mulvany (Illus 6.12), the first director of the National Gallery of Ireland, are amongst the best known.

William Henry Holbrooke (fl 1821–48) portrayed O'Connell as lord mayor, a notable if stylised image of 'The First Catholic who attained that Office after an interval of One hundred & 50 years' (Illus 6.13). It bears O'Connell's crest and his signature, and has an obvious ideological and propaganda purpose. Holbrooke had also portrayed another key moment in O'Connell's career — O'Connell before the bar of the House of Commons in 1829. The Holbrooke of O'Connell as lord mayor might be contrasted with the Charles Grey (1808–92) portrait of O'Connell as lord mayor, which is hanging in the entrance hall of the Mansion House, Dublin. The Holbrooke is so obviously a political icon, whilst the Grey is a formal, full-length, rather dull painting.

According to Gavan Duffy, when O'Connell was in prison in 1844 a daguerreotypist's camera was set up within the precincts.[21] While no copy of this 'photograph' of O'Connell

6.12 Daniel O'Connell by George Mulvany (1809–69), Oil on canvas

A more prosaic portrait than Haverty's shows O'Connell in late middle age, the curly locks finally subdued, a distinct cast of tiredness or disappointment tempering the determination of his features.

National Gallery of Ireland (no 207)

6.13 Daniel O'Connell as Lord Mayor of Dublin, 1841, by William Henry Holbrooke (*fl* 1821–48), Lithograph with watercolour

Politically an important image; O'Connell was the first Catholic for 150 years to wear the lord mayor's chain. The features and hairstyle may be derived from earlier portraits (O'Connell was sixty-six in 1841).

National Gallery of Ireland (no 10,983)

appears to survive, shortly after O'Connell's death in May 1847 advertisements appeared for Beard's patent daguerreotype: 'This faithful photographic likeness of Ireland's departed champion is the only one for which he ever sat', and purchasers could obtain it, as well as lithographs made from it in either black and white or 'coloured by Beard's improved process' from Thomas Delany, Bookseller, No 44 Lower Ormond Quay, Dublin, or Mr T Cranfield, Printseller, 23 Westmoreland Street, Dublin.[22]

A lithograph was published in Paris after the daguerreotype taken in Dublin (Illus 6.14). Others were published in Vienna. The image may be compared with Thomas Heathfield Carrick's (1802–75) watercolour miniature portrait of O'Connell in 1844 (Illus 6.15). Carrick was a celebrated miniaturist, and apparently O'Connell liked this portrait because he sent Thomas Lyons a proof print of it from the Richmond Bridewell on 1 August 1844.[23] The engraving of Carrick's portrait was published in London in June 1844. It was used as a plate for W Cooke Taylor's *National Portrait Gallery*.

In 1843 John Hogan, who according to his biographer John Turpin is 'the sculptor who typified resurgent Catholic Ireland', was commissioned by the Repeal Association to sculpt a statue of Daniel O'Connell.[24] The Repeal Association was taking seriously 'its proper place as the patron of nationality in art' as understood by Thomas Davis. The promoters of the commission, such as the Young Irelander John Pigot, wished to use the O'Connell statue, as did Hogan, 'to express all the power and grandeur of concentrated Ireland'. Hogan desired 'a figure for Ireland, no more of weeping and of weakness, but of pride and command...'

Thomas Davis wrote a poem entitled 'Lines to Hogan' to mark the commission, which began: 'Chisel the likeness of the Chief'.

Hogan idolised O'Connell. He used the finest marble for the colossal statue, conceiving O'Connell as famous classical orator. The statue was exhibited at City Hall, Dublin, in 1846, where it remains today, a monument more to the heroic national vision of its promoters than to the subject it represents. Hogan had firmly established his place as the first Irish sculptor to deal with national themes. He later executed the colossal bronze statue of O'Connell erected at The Crescent, Limerick, in 1857.

INTERPRETING THE EVIDENCE

O'Connell was both the most idolised and the most hated public man of his time. Images of O'Connell lie behind many Irish political and cultural developments since his death; as Donal McCartney has written: 'Irish moods, dreams, aspirations, doubts and anxieties were all reflected in the various images of O'Connell created and invoked.'[25] Images of O'Connell also profoundly affected British attitudes towards the Irish: he was the key transitional figure in the process of simianising the popular images of the Irish in mid and late nineteenth-century Britain. O'Connell as 'The Irish Frankenstein' (for example, in the cartoon by J Kenny Meadows, 1790–1874, in *Punch* on 4 November 1843) illustrates the repulsion and terror conveyed to British public opinion by O'Connell's image. It is important, then, to explore how they were fashioned and to what purpose.

This essay and the essays by James McCord and Miles Chappell on the caricatures of O'Connell, are early explorations of a large body of visual evidence hitherto neglected. Questions remain about the means used to create and distribute the enormous quantities of O'Connellite visual images, about who purchased them, and their meaning to those who bought them. Questions relating to the modes of visual propaganda in the new age of public opinion that O'Connell inaugurated and about the symbolism used in the portraits and the caricatures are as yet unanswered. The popular political iconography used by O'Connell and his political movements awaits detailed study.

O'Connell's keen interest in political uniforms used in the New Catholic Association has already been mentioned, but in the Repeal Association, emblems and symbols became even more pronounced, as a glance at a Repeal Association membership card of the 'Volunteers of 1782 Revived' will reveal.[26] It is important to remember the personal attention to detail demonstrated by O'Connell in his political campaigns. No item was too small to claim his attention, whether in his instructions to local organisers or in the presentation of his image. He knew, as he wrote once, 'the value of attention to details'.[27] Questions might be asked about O'Connell's image-building through study of the allusions in the emblems and symbols and the popular frame of reference to which those allusions could relate: what conventions of literary pictorialism existed and what visual premises are assumed?

Another area for exploration is the portraits of the O'Connell family, from the eighteenth century to the present, as representatives of Catholic family history: do the O'Connell houses, portraits, visual memorabilia such as rings and so forth, cast light on the mentality and aspirations of those represented by O'Connell? A great deal more has yet to be learned about the representation of O'Connell's image in the different phases since his death, as indicated by

6.14 Daniel O'Connell, after a daguerreotype taken in Dublin by M Doussin-Dubreuil, lithograph published by D'Aubert, Paris.

An interesting image of a burly O'Connell in middle age, taken by an early photographic process invented only in 1839. The lack of proper lighting may account for the untypically narrowed eyes.

National Gallery of Ireland (no 10,976)

statues, medals, naming of streets: who was involved in such projects and why?[28] To what extent was there ever a popular cult of O'Connell, producing artefacts such as O'Connell mugs or pottery? Certainly in his lifetime there was an 'O'Connell industry' in respect of exploiting the 'O'Connell market' for images. What effect did this have on the arts and what can we learn about the state of the arts from O'Connell's portraits, monuments, medallions, history paintings, sculptures, prints and other representations?

The pursuit of these questions and others will greatly help our understanding of the emergence and development of popular politics and culture in the nineteenth century. Daniel O'Connell is the great protean figure of modern Irish history, and we will obtain a much clearer focus of his personality and politics if we attend to the available visual evidence.

6.15 Daniel O'Connell in 1844, by Thomas Heathfield Carrick (1802–1875), after a watercolour miniature.

This well-known portrait shows O'Connell towards the end of his life, just before the Great Famine, when his political influence had already begun to wane and his health was in decline. There are no symbols or emblems, just an old man in a chair.

National Gallery of Ireland (no 10,972)

7

Gary Owens

NATIONALIST MONUMENTS IN IRELAND, *c*1870–1914: SYMBOLISM AND RITUAL

istorians have recently begun to recognise the ways in which governments and political movements since the eighteenth century employed an array of symbols and ritualistic devices to mobilise mass support. Public festivals, monuments, national emblems, banners and patriotic songs were not, as they have been commonly understood, superfluous accompaniments to the political process; they were frequently its central components, the very substance of power itself.[1]

From the mid nineteenth century to the outbreak of World War I, one symbolic device in particular — public commemorative monuments — enjoyed extraordinary popularity in western Europe. Statues sprouted up on the public thoroughfares of London at a rate of one every four months during Victoria's reign. The streets and public squares of even modest-sized German towns bristled with patriotic sculpture: in a single decade some five hundred memorial towers were raised to Bismarck alone. Paris seemed so awash in statuary that at one point city officials considered imposing a moratorium on the building of new ones. The term 'statumania', which Maurice Agulhon has coined to describe the almost pathological frenzy of monument-building in France during this period, can be applied to similar phenomena in virtually every country in Europe.[2]

Governments encouraged and often sponsored this effusion of public sculpture because they saw it as a way to strengthen popular support for their regimes and to instil in their societies a sense of political unity and nationhood. Nations, after all, are 'imagined communities'; to

7.1 *William Smith O'Brien memorial, Dublin* 1870

This memorial to a leader of the doomed rising of 1848 was the first monument raised in Dublin to commemorate a person who had stood for armed resistance to British rule in Ireland: a traitor, as the authorities would see it.

National Library of Ireland (Lawrence Collection)

command allegiance they must first be created in the public mind. As Michael Walzer observes, 'the state is invisible; it must be personified before it can be seen, symbolised before it can be loved, imagined before it can be conceived.'[3] Public monuments are ideally suited to this process. Not only can they serve as dramatic symbols of the state, but by their occupation of public spaces, their three-dimensionality and often their sheer bulk, they impose the ideals and aspirations that they represent on the public consciousness in a way that other cultural signifiers cannot. 'Unlike words on a page, always gesturing at something beyond the ink and paper giving them form,' says James Young, 'memorial icons seem to embody ideas, inviting viewers to mistake material presence and weight for immutable permanence.'[4]

Ironically, the qualities that make public statuary so valuable in building support for established regimes also make them useful to groups who seek the overthrow of such regimes. Monuments can sometimes be used to challenge the legitimacy of governments and to objectify the ideals of revolutionary movements.[5] Late Victorian and Edwardian Ireland provides a good example of an attempt to do precisely this. In the half-century leading up to World War I, nationalists erected some forty monuments to honour people and events that represented resistance to British rule. Compared with the magnitude of statumania elsewhere, this was a negligible achievement, and was made worse by the modest size and mediocre quality of most of these memorials. Nevertheless, they sprang from impulses no less powerful than those at work in other countries, and their design, construction and consecration consumed the attentions and energies of Irish nationalists and the public at large to a degree that historians have not fully appreciated. So little have they been regarded, in fact, that as recently as 1975 one scholar could remark: 'before 1921 there was no body of [Irish] art which could be described as unequivocally supporting extreme nationalism...[and] far from there being anything which could be described as a nationalistic art in any strict sense, it seems that there is hardly any art which could be described as nationalistic in any sense.'[6]

This chapter examines some of the means by which public monuments were used to express nationalist aspirations and to transmit political ideas. It is mainly concerned with the way in which symbolism and ritualistic devices were employed to further these ends, particularly in the years around the turn of the century, when statumania in Ireland was at its peak. This was also a time when nationalist politics were in a state of transformation and rejuvenation following a decade of drift and disillusionment. The present study suggests that there was a close correlation between the two developments and that patriotic monuments both reflected and gave shape to a new nationalism that was emerging in the early twentieth century. Before discussing these matters, it would be helpful to examine the history of nationalist monuments in Ireland and to understand what their sponsors believed they could accomplish by building them.

IRISH NATIONALIST MONUMENTS

The first calls to erect patriotic memorials came, not surprisingly, from the ranks of the Young Ireland movement in the early 1840s. *The Nation* newspaper often alerted its readers to monument-building activities in other countries and welcomed the day when such structures would be erected in Ireland. 'The time is coming,' the paper predicted in 1843,

> when, in the streets of Dublin, we will have monuments to Irish patriots, to Irish soldiers and to Irish statesmen. We have now statues to William the Dutchman, to the four Georges — all either

IRELAND: ART INTO HISTORY

German by birth or German by feeling — to Nelson, a great admiral, but an Englishman; while not a single statue of any of the many celebrated Irishmen whom their country should honour adorns a street or square of our beautiful metropolis.[7]

All discussions of monument building in the early 1840s were soon swept aside by the Famine and the social and economic dislocations that followed. It was not until 1862 that nationalists raised the first public statue to a patriotic figure. This was, appropriately enough, the monument to Daniel O'Connell in Ennis, County Clare, which commemorated his famous election victory there in 1828. Two years later, the foundation stone was laid at the bottom of Sackville Street in Dublin of what would become the imposing monument to O'Connell by John Henry Foley and Thomas Brock. A third monument to 'The Liberator' soon went up in Limerick, and another (never built) was planned for Cork.[8]

When, in 1870, a monument was unveiled in Dublin to William Smith O'Brien, a leader of the 1848 uprising (Illus 7.1), the event was said to mark the beginning of a new epoch in Irish history. For the first time since the Act of Union, a monument was raised on a Dublin street to a political figure who represented armed resistance to British rule. This in itself demonstrated Ireland's fitness for self-government for, as John Martin put it at the unveiling ceremony: 'free peoples erect such monuments as this, and only such — monuments to honour the memory of men ... who were loyal to the national cause of their country.'[9]

7.2 *Henry Grattan memorial, College Green, Dublin* 1876, John Henry Foley (1818–74)

Foley's bronze of the parliamentary leader Henry Grattan — leading opponent of the Act of Union — is conventional, but was highly acclaimed: perhaps because by 1876 Grattan's policies seemed to offer something to a wide spectrum of political views.

National Library of Ireland (Lawrence Collection)

The next few years saw other nationalist memorials erected, the most impressive being Foley's statue of Henry Grattan in Dublin (Illus 7.2). The bronze effigy was unveiled in College Green in January 1876 to almost universal praise for its artistic merits and — because Grattan represented a somewhat ambiguous brand of nationalism — its appeal to a broad range of political groups. The same could not be said of two memorials raised outside Dublin in the late 1870s. In 1876, nationalists in Mayo dedicated Ireland's first monument to the insurgents of 1798, in the form of a Celtic cross at French Hill outside Castlebar. A similar memorial was put up two years later at Ballytracy near Boolavogue, County Wexford, to commemorate Father John Murphy and the rebels of '98. But these monuments were not universally popular. Both of them were financed mainly through local contributions and, even then, they received only limited support.

Nationalists hoped to commemorate other figures with public memorials during the 1870s — among them Robert Emmet and Thomas Davis — but most of these projects languished either from lack of funds or poor management. As the Famine had done three decades earlier, the onset of the Land War and the tumultuous events of the 1880s brought monument-building to a virtual standstill.[10] The most notable statues of Irish figures to appear in the 1880s were the products of subscription campaigns launched years earlier. These were the Patrick Sarsfield statue in Limerick (1881) and the O'Connell monument in Dublin (1882). The O'Connell monument was the most outstanding example of public statuary erected in Ireland during this period (Illus 7.3). It was also the most popular: its unveiling in August 1882 brought together probably the largest crowd to assemble in Dublin during the nineteenth century.[11]

To many nationalists, however, such isolated instances of public support for monuments betrayed a general unwillingness to venerate dead heroes with statuary. 'In Ireland we are not a statue-building people', *The Nation* lamented in 1888, 'few of our immortals live either in stone or bronze.'[12] In point of fact, there were approximately fifty public, open-air monuments

7.3 *Daniel O'Connell memorial,*
O'Connell Street, Dublin 1882, John
Henry Foley (1818–74)
Foley's memorial to the Liberator,
Daniel O'Connell, with its attendant
angels and supporting figures, is one
of his most impressive works; its
unveiling in 1882 drew the largest
crowd ever seen in central Dublin in
the nineteenth century.

to political and military figures around the country by the close of the 1880s (excluding a handful of Fenian memorials in graveyards), of which eight were explicitly identified with nationalists. Only two of these — Foley's statues of Grattan and O'Connell in Dublin — compared favourably with political memorials in other countries. Most of the rest were modest in size, off the beaten track, and little regarded outside their localities.

At a time of unbridled statumania in the rest of Europe, Ireland's scarcity of patriotic monuments was a source of embarrassment to many nationalists. Even primitive peoples appeared to surpass the Irish when it came to honouring dead patriots. 'Away up in the north', remarked one observer,

> the Laplanders construct a pile of lichen and snow ... and place it over the remains of their worthy dead... By the banks of their colossal rivers, the American indians plant the weeping willow or the shroud-like Cypress tree around the last resting place of the brave. All times, all nations have honoured their illustrious sons and guarded with a particular veneration their hallowed graves. Shall we alone be ungrateful? To our work, gentlemen, to our work![13]

Ireland's comparative lack of nationalist statuary was made worse by the presence of so many monuments to British military figures around the country. Writers and orators from the 1840s onwards pointed repeatedly to the large number of memorials raised to the memory of British statesmen and soldiers — 'men who had been sent over to slaughter Irishmen' as one of them put it — and, by contrast, to the mere handful of memorials to Irish heroes.[14]

It was not until the closing years of the nineteenth century that nationalists seized upon an opportunity to rectify this imbalance. The 1890s witnessed a growing popular interest in Ireland's history and traditions. It was also a time of disenchantment with Irish parliamentary leaders who, following the death of Parnell, seemed more intent upon waging factional war than on achieving Home Rule. Consequently, many turned to Ireland's past for guidance, and there discovered exemplary heroes whose public veneration seemed long overdue. 'Ireland was appealing to the past to escape the confusion of the present' was W B Yeats's judgment of the popular mood at this time.[15]

In Dublin, Belfast, Cork and a few larger towns, clubs sprang up whose main purpose was to erect monuments to Irish worthies and to stage pilgrimages to places of patriotic significance.[16] By the close of the 1890s, all of these groups joined in planning the most spectacular commemorative event of the nineteenth century — the centenary of the 1798 Rebellion, when the United Irishmen under Wolfe Tone rose up against British rule in Ireland. This year-long indulgence in patriotism and anglophobia was, in its scope and intent, an unprecedented phenomenon. By the time it was over, hundreds of thousands of people in towns and villages across the country had participated in marches and celebrations of all kinds in honour of the rebels of 1798. Only the monster meetings of Daniel O'Connell's repeal campaign and the public gatherings connected with the Land League had brought so many people together for a single purpose over such a long period.[17]

The centenary was more than a colourful celebration; it was also a unique experiment in mass education. It aimed to fix in the public mind an image of Ireland's revolutionary heritage through parades and speeches, books and pamphlets, songs and plays, and, above all, through memorial statuary. In fact, the main goal of the centenary movement was to erect an enormous statue of Theobald Wolfe Tone in a prominent location in Dublin. Though it was never completed, the dedication of its foundation stone at the top of Grafton Street was the central event of the centennial year.[18] Almost as many people turned out for this ceremony as had attended the unveiling of the O'Connell monument a decade and a half earlier. Other communities followed Dublin's lead by putting up monuments of their own over the next decade. Altogether, the centenary produced some thirty memorials in various locations around the country. This was the most concentrated outpouring of commemorative statuary that Ireland had ever seen. Some hoped it was the beginning of a trend. 'When we have done with 1798, we must go back to 1782,' urged one enthusiast,

> from that to 1641 and back still to the days of the Irish kings. No better outcome of the present movement could we secure . . . than the formation throughout Ireland of an association for the erection throughout the length and breadth of Ireland, of monuments to commemorate the great events of Irish history in the places where they severally belong.[19]

Statue-building on such a scale never came about, and within a decade people were asking whether monuments played any useful role in the struggle for national independence. Looking back on the results of the '98 centenary from the perspective of 1906, some members of the newly formed party, Sinn Féin, concluded that the movement to put up monuments had been a 'mistaken policy' and a colossal waste of money and energy. What Ireland now needed, they declared, were more direct methods of obtaining the national goal.[20] By the eve of World War I, the attentions of nationalists were fixed upon more pressing matters than erecting statues. Monument-building in Ireland would have to wait until the events of 1914–22 spawned a new generation of heroes worthy of commemoration.

SYMBOLISM AND PURPOSE

What did nationalists hope to gain from putting up monuments? First, they believed that public effigies of Irish patriots would show the world that resistance to British rule thrived in Ireland. When Dublin's O'Connell monument was unveiled in 1882, for example, one newspaper noted with satisfaction how future visitors to the city would soon be able to stand in the middle of Carlisle Bridge and grasp the essence of Irish history simply by contemplating the statue of 'a Convict [O'Connell] and a Traitor [William Smith O'Brien] on either hand!' Monuments such as these, the paper concluded, preached to everyone 'a lesson of the indomitable spirit of an unconquerable people'.[21]

By the close of the century, the need for such statues seemed greater than ever: the chances of obtaining Home Rule appeared to be remote, the Irish Parliamentary Party was in disarray, and the policies of constructive unionism showed signs of making headway with the general public. To make matters worse, enthusiastic Dubliners turned out in their thousands in 1897 to celebrate that grand apotheosis of the new imperialism, Queen Victoria's diamond jubilee. To concerned nationalists, an obvious remedy presented itself: demonstrations and patriotic statuary would prove that, despite appearances, separatist ideals still lived among the Irish. To one centenary organiser, the whole idea of staging a mammoth celebration in Dublin to lay the foundation stone of the Tone monument was to overshadow the unionist displays of the jubilee year and to show that the heart of the country remained nationalist.[22] The statue itself, declared another, was meant to serve as a public symbol 'in one of the leading thoroughfares of Dublin of the undying attachment of the Irish people to the idea of Irish Nationality ... They

7.4 *1798 memorial, Enniscorthy, County Wexford* 1907, Oliver Sheppard (1864–1941)

The centenary of the rising of 1798 generated many memorials, of which this may be the finest: the rebel priest Father Murphy is shown urging a young insurgent towards distant horizons.

wanted the English visitor to realise when he looked at the statue the determination of the Irish people to rule their own finances and their own affairs'.[23] It was almost with a sense of relief, therefore, that the *United Irishman* newspaper greeted the completion of the first '98 monuments as 'symbols of the return to sense and patriotism' that would save the country. If Ireland were ever to taste liberty, the paper concluded, 'only the spirit which urges the erection of these memorials will gain it for her.'[24]

Nationalists also believed that memorials to dead heroes could teach the country's youth priceless lessons in history. As one monument promoter contended: 'in [the] absence of the systematic teaching of our country's history in the schools, these monuments will be to the child the illustrations of a portion of our national story.'[25] This theme was sometimes embodied in monuments themselves. One design for the proposed Wolfe Tone monument in Dublin depicted a kneeling drummerboy offering Tone a laurel branch, as another boy, gripping a musket, looked expectantly toward the rebel leader.[26] Oliver Sheppard's fine bronze memorial in Enniscorthy, County Wexford, (1907), portrays the insurgent commander, Father Murphy, directing the gaze of a teenage rebel toward a distant objective (Illus 7.4). It is impossible to know how contemporary young people responded to such a statue, but its design suggests the hopes and fantasies of the adults who built it. Here was the materialisation of many a nationalist's dream: that, in the words of one of them, 'the contemplation of such monuments as this may persuade some young Irishmen "to scorn delights and live laborious days" for ... the salvation of their country.' Monuments, after all, were not ends in themselves, as nationalists never tired of pointing out, but means to spur the youth of Ireland into action on behalf of the national cause.[27]

Finally, patriotic monuments were considered to be proof of Ireland's readiness for self-government; tickets of admission to the select club of independent nation-states. This belief was restated in different ways over the succeeding decades. It was implied when nationalist newspapers drew the attention of their readers to statue-building activities in other countries and it was emphasised repeatedly in print and from speakers' platforms whenever new monuments went up. Michael Davitt's comments at the unveiling of a statue in 1905 were typical: 'monuments and memorials', he said, 'are erected in almost every land in honour of those who have deserved well of their country and of their race, and we in common with other people ... are only obeying the impulse of our ... national duty.'[28] Such statements contained an obvious corollary: if the Irish people did not pay sufficient tribute to their fallen heroes, the world would judge them to be unfit for self-government. Every patriot was obliged to honour Ireland's martyrs, claimed Yeats at the time of the '98 centenary, otherwise they would reveal themselves to be a defeated and discredited people.[29]

'LIVING' MEMORIALS

Once monuments were raised, they became reference points in the physical and mental landscape of the communities that built them. They occupied 'sacred spaces' — locations that were effectively nationalist territory. As such, they were incorporated into separatist rituals and became the centrepieces of patriotic demonstrations. Thus, the night that news of the rescue of the Fenian prisoners from Freemantle prison in western Australia reached Dublin in the summer of 1876, a few hundred Fenian supporters paraded with torches through the centre of the city. Beginning at the site of Robert Emmet's execution in Thomas Street, the marchers followed a brass band to College Green, where they made a circuit around the Grattan statue, then headed north to circle the Smith O'Brien monument, before they burned Prime Minister Disraeli in effigy on the north quays.[30] In time, other nationalist memorials regularly served as the focal points of mass meetings or saluting bases for parades.[31]

Once the foundation stone of the Wolfe Tone monument was laid in Dublin in 1898, it figured prominently in many public activities. Wreath-laying ceremonies took place there every year on Tone's birthday. The site also served as the starting point for most of Dublin's nationalist marches. Whatever the occasion — the Parnell and Manchester Martyrs parades every autumn, anti-Boer War marches, the Robert Emmet centenary celebration in 1903, and parades connected with the dedication of other nationalist monuments — all began from the foundation stone. Others, such as the massive funeral procession for Jeremiah O'Donovan Rossa in 1915, made a special point of filing past the stone. They did so in order to forge a symbolic link between each of these events and the separatist ideals that the Tone memorial symbolised.[32]

THE SITING OF MONUMENTS

One of the main concerns of those who organised the building of monuments was where to place them after they were completed. Symbolic considerations weighed heavily in the selection of monument sites. It was essential to erect them in the busiest parts of towns, such as market squares, heavily travelled bridges and the junctions of major streets, so that the ideas they represented received the widest possible exposure. In Dublin, where a comparatively large number of statues competed for attention, this sometimes led to disputes between unionists and nationalists over favoured sites. Selecting ideal locations for monuments could be no less troublesome in provincial towns. The building of the '98 monument in New Ross was delayed for nearly a decade because local nationalists were adamant that it be placed in a central square and not, as some civic officials insisted, on a side street or in a suburb.[33]

Organisers of the Tone memorial in Dublin deliberated for months over a number of possible locations. Some of the places they considered were blatantly provocative, such as the junction of Lord Edward Street and Cork Hill, immediately facing the main guard gate of Dublin Castle. Others were situated in or near symbolic centres such as College Green, where Ireland's parliament once sat and where nationalists were determined it would sit again.[34] The spot they finally chose at the top of Grafton Street had a number of advantages: it was close to College Green, it bisected a major intersection and — most important — it lay in the heart of unionist Dublin. In this section of the city more than in any other, the signs of British domination abounded. Here were such loyalist landmarks as Trinity College, the Kildare Street Club and, as one writer put it, streets populated by 'the essenced tailors and mantua-makers' who served Dublin Castle. During royal visits and on the queen's birthday, this part of Dublin wallowed in red bunting and Union Jacks, but on nationalist holidays green flags were rarely seen.[35] By raising a large statue of Wolfe Tone in the centre of this, the most English part of the capital, nationalists were seizing a symbolic foothold in loyalist territory and issuing a challenge to the country's rulers.[36] They could have easily placed the Tone monument in one of the so-called 'Irish parts' of Dublin, the working-class areas north of the

Liffey or west of College Green, where nationalist support was strongest, but to do so would have diminished its symbolic potency.

When nationalists subsequently used the monument site as the starting point for demonstrations and as a place of annual pilgrimage, they made their challenge even more pointed. Parading through the middle of unionist Dublin on their way to or from the foundation stone became a metaphor for revolutionary action. As John Berger reminds us:

> A mass demonstration can be interpreted as the symbolic capturing of a city or capital... The demonstrators interrupt the regular life of the streets they march through or of the open spaces they fill. They 'cut off' these areas, and, not yet having the power to occupy them permanently, they transform them into a temporary stage on which they dramatise the power they still lack... Demonstrations express political ambitions before the political means necessary to realise them have been created.[37]

In this context, it is worth noting the language that the press sometimes used to describe nationalist demonstrations, especially those connected with the Tone monument. The 'ranks of marching men' who comprised the parades were 'armies' or at least 'men who would make splendid soldiers'; they 'occupied' the city and 'completely choked' its traffic.[38]

When choosing monument sites, particularly those connected with the 1798 Rebellion, nationalists frequently tried to pick locations that were as close as possible to the exact spot where the events they commemorated took place. Battlefields and places of martyrdom were natural favourites because they resonated with patriotic sacrifice and could rouse deep emotions. Thus, nationalists in Tullow, County Carlow, considered it essential to place their statue of Father Murphy on the precise spot where he was executed.[39] Mountmellick's '98 monument was raised at the place in Pound Street where eleven United Irishmen had been hanged. Wexford chose its ancient market square, the Bull Ring, as the place to erect the town's '98 monument because of its many historic associations (Illus 7.5). This was where the town's medieval market cross once stood, where Cromwell's men had slaughtered Irishmen in 1649, and where insurgents had fought and died in 1798.[40]

When monuments could not be placed on sacred spots, parts of sacred spots could sometimes be brought to monuments, and a symbolic link forged in the process. Enniscorthy nationalists were refused permission to erect their '98 memorial on the battle site of Vinegar Hill, so they settled for the next best thing: they quarried a rock from the hill and made it the foundation stone of the statue, which they eventually erected in the town centre.[41] Likewise, the foundation stone for the Wolfe Tone memorial in Dublin was taken from McArt's Fort on Cave Hill outside Belfast, the scene of the United Irishmen's historic 'compact' in 1795. Other monuments, including the Parnell statue in Dublin and the '98 statue in New Ross, County Wexford, were built around stones taken from places that were connected in some way with those whom they honoured.[42]

Wexford's memorial to the 1798 Rising is placed in the old market square: a killing-ground in several Irish struggles, adding to the emotional significance of the memorial.

National Library of Ireland (Lawrence Collection)

MONUMENTS AS SACRED ICONS

The linkage of monuments with hallowed places is but one example of a general tendency to invest them with religious meaning and to treat them as semi-sacred objects. It was also implied in the language used to describe them. Newspapers and public orators typically referred to them as 'shrines' occupying 'sacred spots' to honour the 'martyrs' who had been 'sacrificed' there. Nationalists in Monasterevin, County Kildare, were said to have made 'an altar of the gibbet' when they placed the town's memorial to Father Prendergast close to the spot where he was hanged. When workmen uncovered a fragment of Wexford's medieval market cross as they dug the hole for the town's '98 statue, it immediately became 'a priceless relic', which one enthusiast recommended be incorporated into the monument itself to make it a reminder of the continuity of patriotic martyrdom in Ireland. During a debate among New Ross nationalists over the best location for the town's '98 monument, one speaker predicted that if it were erected at the Three Bullet Gate, where the rebels had won their greatest victory, 'people would kneel down to it and pray'.[43]

The treatment of monuments as quasi-religious icons had a commercial dimension as well. One Belfast jeweller bought up pieces of the Tone foundation stone that were left over after it had been chiselled to shape. These patriotic relics were immediately carved, polished and mounted onto shamrock-shaped scarf pins, harp-shaped brooches and Celtic cross pendants, and sold nationwide. By the turn of the century it was possible to purchase photographs and postcards of nationalist monuments similar to those of holy shrines, churches and cathedrals.[44]

CEREMONIES AND RITUALS

The veneration of memorials as semi-sacred objects was also apparent in the symbolism and rituals that surrounded their formal dedications. These followed the general form of various ceremonies that were familiar to most Catholics in Ireland and included the rites connected with the dedication of stone memorials in churchyards to honour popular priests, the raising of mission crosses at the conclusion of parish missions and, as discussed below, funerals. The general resemblance between these ceremonies and those involved in dedicating nationalist monuments made the latter all the more familiar and stimulating.[45]

When a community erected a monument, it did so in two stages. First, it dedicated the foundation stone in a large public ceremony. Besides being an act of consecration, this event was supposed to drum up support for the monument project and encourage people to contribute money for its completion. It also provided a chance to exhibit civic pride and to demonstrate the intensity of nationalist support. Once the statue was built and paid for — something that could take anywhere from a year to nearly two decades — the community held a second ceremony to unveil the sculpture. Such occasions always attracted huge crowds: the dedication ceremonies of the Tone and O'Connell monuments reportedly drew one hundred thousand and two hundred thousand people respectively. These were among the largest demonstrations to take place in Dublin prior to World War I. Even in small towns, monument unveilings were accompanied by colourful parades, elaborate street decorations and spectacular night-time displays of fire and light. Many of them generated crowds in the tens of thousands.[46]

Every dedication ceremony required months of planning and organisation; some were carefully orchestrated and displayed a remarkable degree of attention to symbolic details. This was best illustrated in the ritualism connected with the laying of the foundation stone of the Wolfe

7.6 The procession to lay a foundation stone for a Wolfe Tone memorial, Dublin 1898

An enormous crowd followed the foundation stone for Theobald Wolfe Tone's memorial through central Dublin, and the city centre virtually closed for the day: though the memorial was never completed on its planned site at the top of Grafton Street.

Tone monument in Dublin in August 1898. Certain of the features of this event are worthy of attention because they illustrate some of the ways in which sponsors of monuments manipulated symbols and rituals to generate public support.

The Dublin commemoration ceremonies actually began in Belfast, where the stone originated. This was a practical act that had symbolic overtones. The political and sectarian make-up of Belfast made it impossible for local nationalists to erect their own commemorative monuments. Donating part of the Tone statue, however, gave them a sense of shared ownership in a memorial icon that was meant to be the most important in Ireland. The stone was also a reminder of the role Belfast had played in the revolutionary events of the 1790s; taking it from Cave Hill linked it directly with Tone, Thomas Russell and the other United Irish leaders.

After it was quarried, finished and inscribed ('1798. Tribute to Theobald Wolfe Tone, Patriot. Belfast Nationalists '98 Centenary Association. 1898'), the granite block received a send-off to Dublin that was worthy of an eminent dignitary. On the day of its departure it was paraded through west Belfast on an elaborately decorated lorry, behind which trooped some twelve thousand people with marching bands and banners. At a colourful dedication ceremony on Divis Street, nationalist leaders gave it their blessings and sent it officially on its way. It was carefully loaded on a train that carried it to Dublin. There, a delegation from the National Centenary Committee waited to escort it to the site of the old Newgate Prison on Harcourt Street, where it lay in state for two nights alongside another foundation stone — that of a monument to the Sheares brothers and other patriots who had died in the prison.[47]

On Monday, 15 August — 'Wolfe Tone Day' as it was popularly called — Dublin officially shut down for the dedication ceremony.[48] That morning the stone was taken from its resting place, lifted aboard a specially decorated lorry, and transported to O'Connell Street behind three bands and costumed members of the Irish National Foresters. It then took its place at the head of an enormous procession that moved solemnly through the city to the monument site (Illus 7.6). In the parade were scores of dignitaries, nearly eighty bands, costumed figures on horseback, and hundreds of banners bearing patriotic slogans and paintings of '98 heroes and battle scenes. Marchers and spectators alike wore badges of green, white and orange; many sported oak leaves or sprigs of ivy taken from Tone's gravesite in County Kildare or heather from Cave Hill. Flags, banners and decorative arches of evergreen lined the route of the procession, and for the first time in years a green flag fluttered from Nelson's Pillar. It was the largest public gathering in Dublin since the unveiling of the O'Connell monument in 1882, and it represented the greatest public celebration of revolutionary nationalism that Ireland had ever seen.

The parade route was chosen solely for its symbolic and instructional value. As one reporter observed, organisers could easily have taken the procession on a more direct itinerary and through wider streets, 'but everything had to give way to claims of historical association . . . and the official route, if long and complex, had . . . the advantage of bringing the processionists into close proximity to many spots of intense interest'.[49] These spots included Tone's birthplace, the building where his body lay after his death, and the site of Robert Emmet's execution.

The mammoth procession took nearly three hours to cover the three-mile route. When it arrived at the north-west corner of St Stephen's Green for the dedication rites, its numbers swelled to a reported one hundred thousand, as it merged with the crowd already gathered

Below

7.7 1798 memorial, Ballina, County Mayo

Ballina's 1798 memorial, instead of a pikeman, presents a symbolic figure of Ireland, which may also be seen as having religious associations.

Opposite top

7.8 1798 memorial, Dundalk, County Louth

In the Dundalk memorial, the religious association of the figure of Erin is made explicit as she holds a cross; the memorial also bears a harp device.

Opposite bottom

7.9 1798 memorial, Thurles, County Tipperary

The Thurles memorial is an unambiguous image of militancy: a boy-soldier bearing a flag and a short sword, seemingly calling his comrades forward.

there. John O'Leary, the aging Fenian and veteran of two uprisings, performed the ceremonial laying of the stone. Before doing so, he drew attention to the way that his very presence in the ceremony represented a living link between the present and the rebels of 1867, 1848 and, by implication, 1798. He was then handed an ornate trowel, the gift of Tone's granddaughter in America who, before she sent it to Ireland, had as many of the patriot's direct descendants as possible place their hands upon it.[50] When O'Leary had finished, he slowly tapped the trowel on the stone six times: once for each of Ireland's four provinces, once for the United States and once for France. Then, at a signal from the platform, a band struck up the theme song of the centenary, 'The Memory of the Dead'. As they began to play, members of the crowd removed their hats and stood silently or sang the well-known lyrics that began, 'Who fears to speak of '98?'

In the intricacy of its rituals and in its focus on specific symbolism, the Tone monument dedication represented a new departure in the staging of mass demonstrations in Ireland. Previous events of this kind — even those connected with the O'Connell monument in Dublin — paid far less attention to ceremony and symbolic detail.

FUNERARY SYMBOLISM

Another distinguishing feature of the Tone monument dedication was its conspicuous use of funerary symbolism. Can the role of the foundation stone be understood as anything other than that of an ersatz coffin in an ersatz funeral? How else can we interpret the veneration that the stone engendered, its public lying in state (a common feature of most nationalist funerals), its place at the head of a solemn procession that slowly wound its way along a circuitous route to the final resting place?[51] Such an overt use of funeral symbols, which also characterised '98 monument dedications in smaller towns, was perhaps unique to Ireland. The reasons for this are not hard to find. They had to do with the political affiliations of the people who planned these events and, most important, with the cultural environment of nineteenth-century Ireland.

Almost without exception, the groups that sponsored '98 monuments were dominated by members of the Irish Republican Brotherhood (IRB), a society that, if nothing else, knew how to stage memorial services. Every November since 1868 the Fenians had organised mass demonstrations to commemorate the executions of the Manchester Martyrs — three IRB members who had been involved in the rescue of IRB prisoners from a prison in Manchester, during which a policeman was shot dead. These typically took the form of mock funerals or solemn marches through the middle of towns and cities to a graveyard. By the 1870s, the IRB began putting up Celtic crosses over the graves of their compatriots. They also poured enormous energy into producing spectacular funerals for their more illustrious dead. When they took on the task of erecting monuments, therefore, they reverted instinctively to the symbols and rituals they knew the best: those of burial and bereavement.[52]

These were also symbols and rituals that were easily deciphered by the Irish people because they were so well acquainted with them. Ireland, it has been said, is 'one of the most funeral conscious countries in the world'.[53] In fact, as Nina Witoszek has argued, the defining characteristic of modern Irish culture is its preoccupation with death. At the heart of Irish culture lies an elaborate funerary code, what Witoszek calls a *theatrum mortis* or 'theatre of the dead', with its wakes, funerals and other rites of death. When, at the turn of the century, republicans began to commemorate the patriot dead with monuments, it was only natural that they presented them in a metaphorical context that was both familiar and powerful. Monument dedications — along with funerals of nationalist heroes, demonstrations at the graves of patriots and, eventually, hunger strikes and executions — became, in Witoszek's words, 'political performances re-enacting the Irish Way of the Cross and providing a medium for national catharsis'.[54]

Many of the monuments themselves reflected the funerary code. A number of '98 monuments were merely large Celtic crosses which, apart from their size, inscriptions and the addition of a few patriotic symbols, were indistinguishable from the kind of tombstones found in most Irish graveyards. Other monuments, such as that in Ballina, County Mayo, featured statues of the figure Erin that were akin to the familiar cemetery effigies of the Virgin Mary (Illus 7.7). The '98 memorials at Monasterevin, Dundalk and Sligo, combined these two images by showing Erin clasping a crucifix or standing beside a Celtic cross (Illus 7.8). At Skibbereen in County Cork, a buxom Erin rests one hand on a Celtic cross, a harp at her feet, while her other hand presses a cluster of shamrocks to her heart.

MILITARY SYMBOLISM

If funerary symbolism predominated on '98 monuments, a hitherto unfamiliar theme is also obvious on many of them: a celebration of armed resistance. Until the 1890s, the subjects of public statuary in Ireland had been monarchs, statesmen, ecclesiastics and other dignitaries, all depicted in static, idealised poses. With the turn of the century a new theme appeared that was at once more aggressive and egalitarian. Erin, a symbol that artists had traditionally represented as a melancholic maiden leaning despondently on her harp, was suddenly transformed into a war-like goddess. On '98 monuments she was sometimes upright and marching, one arm wrapped around a flag bearing the motto '1798', or clasping a sword and flanked by pikes (Illus 7.7 & 7.8).[55] Other memorials to the rebellion, such as those of Thurles, County Tipperary (Illus 7.9), Wexford (Illus 7.5) and Wicklow (Illus 7.10) typically depicted determined-looking peasant soldiers armed with pikes, daggers or muskets. In monuments such as those at Colooney and Arklow (Illus 7.11), rebel leaders beckoned to unseen armies to follow, or, like the statue in New Ross, an anonymous insurgent raised a clenched fist in defiance (Illus 7.12).

Many welcomed this new militancy in memorial symbolism. 'The statue to be erected to Tone [in Dublin] will be no pensive figure', predicted one newspaper in 1898,

> no symbol in bronze of the sorrows of Erin. It will be typical of all that is combative in our race. It will be the figure of a Soldier of Freedom, erect and proud, the embodiment of all that is courageous and bold in a nation that has borne more sorrows and suffered more injuries than any other, and — Lives.[56]

When John Redmond and some of his supporters suggested erecting a one-hundred-foot round tower on Vinegar Hill to honour the rebel dead of 1798, advanced nationalists condemned the project for its ambiguous, if not pacifist symbolism. One of them pointed out that in Glasnevin Cemetery a similar round tower marked the grave of Daniel O'Connell,

> a man who said that liberty was not worth a drop of blood. Why should a like emblem rear its head to honour the memory of patriots who believed that liberty was worth the best blood in the veins of the people, and who shed it in torrents to show that they inherited the instincts of

7.10 *1798 memorial, Wicklow*

Wicklow's memorial combines the two strands of imagery: above, a young farm-boy with a pike waves farewell to his family; below, a Celtic cross and wolfhound flank the pensive figure of Erin bearing a laurel wreath. The tone of this memorial is notably less militaristic than most others.

National Library of Ireland (Lawrence Collection)

7.11 *1798 memorial, Arklow*

The well-executed figure of an armed rebel urging his unseen supporters forward.

freemen?…Vinegar Hill is worthy of a monument which shall be symbolic of civic heroism, and which shall speak from the past to the present and the future with an eloquence to sustain the courage of the patriot and shame the submission of the slave.[57]

Aggressive symbolism was only to be expected on monuments that commemorated armed rebellion. But its appearance and, more important, its public acceptance, also reflected a growing spirit of militarism that was evident throughout the British Isles from the 1880s onward.[58] The militant imagery displayed on '98 monuments was, in part, an Irish manifestation of this phenomenon. As in Britain, it found expression in other forms of popular culture such as quasi-military youth groups, juvenile literature, cheap novels, drama and poetry written for newspapers.[59]

IMPACT AND INFLUENCE

It is impossible to measure popular responses to nationalist monuments with any precision. As we have seen, they were capable of generating enormous and enthusiastic crowds for their dedications. Thousands of people in scores of localities devoted extensive amounts of energy, time and money to their construction. Most of the communities that raised these memorials regarded them with pride and incorporated them into civic activities. As we have also seen, their acceptance and popularity was often enhanced by the rituals and symbolic devices that accompanied their design and consecration.

But monuments were not without their detractors. Nearly all of the ones that commemorated the '98 Rebellion were condemned at one time or another for their artistic shortcomings.[60] Many of their original supporters came to have second thoughts. By 1906, a writer for Sinn Féin denounced the bulk of them as 'abominations' which later generations might justifiably tear down as 'slights to the memory of the men whom they were reared in all their ugliness to commemorate'. Even the revolutionary Maud Gonne, once an enthusiastic proponent of '98 monuments, eventually agreed with Yeats that most of them were simply bad art.[61]

Some critics slighted them for their poor workmanship, but most objected to their design. 'Hardly one of them is an object of real artistic beauty,' sniffed one commentator, 'while several are quite grotesque.'[62] Since Ireland possessed few sculptors of real merit at this time — most nationalist statuary was produced by stonemasons and local craftworkers — such opinions were perhaps to be expected. However, the design of each monument rested ultimately with local sponsors, and their taste, as Gonne observed, was influenced by cemetery monuments and the cheap Italian plaster statues found in most churches.[63] This meant, in other words, lots of Madonna-like figures of Erin, stiffly posed rebels and Celtic crosses adorned with shamrocks, harps, wolfhounds, sunbursts and round towers. These were the familiar emblems of Irish nationalism, which had been popular for decades but which, by the turn of the century, were falling into disfavour in certain circles. To many in the forefront of Ireland's cultural revival, shamrocks and the like represented an outmoded, romantic, English-inspired nationalism.[64] They epitomised what D P Moran condemned repeatedly in the pages of *The Leader* as *raiméis*, or sham patriotism.

Nevertheless, if Moran and others denigrated such symbols, their sheer abundance indicated that the general public liked them. They appealed to popular tastes for the same reasons that the poetry of the Young Irelanders, the histories of A M Sullivan and the novels of Charles

Kickham appealed to nationalist readers. Wolfhounds, harps and figures of Erin, like the monuments they adorned, represented in visual form the traits and preoccupations of what D G Boyce has termed the 'Davisite' tradition in literature (after Thomas Davis). This tradition, as distinct from the Anglo-Irish and Gaelic literary movements, emphasised romanticism and sentimentality. It argued that literature should serve as the handmaiden of politics and that it could best do this in the English language.[65]

The Davisite tradition enjoyed a massive following, particularly among small landowners and the urban middle classes. It came to dominate the political culture of Ireland because it articulated the tastes and self-images of the majority of the Irish people.[66] Patriotic memorials spoke the same language as popular nationalist literature, albeit in symbolic form. They were Davisism in stone and bronze. Monuments and the rituals that accompanied them were no less important than histories, poems, novels, songs and plays, in constructing and articulating a political culture — in inventing, as it were, the idea of an Irish nation.

7.12 *1798 memorial, New Ross, Wexford*
It is notable, and must be significant, that although the 1798 Rising ended in terrible slaughter, not least in New Ross, nearly all the memorial images are of defiance. Here, certainly, there is no hint of regret at the waste of lives.
National Library of Ireland
(Lawrence Collection)

8

Sighle Bhreathnach-Lynch

THE ART OF ALBERT G POWER, 1881–1945: A SCULPTURAL LEGACY OF IRISH IRELAND

*What a true Irishman he was and with what joy his heart was in
any achievement which would bring lustre to the old country.*[1]

On Wednesday, 11 July 1945, a small notice appeared on page seven of *The Times*. It announced simply that 'Mr Albert G Power, sculptor, a member of the Royal Hibernian Academy, died in Dublin yesterday'. On the same day *The Irish Times* published an obituary. It contained a brief biography of the dead man, and the writer concluded 'with him passes one of the most outstanding figures of contemporary Irish art'.[2] Other obituaries were in similar vein. The *Irish Press* stated 'by his death Ireland loses a distinguished sculptor — our greatest since Hogan',[3] and *The Leader*, a strongly nationalist newspaper, proclaimed:

> It is sad to think that this great artist so humble about his genius was taken from us at the age when
> Rodin was beginning his most famous work. Now acknowledged as the greatest sculptor since Hogan
> he has enriched his country by his talents which he gave with a generosity equalled to his patriotism.[4]

The funeral a day later was an impressive one. Aside from his family, relatives and friends, many important dignitaries from the world of art and politics attended. The president of the Royal Hibernian Academy paid his last respects to a fellow academician. So too did Power's peers from the Irish art world, among them the painter Jack B Yeats. The Taoiseach, Éamon de Valera, was present with his minister for post and telegraphs, as was the Lord Mayor of Dublin and a representative from the chief state solicitor's office. A member of the 4th Battalion of the old IRA and the Japanese vice-consul also attended. From this impressive line-up of mourners, it would appear that Albert Power was considered to be a figure of some national importance at the time of his death. Yet within the decade he would be a largely forgotten figure, an artist relegated to brief mentions, if any, by historians of twentieth-century Ireland.

This essay takes a fresh look at Power's career in the context of the great political and social changes that were taking place from the last years of British rule in Ireland to the end of the Second World War. It is this context that is a key factor in revealing not only Power's high artistic standing during his lifetime, but also in explaining his rapid decline in prestige so soon afterwards.

BACKGROUND AND TRAINING

Albert Power was born in Dublin on 16 November 1881. His mother was Mary Atkins, and his father, Henry, a fitter by trade, ran a jewellery and watch-making business. The family, including an older brother and younger sister, lived at 16 Ellis Quay, just off the north city quays, a rather run-down working-class area. As a child, Power showed an inclination to art. A good deal of his time was spent playing in the old clay brickfields near his home, where he modelled portrait heads of his friends in clay.[5] His parents actively encouraged his artistic efforts and allowed him to use the cellar as a studio.[6]

Following a primary education at the Christian Brothers school in North Brunswick Street, the young boy was apprenticed to the carving trade. He spent some years in the workshop of the Smyth family. They were direct descendants of the eighteenth-century sculptor Edward Smyth, who had been employed by the architect James Gandon on his two prestigious Dublin buildings, the Four Courts and the Custom House. As an apprentice, Power acquired the various trade skills, including how to reduce blocks to workable form, lettering, and the carving of sculptural motifs. The scope of Power's training was broadened considerably, however, when in 1894 he enrolled as an evening pupil at the Dublin Metropolitan School of Art, then under the control of the Department of Science and Art, South Kensington, London.

One aspect of the school's training was to be particularly important to Power: life drawing classes. Thus Power acquired 'fine art' skills as well as those needed for the carving trade. He was immensely fortunate in his teachers in this area, who included the distinguished painter Sir William Orpen and the sculptors John Hughes and Oliver Sheppard. Their legacy to Power was to be a stylistic one, and it was their emphasis on a close study of nature that he eagerly embraced. From his earliest student days his progress was impressive, and the annual reports on prizegivings at the school record him as winning many prizes and awards, as well as becoming the Department Art Scholar on three occasions from 1906.[7] By this time he had ceased working full-time for Smyth. Now he taught part-time at the art school and took on odd carving jobs to supplement his income.

From 1906 he began to exhibit publicly with a view to establishing a reputation. The main platform for artists at the time was the Royal Hibernian Academy, which held annual exhibitions in Dublin, and it was to these exhibitions that much of his work was submitted. He did not confine himself to the academy, however. Over the next few years he successfully exhibited at several other venues: the Oireachtas, the Gaelic League, the Arts and Crafts Society, and the

Irish Art Companions, and he took part in the Irish International Exhibition in 1907. Four years later the academy elected him as one of their associate members, a recognition by his fellow artists of his talent and of his achievements to date, which were considerable. Apart from the many prizes and awards he had won, including a gold medal in 1911 for the best sculpture in Ireland, Scotland and the Channel Islands, his work was now attracting favourable notices at the major art exhibitions in Dublin.

Power's years at the School of Art were crucial, not only to the development of his skills as an artist, but to the shaping of his personal artistic beliefs. This was partly as a result of his attending the school during its involvement in the visual aspects of the Celtic Revival. Staff and students participated in important projects, such as the decoration of the Honan Chapel in Cork and Loughrea Cathedral in County Galway. They were also actively involved in the exhibitions of the Irish Arts and Crafts Society, and other organisations such as the Oireachtas and Gaelic League, which were equally keen to promote a distinctively Irish art. This was to have a profound influence on the young student, and his passionately held belief throughout his career that Ireland must develop its own school of art dates from this period. For Power, it would encompass an art of the highest technical quality, using Irish materials where possible, but above all it meant an art produced by those having what he termed a 'national outlook'.[8] He believed that only such artists could treat Irish subjects sympathetically and develop national ideas on appropriate lines.

This view of Irish art was also encouraged by his contact with those teachers and students who were interested in matters nationalistic. Henry Willis, headmaster of the school from 1904 to 1905, was an ardent supporter of the Gaelic League, and enthused the students in everything Irish, including learning the language.[9] Other students were politically active and some would later be involved in the 1916 Rising. The republican Countess Markievicz, along with her husband and his son, attended the school in the evenings at one period. So too did Padraig Pearse, whose younger brother Willie was in the same class as Power and was one of his close friends. Indeed on one occasion both young men went to Paris together on a short visit in order to study and experience at first hand the great works of art on display there.[10] Although Power was not directly involved in political activities himself, he would remain a man of strong nationalist sympathies throughout his life.

Early in 1912 Power and his family moved to his permanent home at 18 Geraldine Street, where he set up his own stone-carving business. The scope of this venture was wide. A business calling-card indicates that the firm was prepared to undertake commissions:

> for all monumental and architectural work in marble, stone or bronze. Altars, pulpits, rails, statues and fonts in stone, marble or alabaster, all work done on the premises.

In this decade Power was to be involved in some major architectural sculptural commissions, many arising from the reconstruction of Dublin following the rebellion of 1916. He carved sculptural motifs on several of the buildings in Lower Sackville Street, now O'Connell Street. Most notable perhaps is the impressive relief over the main entrance of the Munster and Leinster Bank, and a series of heads on each face of the freely styled Ionic capitals on its upper façade.

While his association with major architectural commissions secured Power's reputation as an architectural sculptor, he wanted to establish himself in the fine art arena. With this in

IRELAND: ART INTO HISTORY

mind he continued to show his work regularly at the Royal Hibernian Academy, where he attracted favourable comment, particularly for a series of portrait busts and statuettes exhibited between 1911 and 1920. Those portrayed were among the most prominent figures in artistic and literary circles in the city. His sitters included Sir William Orpen's daughters, Mary and Kit, and the artist Mainie Jellett's two younger sisters (Illus 8.1). These commissions probably resulted from Power's close friendship with William Orpen. Orpen was anxious that his student should establish a reputation in London and he tried to convince Power to send some work for public exhibition there. On one occasion he wrote to him saying 'I think I see a chance of doing something good for you here...now hurry up, it may be a good chance for you'.[11] But Power did not grasp the opportunity. He was only interested in furthering his career within Ireland: first because he saw success exclusively in Irish terms, and secondly because he was temperamentally better suited to the slower, easier pace of the Irish art world, where competition was less cut-throat.

Orpen's Dublin contacts were considerable. On his mother's side of the family he was connected to Sir Hugh Lane, the art dealer and benefactor of the National Gallery of Ireland, and

to the playwright Lady Gregory. Lane was a close friend of Power, as was Oliver St John Gogarty, a leading throat surgeon, writer and poet, a man with a keen interest in both the literary and visual arts. Through Orpen, Power became acquainted with these and other major figures of the Literary Revival: AE (George Russell), James Stephens, Lord Dunsany, W B Yeats, Tom Kettle and Arthur Griffith. With the exception of AE, all of these men would become subjects for portraiture by him. Gogarty especially was taken by Power's easy, witty manner, and the two became firm friends. He was also impressed by the artist's obvious talent and was to become his most important patron. Initially this was confined to portraiture, and through him Power was given the opportunity to do portrait busts of Lord Dunsany and W B Yeats (Illus 8.2). Yeats wrote of the experience in a letter dated July 1917: 'I got here [Coole Park] this morning after spending some days in Dublin where a young man called Power made an admirable bust of me', and then he added, perhaps a touch plaintively, 'I look rather humorous and intellectual than poetical'.[12] This bust was exhibited in the 1918 Academy Exhibition, where it received favourable reviews. One critic declared it to be 'full of life', and another saw it as 'an admirable piece of modelling'.[13]

By 1919 Power's artistic achievements were even more fully acknowledged when he became a full member of the Royal Hibernian Academy. *The Irish Builder* noted:

> Mr Power is one of the most promising of Irish sculptors and his exhibits have formed a striking feature of the Academy Exhibitions for several years past being marked by artistic skill and originality.[14]

CARVING AN IRISH IDENTITY

The following year Power's career changed direction, which added another dimension to his growing reputation as a fine artist and a skilled architectural sculptor. In September 1920, at the height of the War of Independence, Power was approached by Gogarty, who asked him to go to Brixton jail in London, where, posing as a visiting relative, the artist was to secretly draw the features of an Irish prisoner who was in his fifth week of a hunger strike. This sketch from life was to provide the basis for a commission — a portrait of the prisoner in marble. The prisoner was Terence MacSwiney, Lord Mayor of Cork, who was to die on hunger strike on 25 October 1920. Gogarty was deeply involved in politics and was a member of the Sinn Féin party.[15] He had been approached by Mary MacSwiney, who was also actively involved in republican politics and was a sister of Terence MacSwiney.[16] She and her family were determined to have an enduring memorial to her brother, now close to death, and she sought Gogarty's advice.

Power duly set off to London with the relatives. On his arrival he was thoroughly searched, but he managed to secrete a small ball of wax between his fingers, and the tiny wooden tools needed for the job, which were in his pocket, were thought by the prison officer searching him to be no more than matchsticks. Conscious of the prison guard watching him closely from the door, he went over to the bedside, knelt down beside the dying man, and while supposedly in conversation with him, he quickly and deftly recorded his features. On his return to Dublin he carved a marble portrait in the form of a life-mask (Illus 8.3).[17]

Power's depiction of the dying man is interesting. By the time Power met him he was thoroughly emaciated, yet the artist chose not to indicate this. Instead the features recall traditional artistic renditions of Christ's features or those of early Christian martyrs. This quasi-religious portrayal reveals how MacSwiney was perceived by the vast majority of Irish people, including Power. They saw in him a victim of English injustice, a hero ready to lay down his life for his principles.

Power's involvement with the project became publicly known after MacSwiney's death, when a photograph of the original plaster and a report on the visit to Brixton appeared in the *Freeman's Journal*.[18] This served to place the artist in the public's mind as a sculptor sympathetic to the nationalist cause. It also made him vulnerable. There was a real danger that the British authorities in Ireland might raid Power's studio looking for the work. In their eyes, MacSwiney represented treachery and disloyalty to the Crown. As a precaution, Power made several copies of the plaster cast. When the marble was completed, it was hidden for a short time in Dublin before being smuggled to Cork and, when it was thought safe, handed over to the MacSwiney family.

In January 1922 a Treaty was signed between England and Ireland, and the pro-Treaty Cumann na nGaedheal party took over the government of Ireland. Within months Power found employment with the new government. His first commission, thanks to Gogarty, who was now a senator, was to execute two portrait busts. One was of Arthur Griffith (Illus 8.4), first president of the new Free State, the other of Michael Collins (Illus 8.5), chairman of the provisional government and commander-in-chief of the national army. Both men were symbols of the new state: Griffith having been prominent in the negotiations for its establishment, and Collins killed defending its right to exist. The speed of the commission may be read as a symbolic act on the part of the Cumann na nGaedheal party to consolidate its insecure political power base by establishing both men as heroes. The destination of the busts was probably the Dáil chamber, where

Opposite

8.2 *W B Yeats* 1918, Bronze on wood base; height 0.36m
A lively bust, full of character; Yeats himself called it admirable, but 'rather humorous and intellectual than poetical'.
From *W B Yeats*, Exhibition of Books and Manuscripts, Trinity College Dublin, 1956

8.3 *Terence MacSwiney* 1920, Marble; height 0.31m
An idealised portrait of the dying patriot, which does not show the degree of emaciation one would expect after a long hunger strike.
Cork Public Museum

8.4 *Arthur Griffith* 1922, Bronze; height 0.67m
A strong lifelike portrayal of the founder of Sinn Féin, companion to the Collins bronze (Illus 8.5).
National Gallery of Ireland (no 8100)

8.5 *Michael Collins* 1936, Bronze; height 0.67m
First shown at the Royal Hibernian Academy, Dublin, in 1936, this bronze of Ireland's lost leader may initially have been intended for display in the Dáil chamber. It lacks the elegiac simplicity of Power's earlier death mask of Collins.
National Gallery of Ireland (no 8070)

8.6 *The Cenotaph, Leinster Lawn* 1923, Timber, plaster, cement; height 12m
Dominated by an outsize Celtic cross, the official state memorial to Arthur Griffith and Michael Collins links the dead heroes with Catholic and Gaelic tradition.
National Library of Ireland (Lawrence Collection)

8.7 *Coinage designs c* 1926, Plaster; from 16cm to 27.5cm in diameter
Power's models for a new Irish coinage are curiously stiff, lacking the fluidity and grace of the successful designs by the Englishman Percy Metcalfe.
From *Coinage Saorstát Éireann*, Dublin 1928

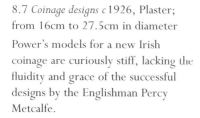

they would serve as a reminder to friend and foe alike that the new state was founded by a party of statesmen of the calibre of Griffith and Collins.

Wishing to commemorate Griffith and Collins in a more public way, the government had a temporary cenotaph set up on Leinster Lawn, in front of Dáil Éireann (the Irish parliament), in 1923, in time to mark the first anniversary of their deaths (Illus 8.6). This consisted of a large Celtic cross with a Gaelic inscription, designed by Professor George Atkinson from the School of Art. Portrait reliefs of both men were set into the base. The reliefs by Power were based on death-masks made by him at Gogarty's request. When viewed in the context of the British monuments placed nearby, those of Queen Victoria and Prince Albert, the cenotaph can be seen to be a celebration of new contemporary Irish heroes, as well as a proclamation of Ireland's independence. The early Irish symbol of a cross with Gaelic inscription can also be interpreted as a declaration of the increasing desire by Irish society to establish a distinctive 'Irish Ireland' identity, one firmly linked to Catholicism and to an ancient and noble pre-conquest past, with its single Gaelic tradition, culture and language.

Power was also involved in another means of declaring a distinctive national identity in this decade: the creation of a new Irish coinage. The new state, anxious to break a further link with Great Britain, decided to produce a separate monetary system. It appreciated that the designs would be of considerable importance: coins are a national as well as an economic symbol. Therefore the imagery settled upon by the government committee was most carefully thought out. It retained only one popular nineteenth-century symbol, the harp, for use on the obverse of each coin. A new iconography was invented in which newly independent Ireland was projected on the reverse of each coin as an agricultural utopia of horse-riding, salmon-fishing and cattle-raising. This concept at once reflected and defined the now dominant ideology: one in which the essential Irish reality was perceived as being located in the unchanging life of the inhabitants of rural Ireland.

Power's designs (Illus 8.7) were not the final choice of the committee (ironically that went to an English sculptor, Percy Metcalfe), but his design for a bronze statuette award for the

Tailteann Games was accepted. These games were held in 1924 and at four-year intervals until 1932. The original Tailteann fair had played an important role in early Irish mythology, being an integral part of the agricultural cycle. Its revival in this period was an enterprising step in attempting to re-establish an even stronger link between the modern state and its ancient past. J J Walsh, the minister behind its promotion, believed that the games would demonstrate to other nation states the determination of the Irish to cling to their roots despite a history of turmoil and upheaval.[19] The secretary of the Gaelic League saw the games as a splendid manifestation of Ireland's culture and nationality.[20]

Power's design of the statuette for the games was appropriate for this kind of cultural ideology (Illus 8.8). He depicted a three-dimensional representation of Queen Tailte, in whose honour the original games had been held. The range of motifs used to describe her apparel can be seen to be a mixture of Celtic designs, generally associated with Irish national identity: a belt containing ogham designs, a Celtic headdress, and a cloak fastened with a brooch based on the famous Tara Brooch. Her regal stance was an expression of an aristocratic race, from which modern Irish society believed itself to have evolved. On the other hand, the relief scenes on the base below, showing nude youths in athletic competition, served as a visual link between these Irish games and those of the Olympiad. Thus Ireland's ancient civilisation was firmly linked to that of ancient Greece.

POWER'S RELIGIOUS ART

The desire in these early post-colonial decades to construct a distinctive Irish identity was not solely confined to the social and political areas of Irish life. Religion, in the form of Roman Catholicism, also contributed in a powerful way: its practices visibly distinguished its members from their Anglo-Saxon neighbours, and historically Catholicism was seen to be truly Irish because its origins lay in an era before the Norman invasion. Although a great deal of religious art was produced in the following decades, much of it was of a decidedly poor artistic quality. Cheap foreign imports of ready-made statuary flooded the home market, and the public seemed content to buy these unoriginal mass-produced works. Artists like Power, when given the opportunity, tried to combat this crass commercialism. An example of this can be seen in Power's carving of a Madonna and Child, placed in the grounds of All Hallows' College, Drumcondra, Dublin (Illus 8.9). The commission came from Fr Tom O'Donnell, president of the seminary, a man with a keen interest in promoting the work of Irish artists. Power was given *carte blanche* in terms of design, and he produced a work that clearly demonstrated his aspiration to promote an easily distinguishable Irish art. He gaelicised the Madonna by depicting her in a Munster cloak, of the type that was presented to young women in this region on their marriage. He also deliberately chose to carve an Irish limestone from Durrow, County Offaly, rather than the popular Italian Carrara marble. The significance of this was drawn out by Fr O'Donnell in his unveiling address, when he reminded his audience that as Durrow was historically associated with early Christian Irish art and Irish saints, this stone was entirely suitable for this most Irish of statues.[21]

At the end of the decade, when another opportunity presented itself to produce quality Irish religious art, Power seized it eagerly. He was asked to design and carve three altars for a small chapel in St Joseph's College, Ballinasloe, County Galway. The patron was Fr Madden, then administrator of the diocese, a man deeply committed to the upgrading of the quality of Irish

8.8 *Queen Tailte statuette* c1924, Bronze; height 0.42m

Made for the revived Tailteann games, a major sporting contest organised by the new Free State, the ancient Irish queen is shown in Celtic dress, while the relief scenes on the base link the event with the ancient Grecian games.

Photograph: David Lynch

church art. He had already involved Power in a major decorative project in the parish church of St Michael in Ballinasloe, County Galway, to which other artists of the stature of Harry Clarke and Mia Cranwill had also contributed. The magnificent works in that church by all concerned are a testimony to the excellence of native Irish artists.

Power's altars in the small chapel at St Joseph's College demonstrated how Irish marbles could be exploited for eye-catching effect at a time when it was considered that their range was too narrow to achieve any kind of colourful results (Illus 8.10).[22] He chose a selection of coloured marbles and then successfully arranged them in a striking way. Stones were chosen from locations that had an historical association with Ireland's Catholic history. For example, Rathlin stone, from which the seven churches of St Ciaran had been built in Clonmacnoise, was used.[23]

When this job was completed, Power went on to other important religious commissions, including the carving of an elaborate memorial to Archbishop Walsh of Dublin, and in the 1930s the carving of the great tympanum of the new cathedral in Mullingar, County Westmeath. He also involved himself in the activities of a Catholic organisation, the Academy of Christian Art, which had been set up in 1929 with the intention of improving the quality of Irish church art. Throughout the next two decades it endeavoured to foster a Catholic religious art through a variety of activities. Members were invited to read papers at its weekly meetings on an array of topics relating to all aspects of the arts.[24] There were illustrated lectures with slides, excursions to places in Ireland associated with Early Christian art, and a collection of illustrations of religious art was made available to members. The academy also published its own journal for a short time. Unfortunately its influence on religious art proved to be a fairly minor one.

THE Ó CONAIRE MONUMENT

The perception of Power as an artist dedicated to an art that sought an Irish form of expression was further confirmed in the public mind when his memorial to the writer Pádraic Ó Conaire was unveiled in Eyre Square, Galway, in June 1935 (Illus 8.11). In 1930 Power had been invited by the Gaelic League to carve the memorial to Ó Conaire, a contemporary writer who had earned his living writing exclusively in the Irish language. Power chose a native limestone for the monument, and from it he carved a full-length seated figure, slightly smaller than life size. Instead of placing him on a plinth, he positioned him on a small mound of stones, symbolic of the stone walls of Connemara. When asked why he had done so by a reporter from *The Leader*, Power explained:

8.11 *Pádraic Ó Conaire monument* c1935, Limestone; height 1.45m
The writer is placed level with the viewer, in a naturalistic setting, emphasising his humanity and simplicity.
Postcard, 1930s

> I chose the old stones of Barna on which Pádraic so often sat during his wanderings. They are the despised stones, like the people the author loved, the common people who for generations were the outcast Gaels. They were his people and it was in them he saw the beauty of Ireland. He wanted no throne of bronze or marble. He would be happy and content with such a resting place, with the view of Galway he loved and the sound of the great bay beyond singing to him.[25]

These words suggest that Power saw certain attractive qualities in the writer: he seems to have regarded him as a gentle, unassuming man, who respected ordinary people, whom many would have considered of little social or political importance, and identified with them in his writings.

ROMANTIC NATIONALISM

Power's view of his creation also gives an indication of his own attitudes to Ireland's history. To him, the ordinary people of Ireland were descendants of 'the outcast Gaels', a dispossessed race. It is this view that informs his design for another monument of this period, a pikeman, unveiled in 1939 in Tralee, County Kerry, by Maud Gonne McBride on behalf of local republican sympathisers (Illus 8.12). It replaced an earlier monument that had been erected as part of the centenary celebrations of the 1798 insurrection, which had been vandalised by the Black and Tans during the War of Independence. The figure of a pikeman represented those peasant leaders who had fought in the '98 Rebellion and it had become the stock design for this kind of monument, which served to remind the Irish people of the past struggle for political self-determination. Power's pikeman however was depicted with one unusual feature: he appeared to stand on large props. In a newspaper article Power explained why this was so:

8.12 *Power working on the Tralee Pikeman* c1938, Limestone; height 2.13m (figure)
Unveiled by Maud Gonne McBride, this tribute to the peasant rising of 1798 was made for a group of republican sympathisers. Power is seen, on the right, working on the statue with his assistants.
Courtesy of Professor John Turpin

> ...this man represents his country, the man who had lost everything. His home has been burnt, everything has been taken away from him. There is nothing remaining to him but the roots of his trees. Yet he is standing on the roots which support his claim to right and justice and faces life sure of conquering. This man is Ireland.[26]

This same kind of romantic nationalist sentiment influenced the design of the Seán Mac Diarmada memorial, unveiled in Kiltyclogher, County Leitrim, in 1940. Mac Diarmada was one of the leaders of the 1916 Rising, and had been executed shortly afterwards. Power was an admirer of Mac Diarmada, and although he had many commissions on hand in the late thirties, he was keen to take on this one. He carved a full-length statue in Irish limestone, depicting the figure in defiant pose awaiting his execution. Mac Diarmada had been injured during the rebellion, and moments before his death was said to have removed the bandage covering his eyes in order to face death directly. This gesture was subsequently interpreted by patriotic Irishmen and women, including Power, as symbolising a 'patriotic idealism and unconquerable tradition'.[27] Around the base of the monument the sculptor cut four rough stones, inscribing on them in Irish the names of the four provinces of Ireland. When queried as to why he had not smoothed or polished the stones, his answer was reported as follows:

> With God's help I will return some day when Mac Diarmada's wish is attained [an independent thirty-two county republic] and I will do a first class job on them. If I die in the meantime I hope someone will carry out both the wishes of Mac Diarmada and myself.[28]

FURTHER POLITICAL COMMISSIONS

The thirties were marked by other commissions, again having a strong political content. For instance, soon after Éamon de Valera's Fianna Fáil party came to power in 1932, Power was requested by it to execute plaques and busts of the dead republican leaders, Cathal Brugha and Austin Stack. In the same way that Collins and Griffith had symbolised the setting up of the state for Cumann na nGaedheal, these two men with their uncompromising republican views, symbolised for the now ruling party the true spirit of republicanism. They were also the heroes of those republicans opposed to de Valera, and when it was learned that Brugha and Stack were being commemorated by the Fianna Fáil party, there were some vehement protests. Cathal Brugha's widow felt strongly that de Valera and his followers had betrayed the republican ideals of her husband by entering the Dáil in 1927. She saw the commemoration of her husband by members of that government as an 'attempt to shelter themselves in the reflected glory of one who died for the republic'.[29] For this reason she forbade Power to use the death-mask of her husband, which he had made when Brugha died, in the preparation of the bust. He was obliged therefore to bow out of the commission, and the government asked Oliver Sheppard to execute the bust of Brugha working from photographs and relying heavily on the memory of those who had known him. Mrs Brugha later allowed Power to execute a portrait of her husband using the mask, but it was a private commission and not for public display (Illus 8.13).

The strength of feeling of the anti-de Valera faction regarding this matter can also be gauged by the events surrounding the renaming of Hammam Buildings in O'Connell Street as Áras Brugha in 1934. This was to mark the bringing of National Health Insurance directly under the control of the state. A plaque with Brugha seen in profile was to be placed over the entrance. Power had duly prepared a plaster plaque and sent it to a local bronze foundry for casting. While there, however, it was stolen by a man who arrived at the premises in a taxi, held up the staff at gunpoint and disappeared with the plaque in his possession. As a result, the renaming of the building had to go ahead without it.[30]

Not all political commissions were government ones. Other republican factions, equally keen to appropriate suitable heroes for their own pantheon of worthy individuals, also erected monuments. What is interesting is that almost without exception they chose Power to carry out the work, in spite of his involvement in government commissions. The main reason for this, aside from the fact that there was only a handful of sculptors in Ireland skilled enough to do this kind of work, was one of artistic style. Power's style was an academic realist one, and

8.13 *Cathal Brugha* 1937, Painted plaster; height 0.67m

This bust was made privately for Brugha's widow, emphasising Power's acceptability to all strands in political life (the Brughas were ardent republicans, at this time opposed both to the Fianna Fáil leader, Éamon de Valera, and to the previous governing party, Cumann na nGaedheal).

Photograph: David Lynch

8.14 *Salmon* 1944, Marble; height 0.48m

An unusual piece which makes impressive use of native Connemara marble, skilfully exploiting its irregularities. The salmon may be seen as a symbol of resurgence.

National Gallery of Ireland (no 8090)

it appealed to the essentially conservative tastes of all Irish political factions. Indeed there was a general distrust of modern art. Conservative Ireland in the twenties and thirties was deeply suspicious of any kind of radical ideas emanating from abroad, and modern art was viewed by many as an alien style, quite inappropriate as the vehicle of expression for the production of a suitable art for the new 'Irish Ireland'.

With this in mind, artists like Power, who themselves distrusted modernist styles, were using a visual language that identified them with the aesthetic demands of most Irish patrons, and this fact helped them to secure employment from a variety of people who would not have seen eye to eye with each other on anything else! One good example of this is that in spite of Power's involvement in monument commissions for republican groups opposed to the Fianna Fáil party in the late thirties, the latter still had no hesitation in choosing him to execute a bust of Thomas Davis, the nineteenth-century poet, journalist and Young Irelander, to mark the centenary of his death. When completed, it was placed in the Dáil.

In spite of his high profile in the area of political sculpture, Power always remained keen to maintain his reputation as a fine art sculptor. During the 1930s and early 1940s he continually exhibited work at the Royal Hibernian Academy. Some of the work was directly connected to his political commissions. For instance, in 1935 he displayed a bust of Pádraic Ó Conaire and a model of a wolfhound that was to be placed on a memorial to the republican Liam Lynch. In 1937 he exhibited his busts of Michael Collins and Arthur Griffith, and in 1940 a bust of Seán Mac Diarmada. The choice of such work for exhibition purposes can be seen as a conscious effort by Power to make the point that political art is a legitimate form of fine art. No doubt he felt also that the art being produced in newly independent Ireland, of necessity must incorporate an overtly political dimension.

'IDEAL' WORKS

Ideal works were generally uncommissioned ones, which permitted sculptors to give free rein to their artistic imaginations. They also served to demonstrate the sculptor's skill in working to a small scale. One of Power's ideal works is particularly imaginative. Using an offcut of Connemara marble lying around the studio, he depicted salmon moving upstream against the current (Illus 8.14). The irregular shapes and natural patterns contained within the piece of stone were fully exploited by him. He used them to suggest fast-flowing water, and the angle and movements of the fish were made to follow the contours that already existed in the block. The carving was full of life, and as a late work it showed that he had lost none of his early promise. Given that he was working in a Connemara marble, that most Irish of stones, and carving a salmon, a fish associated with Ireland and included on its coinage, this work can be seen to have a distinctive Irish dimension.

THE LATER YEARS

Power's last years were ones in which many honours were awarded to him in recognition of his talents. In the early 1940s he was appointed to the Art Advisory Committee at the Municipal Gallery, and as representative of the Royal Hibernian Academy on the Board of Governors and Guardians of the National Gallery of Ireland. In 1944, the year before this death, he was appointed to the selection committee for the Oireachtas Art Exhibition, which included Jack B Yeats and Dermod O'Brien, the president of the RHA. Power, ever keen to promote a distinctive Irish school of art, suggested to the sub-committee that a special prize be offered for a work (painting or sculpture) depicting some aspect of Irish history or mythology. Much to his chagrin, the idea was not accepted; possibly because there were not sufficient funds to cover an annual expense of that kind.[31] Although these same years were marked by many successes, they were not without their share of disappointments. For instance, in 1938, in spite of being regarded as Ireland's pre-eminent sculptor, he was passed over for the post of professor of sculpture in the College of Art. The occasion coincided with a period of change and reform in that institution, and accordingly fresh approaches to teaching were initiated. This resulted in three of the major posts at the college going to foreign artists: a highly unpopular move which provoked a short but passionate debate in the letters pages of the Dublin daily newspapers, as well as a parliamentary question on the matter in the Dáil.

In spite of this major setback, Power went on to complete some further prestige commissions before his death. These included a bust of Éamon de Valera (Illus 8.15) for John L Burke, a solicitor and enthusiastic patron of the arts, who was a close friend of the de Valera family. He also carved monumental statues for the exterior of the dome in Carndonagh Church in County Donegal in the same period, and it is thought that this commission was indirectly the cause of his death. One of the statues slipped its moorings in the studio, and in his attempt to steady it, Power gave himself a double hernia. He refused to have any medical treatment, and some months later he died, aged sixty-four.

One of the obituary writers in 1945 was convinced that Power's work would in time be more and more appreciated as that of 'the outstanding native sculptor of his time'.[32] Several factors were to prevent this from happening. First, modernist styles were increasingly dominating the production of art in Ireland, and Power's strongly naturalistic style seemed decidedly old-fashioned. The advent of the Living Art Exhibitions from 1943 onwards, initiated by up-and-coming young artists, showed that contemporary Irish art was clearly looking beyond a strictly academic style. The second reason for his decline in popularity was that much of his work was located within a nationalist discourse. His art was seen as a clear example of the concept of 'Irish Ireland' attempting to achieve its distinctive political, religious and cultural identity. His political busts, his gaelicised Madonna and Child, the design of the Tailteann Games statuette, and the monument to Pádraic Ó Conaire with its unusual plinth, are testimony to that aspiration. The relationship between Power, his art and the evolution of such an ideology was particularly close because he himself believed in an 'Irish Ireland' as passionately as did his patrons. Both he and his art became inseparable from that particular vision.

In the post-war decades, with economic expansion, the growth of greater social freedom and a better education for all, the drive to establish a rigid Gaelic hegemony in newly independent Ireland became a less attractive idea. Power's art, so closely associated with that world, suffered accordingly. Yet an examination of his works can give us a fresh understanding of this ideological phenomenon, particularly in its visual aspects, and this art, which merited so little attention for so long, can unlock a particularly rich source of historical knowledge.

8.15 *Éamon de Valera* 1944, Plaster; height 0.42m

A fine portrait bust — one of Power's last — which captures de Valera's hawklike features, bearing a typically inscrutable expression, as he guides his country as Taoiseach through the last year of the Emergency (the Second World War).

Courtesy of Terry de Valera

9

Brian P Kennedy

THE IRISH FREE STATE 1922–49:
A VISUAL PERSPECTIVE

The publication of excellent historical surveys of modern Irish history, including that of the Irish Free State (1922–49), has been marked, almost without exception, by ample use of textual documents, but by little or no reference to the abundant and valuable visual documents.[1] With the coming into being of the Irish Free State, the idea that the identity of independent Ireland should be separate and distinct demanded and received recognition in many areas of Irish life, the most obvious perhaps being the new national flag, new postage stamps and coinage, publications in the Irish language, and paintings with Irish subject matter. The visual evidence of Ireland between 1922 and 1949 can tell us much about the Irish Free State and can enable us to place ourselves more vividly and imaginatively in the history of the period.

Teachers of Irish history in secondary schools have, for the most part, followed the poor example of university academics in failing to provide adequate encouragement to their pupils to use their visual capacity. This is a sad reflection on the general lack of appreciation of the power of the visual memory — each of us has experienced moments that are forever etched on our minds. Examples from the recent past in Ireland could include witnessing the visit of President John F Kennedy to Ireland in 1963, seeing television pictures of the aftermath of Derry's Bloody Sunday in 1972, being in attendance among the huge crowd at the Papal Mass in the Phoenix Park in 1979. Such moments help to define national identity and ought to be recorded historically using all available resources, including written and visual records, sound archives and physical objects.

THE BIRTH OF THE IRISH FREE STATE

On Easter Monday, 24 April 1916, a green, white and orange flag was raised above the General Post Office in the centre of Dublin. This symbolic act was recorded in a historic photograph and became a defining moment on the road to Irish independence (Illus 9.1). Patrick Pearse proclaimed the Irish Republic in a stirring message to Irishmen and Irishwomen, which began:

> In the name of God and of the dead generations from which she receives her old tradition of nationhood, Ireland, through us, summons her children to her flag and strikes for her freedom.

After the Proclamation had been read, copies of it were posted in the area around the General Post Office (Illus 9.2). Few mint-condition copies survived for posterity, but reproductions of the Proclamation were to be seen on the walls of many Irish homes in succeeding decades, visual reminders of the charter for which its seven signatories had been executed. Postcards available in Dublin soon after 1916 showed, in the manner of Delacroix's painting *Liberty Guiding the People* (1830, Louvre, Paris), an Irish Volunteer raising the tricolour before the burning ruin of the GPO, and trampling on the Union Jack, the flag of the oppressor (Illus 9.3). On 3 May 1916, the *Daily Sketch* had published a photograph of British soldiers holding the captured flag of the 'Irish Republic' upside-down. During the War of Independence (1919–21), British soldiers scorned republican flags by trailing them in the mud behind their lorries.[2]

9.1 A historic photograph: the Irish tricolour flies over Dublin's General Post Office on 24 April 1916, signalling the start of the rising that led — some five years later — to the establishment of an Irish Free State, of which the tricolour became the official flag.

From *The Capuchin Annual* (1966)

9.2 'Irishmen and Irishwomen: in the name of the dead generations from which she received her old tradition of nationhood…': few Dubliners can have seen copies of the original Proclamation, printed in secret and hastily fly-posted here and there in central Dublin, but its splendid language quickly entered the national folk-mind.

National Museum of Ireland

The Irish Free State (or, in the Irish language, *Saorstát Éireann*) came formally into existence on 6 December 1922. A year before, on 6 December 1921, the War of Independence came to an end with the signing in London of the Treaty, the shortened name for the 'Articles of Agreement for a Treaty between Great Britain and Ireland'. Those in Ireland who rejected the Treaty, led by Éamon de Valera, regarded themselves as the upholders of the Republic that had been proclaimed by Pearse, and they denigrated those who favoured the Treaty as 'Free Staters'. A Civil War began in April 1922 when anti-Treaty forces seized the Four Courts in Dublin. By the time it ended in May 1923, the death toll in the Civil War was not more than seven hundred, but the legacy of bitterness it engendered took decades to begin to dissolve.

In the twenty-seven years of the Irish Free State's existence, before a Republic was finally established on Easter Monday 1949, two major political parties were in power. Cumann na nGaedheal (Fine Gael from 1933), the pro-Treaty party founded by William T Cosgrave, was in government from 1922 to 1932. Fianna Fáil, founded in 1926 by Éamon de Valera, and subtitled 'The Republican Party', came to power in March 1932, and formed successive governments until 1948. Both political parties promoted so-called 'Irish Ireland' policies, a conscious reaction to eight centuries of colonial domination. These policies were considered vital in order to counteract what the Gaelic scholar Douglas Hyde had diagnosed as cultural erosion. Hyde had articulated his views in a most influential lecture, 'The necessity of de-anglicising Ireland', delivered to the National Literary Society in Dublin on 25 November 1892. He called for an end to 'self-destructive and contradictory simultaneously hating and aping of the English' and suggested ways of de-anglicising Ireland, including the promotion of the Irish language and rediscovering its roots in antiquity, employing traditional Irish personal and place names, enjoying Irish traditional music and games, preserving traditional Irish customs and habits of dress, reading Irish and Anglo-Irish literature.[3]

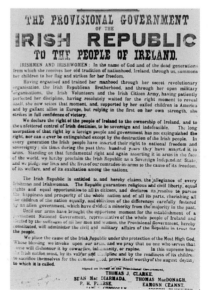

9.3 A postcard issued in Dublin soon after the 1916 Rising shows the symbolic importance of the flag, as the Irish tricolour is raised high and the Union Jack (the British flag) is trampled in the dust. In the background is the General Post Office, headquarters of the rising.

9.4 Wrap the green paint round me boys: imperial postboxes were converted to republicanism with a heavy coat of green paint. It was not thought necessary to obscure the letters VR (Victoria Regina).

A CULTURAL REPUBLIC?

In November 1934, the poet Thomas MacGreevy, who was later to become director of the National Gallery of Ireland, delivered a paper to the Irish Society in London on the theme of 'A cultural Irish republic'.[4] He declared: 'Our first need in Ireland, if we had realised it, was not a political republic, but a cultural republic. We made a mistake. We must rectify it.' MacGreevy lamented that 'There is no Irish cultural republic, no republic of the Irish mind'.

Cultural nationalists like MacGreevy, who shared Hyde's view that Ireland could not be saved 'until the foreign influence of anglicisation is wiped out', were to be disappointed by the Irish Free State. The cultural vision of Pearse and Hyde was increasingly swamped by the efforts of the new political leaders to confront political and economic realities. The nation was now equated with the state, even though as Eoin MacNeill (minister for education from 1922 to 1925) pointed out: 'When a people possesses a form of civilisation which is for it, traditional and distinctive, and when it is conscious of this possession, such a people is a nation whether it be a state or no state or an aggregate of states, or only a portion of a state.'[5] This is what MacGreevy meant: Ireland was now making its cultural existence subservient to its political establishment. Nonetheless, the achievement of a political republic was in itself no small feat. The need for political stability was paramount after years of violence. New economic policies were essential because the Irish Free State was a very impoverished place by today's standards. In 1926, the first census of population after independence revealed that the average size of dwelling had three rooms. Although overcrowding (that is, more than two persons to a room) was severe in certain rural areas, it was not giving rise to high death rates. In the towns, in sharp contrast, overcrowding and high death rates were typical. In Dublin city, 28.7 per cent of the population lived in one-room dwellings, and a further 22.3 per cent in two-room dwellings.[6] The statistics of the census of 1946 showed that emigration was 8 per 1000, unemployment 7.3 per cent,[7] 61 per cent of all private dwellings had no piped water supply,[8] 62 per cent had no fixed bath, 62 per cent had no flush lavatory and nearly one half had no special sanitary facilities.[9] The numbers of persons living in overcrowded conditions was high despite a decrease from 27.2 per cent of the total population in 1926, to 22.5 per cent in 1936, to 16.8 per cent in 1946.[10] While keeping this harsh economic background in mind, some of the most visible attempts to develop a distinct identity for independent Ireland will now be detailed.

POST-BOXES AND STAMPS

Among the first commissions of the new state was the painting green of all the post-boxes. From a nationalist viewpoint, there was something satisfying about seeing the letters V R (Victoria Regina) or E R (Edwardus Rex) painted green (Illus 9.4). In terms of identity formation, the psychological impact of independence was made most apparent in such minor yet significant alterations.

The first stamp produced in December 1922 for the first definitive series was green in colour, and showed a map of Ireland set against a green background (Illus 9.5). No division was shown on the map to indicate the existence of the six counties of Northern Ireland, which had remained part of Great Britain under the terms of the Treaty. This stamp firmly established itself in public consciousness, because it remained in circulation for forty-six years. The

Left

9.5 The first stamp for the new Irish postal service: green in colour, naturally, and showing an island resolutely unpartitioned. This image had political as well as symbolic importance.

9.6 The national colours of green, white and orange are emphasised in this special-issue stamp, issued in 1941 to commemorate the 1916 Rising. The use of an overprint also echoes the beginnings of the Irish postal service, when British stamps with an overprint were used for a time.

Left

9.7 A selection of Free State postage stamps shows a widespread use of Celtic and Catholic symbols (the cross, harp and shamrock), as well as celebrating national achievements like the harnessing of the River Shannon for electric power.

9.8 A delicate distinction is made in this Olympic postage stamp of 1988. The cyclist represents *Ireland* — the team was chosen from all thirty-two counties — whereas the stamp is issued by 'Éire' — the state comprising the twenty-six counties of the Republic.

use of green, white and orange as a motif on Irish stamps became commonplace. A notable example was the stamp issued in 1941 to commemorate the twenty-fifth anniversary of the Easter Rising (Illus 9.6). Acutely political in tone, it was printed in orange and showed a white map of Ireland (no border indicating Northern Ireland) with the following words in Irish printed over the map in green letters: '*1941 i gcuimhne aiseirghe 1916*' (1941 in memory of the Rising of 1916). The traditional notion of Ireland as 'a land of saints and scholars' was also reinforced on stamps of the Irish Free State period. Many are richly symbolic, employing motifs like the Irish harp, the shamrock and the Celtic cross. David Scott, in his examination of Irish postage stamps, comments that Irish stamp design during the years of the Irish Free State 'promoted a strongly nationalist and religious picture of the Irish cultural identity, with a strong emphasis on the Irish language' (Illus 9.7). Following the declaration of the Republic of Ireland in 1949, the more general theme of 'cultural identity' was adopted on Irish stamps, an emphasis on literary, historic and economic, as opposed to specifically political and religious images. Of the thirty-four commemorative stamps issued between 1922 and 1959, twelve celebrated Irish political/nationalist events or anniversaries, nine marked religious festivals or days, six commemorated cultural topics (including the Gaelic League, the Gaelic Athletic Association and the Catholic University), and sixteen were inscribed in the Irish language.[11] Although the English title 'Republic of Ireland' appeared on two stamps in 1949 (the issue marking the declaration of the Republic, and the commemorative stamp for the centenary of the death of the poet James Clarence Mangan), the single word 'Ireland' did not appear on any stamp until 1988, when it was used on one of the Olympic commemorative set; but as on all the other stamps, the word 'Éire' also appeared (Illus 9.8).[12]

THE 1948 OLYMPICS

It was appropriate that an Olympic stamp should have been the first to feature the word 'Ireland', because the issue of the country's correct name and the definition of its political boundaries had led to the non-participation of the national team at the Berlin Olympics in 1936 and to an extraordinary debacle at the next Olympics in London in 1948.[13] In 1936 the Irish Athletics Association was suspended from the international athletics movement because it refused to accept a new rule of the International Athletics Federation confining countries to their political boundaries. The British-dominated organising committee of the 1948 Olympics insisted on listing Ireland as 'Éire', because this was the title by which they knew the country. Furthermore, they argued, this was the name on Irish stamps, and it also featured on the letterhead of the Irish minister for external affairs. The Irish Olympic Council argued that the official languages of the Olympics were English, French and Spanish, and the name of 'Éire' in English was 'Ireland'. The Irish swimming and diving team was withdrawn in protest, and Irish teams in a number of events had to lobby shrewdly to avoid disqualification because they included participants from the six counties of Northern Ireland. The Olympic organisers had further bureaucratic difficulties in recognising that many Irish sporting organisations had all-Ireland status, such as those responsible for boxing, cycling and rowing.

The 1948 Olympics episode was an extreme example of the problem of asserting national identity, but it highlights the difficulty arising from Ireland's constitutional claim over the island's thirty-two counties. Ireland, under the 1937 Constitution, is a country where the state

IRELAND: ART INTO HISTORY

is not coterminous with 'the national territory'. It has been observed that 'few citizens of the twenty-six counties can have a clear map-image of their state'.[14] When most citizens of the twenty-six counties think of the map of Ireland, it will invariably be a map of the whole island. Few citizens, excepting some perhaps in the border counties, would be able to draw the shape of Northern Ireland. This may be the legacy of the consistent refusal of the Irish Free State to represent the boundary line drawn up in 1922. The masthead of many Irish publications included the map of the island of Ireland, with no border indicated, for example that of the Fianna Fáil-controlled *Irish Press*, which was founded by Éamon de Valera in September 1931. De Valera's manner of underlining the existence of partition to his visitors was impressive. Sir John Maffey, the United Kingdom Representative to Éire, noted how one of his first meetings with de Valera, in September 1939, ended with a dramatic flourish: 'As I left the room he led me to his black map of Éire with its white blemish on the north-east corner and said: "There's the real source of all our trouble." He could not let me go without that.'[15] It is significant that de Valera had cleverly altered the proposed wording of Maffey's title from the suggested 'United Kingdom Representative in Éire' to 'United Kingdom Representative to Éire'.[16] Issues such as this were crucially important to de Valera in emphasising the independence of the Irish Free State.

PASSPORTS

The introduction of an Irish Free State passport was a cause of controversy during the 1920s.[17] The question of citizenship arose during the Anglo-Irish Treaty negotiations in 1921. The British government wanted the citizens of the Irish Free State to be British subjects. Lloyd George, the prime minister, could not understand how the Irish negotiators could accept membership of the British Commonwealth and yet not wish to be British subjects. The alternative was that they should be foreigners, who would not enjoy any of the privileges of Commonwealth membership. The members of Dáil Éireann (the Irish parliament) were certain that the Irish people would not accept being known as British subjects. When the Irish Free State was established in December 1922, the new minister for external affairs, Desmond FitzGerald, took immediate steps to issue Irish passports, and proposed the wording 'imperial British citizenship' as an alternative to 'British subject'. Although the British Colonial Office was conciliatory in the effort to find a solution to the issue, the British Foreign Office was resolute and insisted on the words 'British subject', for fear of establishing a precedent for other emergent states in the empire. The issue remained unresolved, and on 4 March 1924 FitzGerald proposed the Irish government's final wording 'citizens of the Irish Free State and the British Commonwealth of Nations'. The British government failed to respond quickly to the Irish proposal and, faced with legislative difficulties, the Irish government began issuing passports using its formula of words on 3 April 1924. The British response was to refuse to recognise Irish passports, and the matter was not finally resolved, from the Irish viewpoint, until the enactment of the Irish Nationality and Citizenship Act, 1935, which established Irish citizenship and gave legal basis for the symbolic removal from Irish passports eleven years earlier of the term 'British subject'.

9.9 The Great Seal of the new Free State, featuring an old Irish harp, was actually made by the Royal Mint in London, without the prior approval of the British Colonial Office.

9.10 'The silent ambassadors of national taste': the new coins were chosen by a committee that included the poet W B Yeats. The symbols used were chosen by the committee, but the actual designs selected were by an English sculptor, Percy Metcalfe.

STATE SEAL

The Irish Free State government decided early in 1923 to ask the Royal Mint in London to engrave a Great Seal and a number of other seals to be used to endorse documents issued by government ministers and the courts. The first design proposed for the state seal incorporated a heraldic shield and crest, but the Royal Mint, while seeking not 'to interfere in any way with what is purely the concern of the Free State Government', proclaimed that the design 'would really be a disaster for the new seal'. The Royal Mint advised: 'Indeed, it is questionable whether heraldry itself as being the product of purely Norman origin is entirely suitable for introduction into the seal of the Irish Free State.'[18] It was decided instead to use a design based on the Irish harp in the collection of Trinity College Dublin, which was reputed to have belonged to the great Irish king, Brian Boru, who was killed fighting the Vikings at the Battle of Clontarf in 1014. The Royal Mint pronounced itself pleased with the harp image and 'delighted' that the Free State had been saved from the 'calamity' of the first design.[19] The seal was delivered to the Free State government on 15 June 1925 (Illus 9.9). Three years later, the British Colonial Office expressed concern to the Royal Mint that the Irish seal had been commissioned by the Irish government without their permission. The Royal Mint agreed that the Colonial Office guidelines would be adhered to in future and 'in the case of the Free State seals it was thought politic to avoid any official cognisance of what actually happened'.[20]

COINAGE AND PAPER CURRENCY

In contrast to the first definitive series of stamps, the advisory committee on the selection of a new coinage scrupulously avoided what its chairman, W B Yeats, called 'outworn so-called national symbols, such as the shamrock, the sunburst and the round tower'.[21] The only traditional symbols retained on the coinage issued in December 1928 were the harp (the Brian Boru harp, as used on the state seal), which appeared on the obverse of all coins, and the wolfhound, which appeared on the 6d coin. The designs of the Englishman Percy Metcalfe, who won the coinage design competition, were agricultural in theme, in accordance with the Irish Coinage Committee's brief. The committee's decision to employ birds and beasts as the iconography for the coinage was controversial. Only the determined independence of the committee succeeded in overruling public indignation. Yeats, the confident aesthete, was pleased with the new coins (Illus 9.10). He called them 'the silent ambassadors of national taste'.[22] He was indeed correct: the coinage was an excellent advertisement for independent Ireland.

The new Irish paper currency carried an important national image on its watermark. In early Irish literature Ireland was represented allegorically as a woman. In ancient tradition, the name most often ascribed to this woman was 'Éire'; other names for her were 'Banbha', 'Fodhla', 'Róisín Dubh' and 'Caitlín Ní hUallacháin. The last-mentioned name, anglicised as Kathleen Ní Houlihan, was used as the title of an important play by W B Yeats. The Note Committee, established to determine a design for the Irish paper currency, decided in December 1927 to ask the artist Sir John Lavery to paint a head and shoulders portrait of his beautiful wife, Hazel, for use as the watermark on all Irish notes (Illus 9.11). This was in recognition of the Laverys' assistance in acting as intermediaries for the Irish delegation during the Anglo-Irish Treaty negotiations in 1922. Thus it was that the image of Mother Ireland, the beautiful and noble guardian of the Irish soul, came to feature in every citizen's commercial transactions (Illus 9.12).

9.11 *Lady Lavery as Kathleen Ní Houlihan* 1928, John Lavery (1856–1941), Oil on canvas

The beautiful Mrs Hazel Lavery, American-born wife of the Belfast artist Sir John Lavery, in a portrait specially commissioned for the new Irish currency: a surprisingly cosmopolitan choice, though the Laverys had shown themselves to be good friends of Irish independence.

Central Bank of Ireland, Dublin

9.12 Banknote featuring a portrait of Lady Lavery

THE IRISH LANGUAGE

One of the most significant identity marks of the Irish Free State was the concerted attempt to introduce Irish as an everyday medium of speech throughout the country. Many of those who promoted the language policy had all the zeal of the convert — de Valera, for example, was twenty-five when he began to learn Irish. In a variation of de Valera's wall map of Ireland, Ernest Blythe, while he was minister for finance (1923–32), demonstrated his commitment to the Irish language by having a map of the Irish-speaking Gaeltacht areas adorn his office.[23] A basic element of the language policy was the need to confront citizens with the visual presence of the language. Irish language titles were often used for new state agencies. De Valera considered that 'the introduction of the words does help to familiarise people with the language'.[24] Key words were established in Irish, such as the use of the title 'Taoiseach' instead of 'Prime Minister'. De Valera favoured the use of Irish words in official letters. He argued:

> It is patchwork — I am quite willing to admit that — but is it not better for us to begin a letter with 'A Chara' and end it with 'le meas' than to use the English forms? Of course, it would be very much better if we could have it the other way, if the substance of a letter were in Irish and the introductory and concluding phrases in English but, until we reach the stage in which the letter as a whole is written in Irish, why not introduce it in this way, as is done in the case of street names, or other short phrases?[25]

The Irish language was a potent agent for change. Although the policy of making Irish the first spoken language failed dramatically, it nevertheless achieved a deep impact. A number of government initiatives helped to promote the Irish language and native culture. De Valera was especially proud of the work of the Irish Manuscripts Commission and the Irish Folklore

9.13 A tourist poster proclaims 'Old Erin still survives... The ancient values remain unchanged in Ireland' — but hastily goes on to say that catering and transport fully match up to modern requirements.

Bottom right

9.14 *Lakeside Cottages* c1930, Paul Henry (1876–1958), Oil on canvas

Paul Henry's images of an idyllic, uncluttered west of Ireland landscape were a shrewd choice for a widely distributed poster campaign aimed at tourists.

Hugh Lane Municipal Gallery of Modern Art, Dublin

Commission, which were established in 1928 and 1935 respectively. His attempts to establish an Institute of Irish Historical Studies failed in 1938. Two years later, however, he guided the legislation to establish the Dublin Institute of Advanced Studies safely through the Oireachtas (the Irish legislature). The institute had two constituent schools, the School of Celtic Studies and the School of Theoretical Physics (the School of Cosmic Physics was added later). The Irish Placenames Commission, founded in 1946, assisted the promotion of the Irish language by finding Irish names for streets and towns, for use on maps and signposts. Irish placenames certainly put the language visibly on every street in the country. Tourist literature promoted the clean, untrammelled, quaint image of a country untouched by urban difficulties. 'Old Erin survives in Modern Ireland', one poster advised, 'The ancient values remain unchanged in Ireland' (Illus 9.13). Promotional posters depicting paintings of the west of Ireland, with an isolated thatched cottage set in a magnificent landscape, helped to reinforce the country's international reputation for unsophisticated charm (Illus 9.14).[26] Paul Henry's paintings became so hackneyed that a cartoon in *Dublin Opinion* had a visitor exclaiming before a western landscape, 'Darn it, Paul Henry's been here already!' (Illus 9.15).

ART AND ARCHITECTURE

That a political republic and not a cultural republic was created in the first decades of independence is illustrated by an incident cited by Dr George Furlong, director of the National Gallery of Ireland 1935–50:

Below

9.15 A *Dublin Opinion* cartoon: 'Darn it, Paul Henry's been here already.' Although the elements appear simple, Henry's landscapes are highly organised and not easily reproduced.

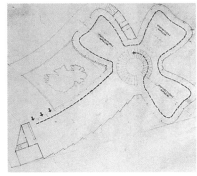

De Valera never came to visit the National Gallery. The only time he requested advice from me was in connection with his Christmas card which was sent to foreign Heads of State. In 1936 I proposed that a new design should be used instead of the stock designs like the Rock of Cashel. I suggested a 'Greetings from Ireland' card with the heraldic shields of the four provinces. Dev's initial reaction was favourable. He thought it looked well but after some discussion he asked me what was the origin of the heraldic designs. I told him they were probably of Norman origin. He immediately cooled on the idea and a stock design was used again that year. I was surprised when the next year, he called me to see him. He asked me did I remember the design I had proposed with the heraldic shields. He thought it would be very appropriate for 1937. The new Constitution had laid claim to the four green fields.[27]

The power of the map motif to emphasise a distinct identity for Ireland was ably employed by Michael Scott when he was commissioned to design the Irish pavilion for the New York World Fair in 1939 (Illus 9.16). Scott explained how he evolved his innovative design:

The site was irregular and small, rather difficult in fact. I tried a whole range of different forms which were recognisably Irish, starting with beehive huts! I thought of the shamrock as one of the first, of course, but rejected it. Then suddenly I thought of the Fair's theme — 'a new world of tomorrow' and of how the aeroplane had given architecture a new, top elevation. So I started work on the shamrock plan...it became very popular as 'the shamrock building' and these words used to boom out as the bus tours went past the building.[28]

The only colours adorning the steel and glass building were the white of the top and end faces, the green of the door uprights, and the orange of the hood that the uprights supported (Illus 9.17). Furthermore, to the left of the door was a pool in the shape of the map of Ireland — thirty-two counties — which was lit from underwater at night, thereby silhouetting the map.

Left

9.18 'The Four Green Fields', a stained-glass panel made by Evie Hone (1894–1955) for the New York World Fair. The title refers to the four provinces of Ireland, of which Ulster was one.

Government Buildings, Dublin

Right

9.19 *Achill Horses* 1939

Mainie Jellett (1897–1944)

Oil on canvas

A semi-abstract design specially chosen by the Department of Industry and Commerce for the 1939 World Fair. The horse was of course a significant part of Ireland's image for tourists.

National Gallery of Ireland (no 2185)

Near right

9.20 Perhaps the best-known of all Irish sculptures, the representation of the dying Celtic hero Cuchulainn, by Oliver Sheppard (1864–1941), chosen as a memorial to those who died in Ireland's struggle for independence.

General Post Office, Dublin

Far right

9.21 There were limits to official toleration in artistic matters. This stained-glass window (detail) by Harry Clarke (1889–1931) was officially commissioned for the International Labour Office in Geneva, but was rejected, and is now in Florida.

Mitchell Wolfson Museum, Miami

The motifs of the map garden, the shamrock and the colours of the national flag clearly established the Irish presence at the World Fair. The building was adorned with a vigorously monumental sculpture of 'Mother Éire' by Professor Herkner of the National College of Art. It is noteworthy that the government directed that the word 'Ireland' should be inscribed on the building instead of 'Éire', which was considered to be inadequately known in the United States.

Pragmatism was a typical trait of the governments of the Irish Free State. Despite economic deprivation, it was during the 1920s that most of O'Connell Street in Dublin was rebuilt.[29] After the Easter Rising in 1916, the Dublin architect Horace O'Rourke, and the British government's chief planning inspector, Raymond Unwin, conspired fruitfully to design a magnificent street frontage for O'Connell Street. The Dublin Reconstruction Act 1916 was followed in the post-Civil War period by the Dublin Reconstruction (Emergency Provisions) Act 1924, which enabled O'Rourke to design an imposing frontage, with the Savoy Cinema as its centrepiece. During the 1920s also, the government spent considerable sums from scarce public funds on rebuilding the Four Courts, the General Post Office and the Custom House. It is difficult to understand why these buildings, which had housed key elements of British authority in Ireland, were thought worthy of preservation when many other buildings were allowed to fall into ruin through neglect. The Custom House reconstruction was completed in 1929 at a cost of £300,000. In 1933–4, in stark contrast to the preservationist tendencies indicated by these initiatives, the Irish government gave detailed consideration to a proposal submitted by the minister for finance, Seán MacEntee, that large numbers of Georgian buildings in Merrion Street, Merrion Square and Lower Baggot Street, Dublin, should be demolished to facilitate the construction of an extensive complex of purpose-built government offices.[30] Fortunately, this incredible plan had to be abandoned in 1937 when the government decided that arterial drainage in rural areas was a higher national priority.

It is also an intriguing fact, one worthy of further research, that, on occasion, Irish governments saw no difficulty in employing a radical architectural design and in exhibiting innovative and even abstract art works when they were to be erected or shown abroad, whereas when employing the work of Irish artists at home, the government tended to be quite conservative. Evie Hone's stained-glass window, *The Four Green Fields* (Illus 9.18), which was commissioned for the New York World Fair and won first prize for stained glass there, was quite modern in conception, although its title carried a potent political message. Mainie Jellett's semi-abstract painting *Achill Horses* (Illus 9.19) was specifically requested by the Department of Industry and Commerce to be shown at the same World Fair. In contrast, at home in 1934 the government had selected Oliver Sheppard's finely modelled but rather traditional sculpture, executed 1911–12, *The Death of Cuchulainn*, (Illus 9.20), for erection in the General Post Office as a national memorial to those who died in the Easter Rising of 1916. The image of Cuchulainn was no doubt considered to be appropriate for such a memorial because it evoked heroism and self-sacrifice.

As with most issues in the years of the Irish Free State, it is dangerous to generalise, because the Irish government was not always prepared to promote progressive Irish art on the international scene. In 1927 the government commissioned Harry Clarke to design a stained-glass window for presentation to the International Labour Office of the League of Nations in Geneva as a gift from the Irish Free State. Clarke's designs for the Geneva window illustrated fifteen scenes from contemporary Anglo-Irish literature. Although it was an artistic masterpiece, it was rejected by the government and was eventually bought back by the author's widow. Problems arose with one illustration in particular, a sensuous, almost nude girl dancing before the fat and drunken figure of Mr Gilhooley, a scene from a book by Liam O'Flaherty (Illus 9.21). The fact that O'Flaherty was a banned writer and espoused communist views at this time probably exacerbated the situation. President Cosgrave informed the artist 'that the inclusion of scenes from certain authors…would give grave offence to many of our people'.[31] It was clear that the government had no intention of sending the window to Geneva if it contained 'subjects that would displease'. Despite valiant efforts by concerned individuals to place the Geneva window in an appropriate Irish national institution, the government and the institutions proved unwilling or unable to secure it and, finally, in 1988 the window was acquired by the Mitchell Wolfson Museum in Miami, Florida, where it now resides.[32]

IRISH PUBLICATIONS

Perhaps the best examples of the type of painting that was politically acceptable were those used to illustrate the *Saorstát Éireann Official Handbook*, which was published in 1932. To leaf through this publication is to be offered a window into the philosophy underlying the Irish Free State, the philosophy of an Irish Ireland uncontaminated by its colonial past. In de Valera's opinion, the *Official Handbook* was: 'a valuable book in many respects. It was very well produced. It was, in fact, a splendid specimen of Irish printing and Irish production.'[33] It was a point of pride that publications such as this one should be all-Irish productions, employing native printers, engravers, photographers and publisher. The Celtic-style cover of the *Official Handbook* was designed by the talented manuscript illuminator Art O'Murnaghan (Illus 9.22),[34] and the illustrations included works by Seán Keating, Paul Henry, Harry Kernoff, Seán O'Sullivan, Maurice MacGonigal and Estella Solomons. These works indicated the beauty of the Irish landscape, the importance of the Irish heritage, the treasures of the

IRISH TRADE JOURNAL
AND
STATISTICAL BULLETIN

IRISLeaḃar Tráḋála aġus ḟeasaċán
STAITISTIḋeaċta na héireann

VOL. XIII. No. 4.   DECEMBER, 1938   PRICE 4D.

9.25 A charming image: but is this pastoral design really what was needed to promote Irish trade, in a journal mainly read by hard-headed businessmen and economists?

National Museum, the country's historic architectural masterpieces, and new construction projects such as the Shannon Hydro-Electric Scheme.

Similar visual manifestations of the emphasis on Irish cultural identity are provided by the *Catholic Emancipation Centenary Record* (Illus 9.23), printed in 1929 by Colm O'Lochlainn of The Three Candles Press, by the *Catholic Emancipation Centenary Celebrations Pictorial Record* (1929), and by any edition of *The Capuchin Annual*. The documentary value of *The Capuchin Annual* (1930–77) cannot fail to impress historians: the cover illustration by Seán O'Sullivan (Illus 9.24), the masthead dedicated in the manner of the seventeenth-century Franciscan composers of the Annals of the Four Masters 'To the Glory of God and the Honour of Ireland', the informative advertisements, the nationalistic tone of many of the articles, the interest in Irish art, the sheer quality of the production.[35]

A sense of defined identity is also apparent from many of the publications of An Gúm, the publications branch of the Department of Education. In 1893 Douglas Hyde lamented that there were a mere six Irish language books in print. Between 1926 and 1964, An Gúm produced 1465 publications (1108 general literary works, 230 pieces of music and 127 text-books).[36] An Gúm established high standards of printing, layout, illustration and jacket design. At times, however, the nativist quality inherent in the cover illustrations of official publications achieved outstanding excess. The cover of *The Irish Trade Journal and Statistical Bulletin* is ambiguous to say the least (Illus 9.25). The viewer would have to ask how this quaint image is intended to convey a spirit of commerce and industry. There is no hint of modernity: lethargy appears to have won a clear victory over industrialisation.

THE WORKS OF SEÁN KEATING

In a picture entitled *Night's Candles are Burnt Out*, the artist Seán Keating demonstrated the emerging conflict between the struggle for an Irish Ireland and the need to enter the age of technology (Illus 9.26). Although Keating was, to an extent, the official artist of the Irish Free State, and this painting was one of a series commissioned by the Electricity Supply Board to record the construction of the hydro-electric scheme on the River Shannon, the artist succeeded in creating a most significant and critical visual meditation. The picture is an allegory showing Ireland emerging from economic deprivation, enduring the War of Independence and the Civil War, and progressing to economic prosperity. The businessman contractor looks at the gunman with disdain. The big dam generating electricity will supplant the oil-lamp held by the workman and the candle used by the priest (seated at the bottom right of the picture). The young family (on the right), who point towards the dam, represents the new era, while the skeleton (top left) represents the old redundant past. The bearded man is a self-portrait of the artist.

The espousal of nationalism, overt in works like *Night's Candles are Burnt Out*, was an understandable characteristic of the work of artists who had grown up in a time of tumult, war and deprivation, but also intense excitement.[37] The idea that a new Ireland was in the making encouraged many individuals to tolerate further economic difficulties, safe in the knowledge that the country had control over its own affairs. The influence of the writings of Thomas Davis (1818–45) was strong; he had written of the need for the widespread use of the Irish language, for publications in Irish, Irish games, Irish festivals, native folk traditions, for a school

9.26 *Night's Candles are Burnt Out* 1928–9, Seán Keating (1889–1977), Oil on canvas

An allegory showing the conflict between business, church, revolution and traditional values against the backdrop of the Shannon hydroelectric scheme.

Oldham Art Gallery, Lancashire (on loan to the Electricity Supply Board)

Far left

9.27 *The Holy Well* 1916, William Orpen (1878–1931), Tempera on canvas

A strange picture based on a somewhat highly coloured representation of ancient pilgrimage customs, presumably with an allegorical significance.

National Gallery of Ireland (no 4030)

Left

9.28 *The Man from Aranmore* 1905, Jack B Yeats (1871–1957), Chalk and watercolour on board

The simple dignity and strength of the west-coast fisherman is evident in this watercolour.

National Gallery of Ireland (no 6317)

9.29 *Men of the West* 1915, Seán Keating (1889–1977), Oil on canvas

An iconic painting of the Irish independence movement, one of a series commemorating the men who fought for Irish freedom.

Hugh Lane Municipal Gallery of Modern Art, Dublin

9.30 *Economic Pressure* c1930, Seán Keating (1889–1977), Oil on board
This painting shows another side of the reality of Irish independence: a shortage of work at home forced many young people to embark for foreign shores.
Crawford Municipal Art Gallery, Cork

9.31 *Allegory* 1925, Seán Keating (1889–1977), Oil on canvas
Gravediggers prepare a resting place for a tricolour-clad coffin, while a priest and businessman stand by and a woman nurses her child. The apparent message (the burial of the revolution) would not have been popular in official quarters.
National Gallery of Ireland (no 1236)

of art in each major city, and for national subject matter in painting and literature.[38] The obstacle to delivering Davis's agenda following the foundation of the Irish Free State was that, in the opinion of Fr Timothy Corcoran SJ, professor of the theory and practice of education at University College Dublin, 'we have in this country been viewing all history, all literature, all art, through the medium of the English mind'.[39] It was necessary to identify with the traditions of the true native Irishman, the peasant. One commentator in the short-lived but lively journal *Ireland To-Day* (1936–8) elaborated:

> If there is one country in the world where one man symbolises nearly all national life and nearly the whole content of the national struggle, that country is Ireland, and that man is the Irish peasant ... all art and all culture in a primitive society such as ours arose from the people; from the great yeomen, from folk music and folklore, from communities and craftsmen in contact with the peasant and the soil.[40]

The dignity of the single-minded Irishman had been depicted by William Orpen in his strange picture *The Holy Well* (Illus 9.27) and by Jack B Yeats in his *The Man from Aranmore* (Illus 9.28). But it was Keating who provided the most dramatic and rhetorical visual icons of the Irish Free State. His *Men of the West* (Illus 9.29) set the tenor of national painting. His Irishmen were proud, not afraid to fight, resolute and determined. Keating's *The Race of the Gael* (IBM, New York), which won first prize in an international competition of contemporary painting sponsored by the corporate giant IBM in 1939, offered another prime example of the strength of character of Irish men and women. The emotive picture *Economic Pressure* (Illus 9.30) and his provocative *Allegory* (Illus 9.31) mark Keating out as the Irish painter who produced the most powerful visual documents of the Irish Free State.

Although they did not constitute an organised nationalist school of painting, the works of artists like Seán Keating, Paul Henry, Maurice MacGonigal, Charles Lamb, James Humbert Craig and Patrick Tuohy helped to create, in visual terms, 'a corporate identity' for independent Ireland.[41] In 1937, just two years before his death, W B Yeats visited the Municipal Gallery in Dublin. He sat before John Butler Yeats's portraits of famous Irish leaders, Keating's

Below right

9.32 Celtic designs are brought out again for the record of the Eucharistic Congress, which was held in Dublin in 1932: a focal point for Catholic sentiment in the new state.

Below left

9.33 The Eucharistic Congress of 1932: this huge structure was built to house an open-air altar in the Phoenix Park.

Men of the West and Lavery's *Blessing the Colours*, and found himself 'overwhelmed with emotion'. This was the essential Ireland '...not as she is displayed in guide book or history, but, Ireland seen because of the magnificent vitality of her painters...'.[42]

IMAGES OF IRISH CATHOLICISM

A visual perspective of the Irish Free State would be lacking if it failed to demonstrate that the early decades after independence were marked by Catholic triumphalism. The high point was the remarkable week of celebrations to mark the thirty-first International Eucharistic Congress, held in Dublin from 22 to 26 June 1932. *The Eucharistic Congress Pictorial Record* (Illus 9.32) provides a wealth of images that make the point more strikingly than written documents can ever do — the scale of the structure created to house the altar at the Phoenix Park (Illus 9.33); the image of six Air Corps planes flying in crucifix formation over the ship bringing the Papal Legate (Illus 9.34), His Eminence Cardinal Lorenzo Lauri, into Kingstown Harbour (Dún Laoghaire); the sight of the lord mayor, the ceann comhairle (speaker) and members of the government kneeling on the grass of the Phoenix Park on Men's Day (Illus 9.35); the decorations at the Earlsfort Terrace premises of University College Dublin; the artificially constructed round tower at College Green (Illus 9.36); and the one-thousand-year-old St Patrick's Bell, which was rung at the consecration of the Pontifical High Mass. The congress was a pivotal point in the history of the Irish Free State and was a testimony to the homogeneity to which the political republic aspired.

Widespread devotion, religious practice and sincere faith characterised Irish Catholicism, which became a distinguishing mark of identity. De Valera declared in a St Patrick's Day broadcast to the United States of America in 1935:

> Since the coming of St Patrick, fifteen hundred years ago, Ireland has been a Christian and a Catholic nation. All the ruthless attempts made down through the centuries to force her from this allegiance have not shaken her faith. She remains a Catholic nation.[43]

This self-conscious Catholicism inspired the governments of Cosgrave and de Valera to enact laws that exercised strong social control over the population. The most significant of these laws were: the Censorship of Films Act, 1923 (a film censor was appointed to cut or ban films judged to be 'subversive of public morality'); the Intoxicating Liquor Act, 1924 (which reduced the opening hours of licensed premises); the legislative ban on divorce, 1925; the Intoxicating Liquor Act, 1927 (which reduced the number of licensed premises by curbing licences); the Censorship of Publications Act, 1929 (a Censorship Board was established with powers to ban obscene literature and birth-control propaganda); the 1933 Budget tax on imported daily newspapers (designed to limit the sale in Ireland of the British yellow press); the Criminal Law (Amendment) Act, 1935 (which prohibited the sale and distribution of contraceptives); the Public Dance Halls Act, 1935 (which made it necessary to obtain a licence for public dances and thus curbed the number of country dances); and the Constitution of Ireland — Bunreacht na hÉireann — enacted in 1937 (which defined the rights, obligations and duties of Irish citizens). Catholicism, the declared religion of 93 per cent of the population, was the inspiration and fundamental basis for these laws. England was usually cited as the cause of Irish ills. Fr Timothy Corcoran SJ praised the Catholic Middle Ages which had produced the great cathedrals of

9.34 The Eucharistic Congress: planes of the Irish Air Corps flying in the form of a cross as they escort the ship bringing the papal legate to Ireland.

9.35 An image of respectful genuflection, as Irish public representatives kneel in the Phoenix Park, Dublin, during the Eucharistic Congress of 1932.

9.36 Decorations at Earlsfort Terrace for the Eucharistic Congress (above) and (below) a newly constructed round tower at College Green made it impossible for any citizen of Dublin to ignore the Congress and its historic resonance.

9.37 The old order changeth: a great statue of Queen Victoria by the Dublin-born sculptor John Hughes (1865–1941) is removed from the precincts of Leinster House, seat of the Irish parliament, in 1948. The sculpture is now in Sydney, Australia.

Europe. In contrast, 'the true symbol of modern industrial England ... is the workhouse'. History as taught in Irish schools had excluded Catholic culture and, Fr Corcoran concluded,

> The true corrective for all these derivations from the sound way is therefore to be found in the integral, and not partial, teaching of History in our Catholic schools. Religion and its natural connections and influences should be put back in its true place, at the heart of the subject.[44]

Alfred O'Rahilly, professor of mathematical physics at University College Cork, agreed: 'The teaching of history must, in Irish Catholic schools, be frankly and fully Catholic.'[45] In 1922 the Central Catholic Library was established in Dublin 'to surround the reader with Catholic books' and 'for the promotion not of merely wholesome reading, but of expressly Catholic reading, provided, of course, that it is wholesome.'[46] Fr P J Gannon SJ praised the Irish censorship laws and found it difficult to understand why writers should protest against them. The laws were but 'a simple measure of moral hygiene, forced upon the Irish public by a veritable spate of filth never surpassed, perhaps never equalled in the past history of English literature'.[47] Rigid censorship left some peculiar legacies. For example, it allowed few paintings of nudes by Irish artists. The standard images were landscapes, peasant scenes and portraits. The most renowned Irish painter of the period, Jack Butler Yeats, in the opinion of his friend Terence de Vere White, had 'no desire to paint even an academic nude ... there was nothing effeminate about him, nor did he suggest undue squeamishness. His personality was essentially masculine.'[48] That Yeats should have emphasised his masculinity highlights the sex stereotyping that marked the arts in the Irish Free State. Male artists painted and sculpted subject matter that was bold, vigorous and in keeping with a state founded on physical struggle.

CONCLUSION

The isolationism of the Emergency (as the Second World War was officially known in Ireland, to reinforce the policy of neutrality) marked the end of an era. The inward-looking rhetoric of the Irish Catholic nationalist became something to scorn. The disenchanted nicknamed the *Saorstát* (Free State) the 'Sour State'. The writer Seán Ó Faoláin argued that 'we are snoring gently behind the Green Curtain that we have been rigging up for the past thirty years'.[49] He considered it was Ireland's misfortune to be gripped by a combination of forces:

> the Gaelic Revivalist who fears the influence of European, and especially English literature (for nationalistic reasons) and the Catholic Actionist who fears the same (for pious reasons). Their motives are the best. Their methods are the worst.[50]

The removal of the sculpture of Queen Victoria from the grounds of Leinster House in 1948 was indicative of a changing Ireland (Illus 9.37). The declaration of the Republic of Ireland marked the beginning of a new period of national development. The Irish Free State had served its purpose by establishing a series of identifiable national symbols based on native traditions. This was a valuable legacy which should neither be derided nor forgotten, and many historians have tended to do one or the other. A visual perspective of the Irish Free State provides an immediate and stimulating depiction of the process of identity formation. To fail to employ visual images when documenting, researching and teaching history is surely to miss the element that impacts most on the memory.

PART THREE

PUBLIC AND PRIVATE FASHIONS

10

Raymond Gillespie

IRISH FUNERAL MONUMENTS AND SOCIAL CHANGE 1500–1700: PERCEPTIONS OF DEATH

Reflecting on the life of William Bedell, bishop of Kilmore, who died in 1642, his chaplain and son-in-law Alexander Clogie observed that he had 'always in readiness wonderful ability to discourse, to pray, to preach, to write, to dispute, to comfort and at last to die'.[1] The inclusion of the ability to die among the bishop's attributes was not unusual. While few memoirs and contemporary biographies exist from sixteenth- and seventeenth-century Ireland, almost all have accounts of the death scenes of their subjects. A good death was seen as the reflection of a good life and a promise of eternal reward.[2] The reasons why death was an ever-present reality in most people's minds were not only theological. High infant mortality, a relatively short life expectancy compared to today, and occasional outbreaks of plague, all ensured that the reality of death was close. Travel, for example, was fraught with hazards so that people sometimes made wills before setting off on a journey. James Browne Fitzandrew, a Cork merchant, made his will on 10 October 1578 on the occasion of a journey to Bordeaux; significantly, he made no provision for the disposal of his body since it would not be found after a shipwreck. Even short journeys could inspire fear. Richard Boyle, later first Earl of Cork, noted in his diary for 1613: 'I being advised by letters from the lord deputy to make my repair to his Majesty in England made my last will and testament.' A less adventurous soul, Garret Fitzgarret, archdeacon of Emly, made his will in January 1636 'for fear of any sudden death being now to take my journey towards Dublin'.[3]

10.1 'I was as thou art, and thou shalt be as I am now': the carved images of decomposing cadavers on the sixteenth-century Goldyng tomb at St Peter's Churchyard, Drogheda, County Louth, carry a potent reminder of human mortality.

10.2 At Youghal parish church, County Cork, the tomb of the Great Earl of Cork, Richard Boyle, was built to his own design twenty-four years before his death. The earl awaits judgement, serene in his robes of office, while his two wives kneel at either side.

This environment led many people to give much thought to their mortality. Patrick Mynagh from Cork noted in his will of 16 September 1570: 'I Patrick Mynagh being of perfect understanding with knowledge and perseverance in mind as well as health, by reason that all men are mortal and always under the fear of the thraldom of waves of fortune, therefore will and ordain these articles following.' The will was not proved until 26 November 1571. Sickness could also concentrate the mind on mortality, as is evidenced in the will of one Andrew Gawley, a Cork alderman, which was made on 18 November 1579 and proved on 8 February 1580: 'In the name of God and his holy blessed mother Mary and all the company of heaven, I, Andrew Gawley … being weak of body yet sound of mind and reason, God be praised, considering that the end of life in all creatures is death and that every Christian man ought to be in readiness to prepare himself thereunto do make my last will.'[4]

FUNERAL MONUMENTS

This strong realisation of the inevitability of death was reflected in the burial monuments of the time, and in early modern art and architecture. The Lynch doorway in Galway, for instance, incorporates a 1625 panel showing a skull and crossbones and the inscription: 'Remember death, vanity of vanity, all is but vanity.'[5] Charles Byrne's tomb at Tullow, County Carlow, recorded, 'I was once earth, I am earth again, I am nothing else, farewell frail earth, hail o worms I lay me down', and in St Brigid's Cathedral in Kildare, a Fitzgerald tomb of 1618 was inscribed, 'Pity me, pity me, you at least my friends. Jesus. For today it is me [who has died] tomorrow to you.'[6] This derived from a medieval legend in which three dead kings met three live kings and addressed them 'you will be as we are', and advised them to prepare for death.[7] This tradition is also represented by cadaver effigial monuments, which flourished in Ireland from the late fifteenth century to the 1630s. These typically show a corpse in the course of decomposition, and often, as on the early sixteenth-century Goldyng tomb at Drogheda, with vermin eating the decomposing body and the inscription 'I was as thou art, and thou shalt be as I am now' (Illus 10.1). Into the eighteenth century, people continued to decorate their tombs with such reminders of mortality as the skull and crossbones, the hourglass, a coffin and a bell.[8]

One way in which people prepared for their coming demise was to design their own funeral monuments. Many stipulated that they were to be buried with their deceased family. Where a new tomb was to be built, some left elaborate instructions in their wills as to its form. John Hamlyn of Smithstown, County Meath, stipulated in his 1589 will that his graveslab was to be eight feet long, five feet wide and one foot thick, it was to be taken from a quarry at Ardbracken, and was to have his name and arms carved on it. All this was to be done within six months of his death. Maurice Fitzgerald of Newcastle, County Longford, instructed that his tomb was to be in the abbey of Athlone, was to cost £20, which was to be paid by his sons in proportion to their inheritance, and this was to be done within three years.[9] A more reliable way of ensuring that a tomb was to one's satisfaction was to have it constructed before death. Sir Arthur Chichester's tomb in Carrickfergus, County Antrim, already existed before his death, as did the tomb of the Earl of Cork in St Patrick's Cathedral in Dublin. In some tombs, the inscriptions have no date of death, a blank having been left to be filled in when the patron died.[10]

This concern with a satisfactory design indicates that the tomb was an important public structure. Richard Boyle, in fact, created two tombs in Ireland. Although he did not die until

1643, he entered into an agreement with the tombmaster Alexander Hylls of Holborn in London in 1617 for the construction of a tomb in Youghal parish church, Cork (Illus 10.2). This tomb depicted the state of the Boyle fortune in 1619. Of Boyle's fifteen children, ten are represented; the others were born after 1619. Boyle himself occupies the centre of the monument and is shown in the robes of an earl, holding in his right hand the purse of office of the lord treasurer. On either side of the effigy are Boyle's two wives. His mother is shown above the monument, with the children below, all adding up to a visual genealogy. The genealogy was also inscribed on the tomb.[11] With Boyle's rapid rise in social status, it was necessary to alter the iconography. In 1630 he entered into an agreement with Edward Tingham of Chapelizod, Dublin, for the construction of another tomb in St Patrick's Cathedral for himself, his second wife and her family (Illus 10.3 & 10.4). All thirteen children who were alive when the tomb was constructed are shown, and those who had acquired titles are dressed in the appropriate regalia. The tomb reflects a more complex and prestigious genealogy, ignoring Boyle's first marriage and his own relatively humble lineage, and traces the descent of the family through his second wife's family. At the top of the tomb is his wife's grandfather, Robert Weston, dean of St Patrick's and lord chancellor between 1567 and 1573. The next level shows Weston's daughter (Boyle's mother-in-law) and her husband, Sir Geoffrey Fenton, who held a wide range of offices in Ireland under Elizabeth, including secretary of state from 1580 to his death in 1608. The inscription also included Boyle's new offices, most importantly that of lord justice, which he held at the time of the construction of the monument.[12]

The Boyle monument of 1630 was not a haphazard collection of statuary. The images were carefully selected and arranged, with professional heraldic advice, to make a social statement. Boyle's claim to be an important magnate was reflected in the size of the monument, its

10.3 Sir Richard Boyle had a second tomb built in St Patrick's Cathedral, Dublin, in case death should look for him there. His first wife, whose parentage was disappointing, is given no place here. The drawing was executed by Thomas Dineley in 1680. National Library of Ireland (Ms 392)

10.4 An engraving of Sir Richard Boyle's Dublin tomb, published in 1818, shows some changes to the upper portion compared to Dineley's drawing of 1680 (Illus 10.3), (or else Dineley's drawing was inaccurate).

demonstration of wealth and office, and its symbolic genealogy, which added the sanction of age to these attributes. These statements led the new lord deputy, Thomas Wentworth, Earl of Strafford, to force Boyle to move the monument from behind the high altar to a more discrete part of the church.[13]

The example of the Boyle tomb is not unique. The creation of a funeral monument was more than the making of a grave; it was as much for the living as for the dead, since it made a statement about the status and power of the individual and his/her family. For this reason the destruction of tombs was regarded more as revolution than sacrilege. At the end of March 1643, for instance, Sir Thomas Meridith smashed the tomb of a Mr Eustace at Castlemartin in County Kildare. His ensign, Edward Roe, later deposed that he did this because 'Mr Eustace of Castlemartin had burnt the house of Sir Robert Meridith, who was brother to the said Sir Thomas and sayeth that the said Sir Thomas sayeth further that he knows this [the destruction of the tomb] would vex the said Mr Eustace more than anything else he could do unto him'.[14]

FUNERAL IMAGERY AND SYMBOLISM

Funeral monuments can provide an index to the changing social attitudes and priorities in six-teenth- and seventeenth-century Ireland, and when decoded can reveal patterns of social change among the gentry over a long period of time, which are almost impossible to obtain from documentary sources alone. Such decoding is not easy, since monuments contain many elements whose rate of evolution differs. One of the features of funeral customs and practices is their complexity. While the act of dying may have been an individual one, the rituals and images of the funeral were intended to preserve social stability in the face of dramatic change, and thus were rarely innovative. Rituals such as a religious service, which could be matched to official religious belief, tended to change more rapidly than images representing social structures and political hierarchies. At any one time there were overlapping layers of belief expressed through the images and rituals of death and dying. The will of Jenico, third Viscount Gormanston, who died in October 1569, provided 'that my son shall yearly have a memorial of me and give always to the poor', which resembles strongly the Catholic tradition of a memorial service, the year's mind, yet Gormanston was almost certainly a Protestant.[15] The will of Sir Thomas Cusack of Lismullen in County Meath, a staunch Protestant, contained a similar inconsistency, proclaiming himself in a long theological preamble to be a member of the elect, but providing money for a year's mind. He also allocated funds for a chapel at Trevet, County Meath, where he wished to be buried, and a priest was to be paid £4 a year for ever to sing the service, a stipulation that resembles the foundation of a Catholic chantry chapel.[16] New religious beliefs clearly proved no substitute for the social practices of the traditional world. Similarly, in the world of imagery there were discrepancies between the stated position and reality. In 1563, for instance, the symbols of the Passion were removed from many Irish churches, including Christ Church Cathedral, as 'popish', yet they were used on the tomb of Bernard Adams, the Protestant bishop of Limerick who died in 1625.[17] Again the box-tomb with sculptured recumbent figures can be traced from the Middle Ages into the early eighteenth century, indicating the slowness of changes in some areas, but the types and combinations of images on that tomb, and on other memorials associated with it, changed radically over the same period.[18] This essay attempts to decode the changes in

funeral imagery and, since it was created as much for the living as for the dead, to relate it to the social changes it documents.

Various elements were combined in the sculptured Irish tombs of the early sixteenth century, but the predominant theme among them is religious. To contemporaries, however, the division between sacred and secular themes was less obvious. The Church was not only a spiritual body, but an important force in political, administrative and economic life, and many religious symbols had a secular importance. At its simplest, a grave-covering consisted of a cross-engraved slab, the cross often segmental, with intricate interlacing rising from a stepped base, representing Calvary. There was usually a short Latin inscription recording the name of the departed, with a request for prayers for the soul, possibly conferring indulgences. More dramatic, and reserved for the upper social order, was the box-tomb, on which lay a slab, often with a sculptured image of the deceased. Men were clad in armour, unless a cleric, and women were depicted in contemporary costume (Illus 10.5). The side panels of the box often contained niches, in which were 'weepers' who represented the apostles or other appropriate saints, unusual in European tradition by the early sixteenth century. In the case of the apostles, they were not randomly arranged, but often followed the order in the prayer 'Communicantes' in the canon of the Mass, or the order assigned to them in the different parts of the Creed.[19] Other saints with local significance were sometimes represented, such as St Francis, or St Denis of France, in Franciscan churches.[20] The end panels of the box were reserved for less formal treatment, displaying a crucifixion or perhaps a personal or family saint. In such tombs heraldic detail was subsidiary to the religious imagery, although often present. Within Gaelic Ireland a similar set of images existed, though the form tended to be that of a niche tomb, with tracery filling in the upper part of the niche. Images of saints featured on the front panels (Illus 10.6). Within the architecture of the church the arrangement of these tombs was not random, but reflected the intertwined social and religious structures of the community. Burial close to the high altar was a sign not only of sanctity, but also of social standing.

10.5 The altar-tomb (or box-tomb) of the Grace family in St Canice's Cathedral, Kilkenny. The saints standing below the prostrated figure are invoked according to precise rules.

10.6 A fifteenth-century Gaelic niche-tomb at Kilconnell friary in County Galway shows a similar arrangement of saints to that in Illus 10.5, invoked to assist the deceased in attaining salvation.

10.7 The tomb of an unknown woman, probably a widow, in St Canice's Cathedral, Kilkenny (first half of sixteenth century). Apart from a bishop on the left, all the saints featured in the side-panel are female, including the Magdalen, second from the right.

The division between the religious and social structures brought about by the Reformation saw the dissolution of these arrangements. In the 1640s the Cistercian Malachy Hartry noted some of the confusion wrought by this change: 'when the new religion of Protestants sprang up about sixty years ago ecclesiastical immunity was violated by abuses ... and each one chose a place of burial for himself in whatever part of the church he pleased, thereby an unheard of scandal took place owing to the sacrilegious abuses that were introduced.'[21]

The religious significance of such tombs is clear. The deceased was committed to the care of the saints, who would intercede for him/her, and the figures, if arranged in the form of the litany, would act as a continual prayer for the deceased's soul. Thus most late fifteenth- and early sixteenth-century wills began with the formula 'I bequeath my soul to Almighty God and the Blessed Virgin Mary and all the Saints'. The native Irish annals recorded similar invocations of the protection of saints for the deceased. This practice continued as late as 1636, when Brian Mac Diarmada 'was interred nobly, honourably in Clonmacnoise under the protection of God and Ciarán on the festival day of Brigid'. This theme of protection is evident in the O'Connor tomb at Roscommon friary, or the tombs at Dungiven priory, or Tralee, where the body is guarded not by saints but by statues of gallowglass soldiers.[22] Women also sometimes preferred to be protected by other females who would intercede for them (Illus 10.7).

Such monuments provided the bridge between the living and the dead, and helped to minimise the social disruption caused by the death of a powerful figure in the local community. The sculptured figure of the deceased was shown in a state of suspended animation between the earthly and heavenly world. This connection between the dead and the living is also apparent in the funeral ritual, which began before death and continued after it. A notarial instrument of 1514 recorded how John Kerny, parish chaplain of Dundalk, County Louth, went to Christopher Dowdall's house in the town 'wherein the said Christopher lay sick, to whom Sir John administered the sacraments of the Eucharist and Extreme Unction. And he heard Christopher declaring and disposing of the lands and tenements of his inheritance'. The instrument adds that Margaret Plunket, Christopher's wife, the parish clerk of Dundalk 'and many other good men of that town whose names he knows not' were present: death was a public event.[23] Following the death came the funeral Mass, accompanied by a series of communal events, such as the wake and the funeral feasting, with the grief of the community being ritualised in the keening women who followed the corpse. Once the immediate events of the funeral were over, the dead were not forgotten. The prayers for the dead, formalised in the month's mind and the year's mind, often with great feasting, would continue for some time. The Catholic will of Richard Netterville of Corbally in County Dublin made provision for his funeral, a month's mind and a year's mind to be kept in good state for his friends, charging his estate with bread, beer, mutton, pork and drink for the occasion. Henry Shee of Kilkenny made a similar provision in his 1612 will, adding that he was 'to be prayed for ... as is usual among good Catholics in God's church as often as she [his wife] can procure the same.'[24]

These funeral customs point to an extended family or lineage society, which characterised early sixteenth-century Ireland. The funeral encompassed not only the immediate family of the deceased, but the broader community, including a lord's servants and followers. The array of saints on the tomb represented the extended family of heaven, bound together by their sainthood and reflecting the ties of lordship on earth. Thus a person passed from one extended

IRELAND: ART INTO HISTORY

family to another. The strength of the lineage society varied from region to region. Within Gaelic Ireland the lineage society was predominant.[25] Here the appearance of saints or members of the earthly household, the gallowglasses, was nearly universal. Within the area known as the Pale, which comprised parts of Counties Dublin, Meath, Kildare and Louth, there were more subtle distinctions. In the outer Pale, mainly the lordships of Ormond and Kildare, the tomb adorned by saints was almost universal. This was march land, where warfare was common, and the great lineage families of Kildare and Ormond supported many retainers by exactions on the tenantry, which prompted frequent complaints.[26] In the inner Pale, around Dublin and Meath, estates were smaller, and the lords less powerful, and unable to muster great extended lineages. Here there was a different emphasis in the imagery of the funeral monuments, with blind arcades embellished with coats of arms replacing the saints on many tombs.[27] Thus the differences in the iconography of early sixteenth-century Irish tombs point to subtle differences of social organisation within the country, emphasising the lineage society in some areas and playing it down in others, but always reflecting the connection between the earthly and the heavenly worlds.

CHANGING ICONOGRAPHY

In the latter part of the sixteenth century the balance of the elements within the iconography of tomb construction began to change. Among the Anglo-Irish of the Pale, the saints began to be replaced with other religious symbols, most importantly the symbols of the Passion. These were of considerable antiquity and had featured on Irish tombs of the fifteenth and sixteenth centuries, often in a heraldic form, but were usually subsidiary to other religious symbols.[28] The more frequent use and prominence of these symbols reflects the increasing penetration of the religious ideas of the European *devotio moderna* and the Counter-Reformation into Ireland, mainly into the Pale and Munster. These ideas revitalised the Mass as a central part of Catholic devotion and tried to suppress local cults of saints. The Passion was intimately linked to the Mass, and some chalices from the late sixteenth century are engraved with the Passion symbols and scenes of the Crucifixion (Illus 10.8).[29] Indeed from the early seventeenth century many Catholic tombs were modeled on altars, at which Mass could be celebrated. The religious symbols on tombs indicate that in some parts of Ireland from the late sixteenth century, people were beginning to entrust their salvation to the Passion rather than to the intercession of saints. This change is mirrored in the opening formularies of wills, in which Catholic testators no longer committed their souls to God, Mary and the saints, but to God alone, and expressed their trust in Jesus for salvation.[30]

More significant than the change in the religious imagery was the secularisation of the symbolism on many tombs. Increasingly, the imagery on Catholic tombs of the late sixteenth and early seventeenth century was that of the family. On the mid-1580s' Barnewall tomb at Lusk and that of the Dillons at Trim, the niches have become arcades in the classical tradition, with complex heraldic detail. The Lusk tomb also lists the five sons and fifteen daughters of Sir Christopher Barnewall in four columns on the north side of the box (Illus 10.9).[31] This concentration on armorial detail and remembrance within the family is also paralleled in the bequests contained in wills. While fifteenth-century Catholics made bequests of goods and chattels to the Church to pray for their soul, sixteenth and seventeenth-century Catholics made bequests to their relations to remember them.[32]

10.8 The tombstone of William Galwey, 1628, at St Multose Church in Kinsale, County Cork, shows a remarkable profusion of symbols of Christ's Passion, reflecting the influence of the Counter-Reformation.

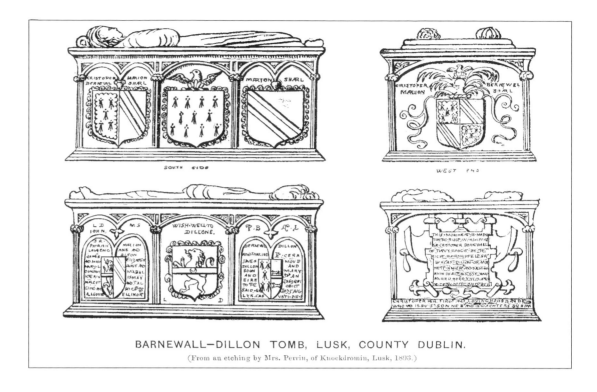

BARNEWALL–DILLON TOMB, LUSK, COUNTY DUBLIN.
(From an etching by Mrs. Perrin, of Knockdromin, Lusk, 1893.)

10.9 The Barnewall-Dillon tomb at Lusk, County Dublin (late sixteenth century) shows secular and heraldic designs taking over from specifically religious images.

This apparent disappearance from tombs of religious symbols and requests for prayers for the dead is explained in part by a relocation of this imagery. Jenico, fifth Lord Gormanston, for instance, specified in his will of 1629 that 'four or five pictures be drawn on canvas or otherwise as near as they can to my stature, one whereof to remain in this chapel [Gormanston], the rest to be placed in chapels of the friars preachers with the words under them "Pray for Gormanston" '.[33]

The disappearance of religious symbols from tombs is roughly contemporary with the increase in popularity of the wayside and churchyard cross. Some one hundred stone examples of these have survived from the seventeenth century, but there were many more, often erected in wood. The Jesuit annual letter of 1617 refers to County Meath where 'crosses of wood are put on the road near the house of a dead person with an inscription asking for prayers for the souls of the faithful departed', and the maps of the Farney estate in County Monaghan by Thomas Raven also show roadside crosses as a common feature.[34] The surviving stone wayside crosses usually ask for prayers for the deceased, supply a date of death, and give the name of the donor. The iconography of these crosses is usually simple, the Crucifixion being the most common image, with some depictions of the Virgin and Child. Saints are seldom featured, but they do occur at Duleek and Baronstown in County Meath and at two other locations. Unlike the use of saints on the tombs, the saints depicted on the crosses do not appear to have any formal liturgical significance.[35] At Duleek, for instance, only four apostles appear, St Peter, St Andrew, St James and St Thomas. St Cianan, who founded the first church at Duleek in the fifth century, is also shown, and St Patrick, a rarity on sixteenth-century tombs, is featured with St George and the dragon and St Mary Magdalene. The instruments of the Passion are arranged heraldically on the collar of the cross. This separation of the religious symbolism from the formal public monument to the deceased and the transfer to more personal and informal locations reveals an

IRELAND: ART INTO HISTORY

innovative separation of Church and secular society. Indeed this parallels the political stance that the Old English of the Pale were to adopt from the late sixteenth century: they could be loyal to the king as subjects in public matters, but in the private matter of religion their allegiance lay with the papacy and the Catholic Church.[36]

The religious changes of the late sixteenth and early seventeenth centuries produced a new set of Protestant ideas about death and the images chosen to represent the deceased. Protestant sensibilities regarded the tombs fashioned in the early sixteenth century as idolatrous. They preferred a purely memorial monument representing the achievements and family of the deceased. One of the earliest Irish examples is the tomb of Sir Thomas Cusack of Trevet in County Meath who died in 1571, having held most of the prominent offices in the country. The tomb is now destroyed, but the main elements of the iconography can be reconstructed from the remains (Illus 10.10). One of the main panels shows Sir Thomas and his second wife kneeling at a prayer table, on which lies an open book, probably the Bible. Behind Sir Thomas are his four sons, and behind his wife are the couple's six daughters. The two youngest daughters stand at either end of the tomb, one holding the purse of the lord treasurer and the other holding the mace of lord chancellor, both offices held by Sir Thomas. One other element of the tomb, added much later, comprised a family 'tree' springing from a heraldic shield, with the Cusack arms on one side, and with branches showing the marriages of Sir Thomas's sons and daughters.[37] This sort of representation of the family gathered around the prayer desk became almost universal among Protestants in the late sixteenth and early seventeenth centuries.[38] It would be wrong, however, to portray this type of sculpture as a purely Protestant tradition. The Catholic Dillon tomb at Trim, County Meath, has a representation of a family group at the west end (Illus 10.11), and the Aylmer monument at Donadea in Kildare shows the family of Sir Gerald above figures of Saints Jerome, Augustine, Gregory and Ambrose. How quickly these new ideas penetrated into the Gaelic Irish community is unclear, but certainly by the early seventeenth century the tomb

10.10 A side panel of the tomb of Sir Thomas Cusack at Trevet, County Meath (c1571), shows a new Protestant preference for memorials focused on the family of the deceased: a tomb featuring bishops and saints (Illus 10.5 and 10.7) could be seen as idolatrous.

10.11 A Catholic tomb (Dillon family) at Trim, County Meath, shows a family group at prayer, similar to that on the Protestant tomb in Illus 10.10.

of O'Connor Sligo in Sligo Abbey was similar in design, with O'Connor Sligo and his wife depicted kneeling on each side of the wall tomb.[39]

While Protestants and Catholics during the late sixteenth and early seventeenth centuries chose to put rather different visual images on their tombs, the basic message was the same: the emphasis was on the immediate family of the deceased and his/her genealogy, in contrast to the extended lineage to which the tombs of the early sixteenth century had appealed. To some extent the changes in tomb architecture and iconography were imitative of English styles which had evolved to meet changes in that society, but it was not simply a stylistic matter, since there are other indications of a greater preoccupation with status and genealogy. The creation of the office of Ulster King of Arms in 1552 points to an increased concern with genealogy and heraldry. This office produced funeral certificates and regulated the increasingly common heraldic funerals. The funeral certificate preserves, in a different form, the information often given on tombs, the names of the deceased and their children, and often gives coats of arms.[40]

The reasons for this change from a lineage-dominated society to one dominated by more restricted family structures are complex. The Counter-Reformation in Ireland, for instance, was as concerned with social reforms as it was about spiritual regeneration, and it produced a concerted attack on the extended lineages of both Anglo-Ireland and Gaelic Ireland. In the area of funeral customs, the communal wake, the feasting and the ritual weeping, or keening, were all condemned by the Irish Counter-Reformation synods.[41] While the 1571 funeral monument of Richard Butler, Viscount Mountgarret, in St Canice's Cathedral, Kilkenny, is architecturally in the traditional Gothic style, its iconography displays the twin concerns of the new order in the symbols of the Passion and the arms of the family (Illus 10.12). The social aims of the Counter-Reformation were also aspired to by the English administration in Ireland, who sought to destroy the extended lineages of 'over mighty subjects'. Indeed, this became an underlying principle of sixteenth- and early seventeenth-century government policy towards Ireland.

As well as being mediated through England, many of the new ideas on the organisation of society were imported directly from the Continent, especially among the Old English and native Irish. The Barnewall tomb at Lusk and the Dillon tomb at Trim both show European influences

10.12 The funeral monument of Sir Richard Butler (1571) in St Canice's Cathedral, Kilkenny, is in traditional Gothic architectural style, but images of the Passion appear instead of extended family lineage.

in the dress and armour of the figures carved on them, and both have architectural features that are recognisably Renaissance in style. Again on one of the surviving end panels of Sir Peter French's tomb in the Franciscan friary in Galway, the image of the Trinity is of a more modern type than the sixteenth-century 'throne of grace' type images.[42] This interchange of ideas gave rise in the late sixteenth century to a society in some parts of the island where education was becoming more important than military strength in determining a man's status, and the process of law rather than violence emerged as the way of resolving disputes. The family moved closer to the humanist idea of a small unit, rather than that of a mighty lineage.

One other important reason for change is indicated by the rise of the heraldic funeral among the Old English and the newcomers. The heraldic funeral was an indicator of social status in a society where rapid social mobility was the norm, and it also provided a symbolic display of the passage of land from one generation to another.[43] The transfer of land from the Gaelic Irish to the Old English and the newcomers in sixteenth- and seventeenth-century Ireland, was an uncertain and often difficult process, and to consolidate these new acquisitions a smooth passage to a second generation was required. The symbols carved on tombs, whether in the form of heraldic devices or a representation of the family, served to identify the inheritors and emphasise the continuity of new-found wealth. Recently acquired wealth was underpinned by indications of status, usually office, and hence the detailed representation of the offices held by the deceased.

THE RISE OF THE EPITAPH

From the middle of the seventeenth century the balance between the various elements of the funeral monument began to change again. With the rise of classical learning came formal classical architecture. This had become an integral part of the design of most tombs by the early part of the seventeenth century, especially in the Kilkenny area, with the consequent decline in sculptured monuments. Between 1571 and 1603 twenty-two sculptured monuments were created; this figure rose to eighty-one over the next forty years, but fell to twenty-nine between 1641 and 1689. This drive for classical models included increased emphasis on the epitaph, which Thomas Dineley, for example, saw as one of the most important elements on the classical Roman tomb.[44] By the end of the seventeenth century the normal form of memorial was an epitaph with an architectural surround, often using different colours of marble for effect. The written epitaph became the most prominent feature on the tomb. Increasing literacy during the seventeenth century, with many people learning to read if not write, made the epitaph more accessible, and the normal language of the inscription changed from the Latin of the sixteenth century to English, or in some cases Irish.[45]

The rise of the epitaph affected the nature of the message the tomb was intended to convey. New attributes of gentility, such as a classical education, knowledge of the law and wide learning, were not easily shown in symbolic form: they were more appropriately portrayed in words. The inscription on Sir Thomas Cusack's tomb is in Latin, in classical metrical and iambic metre, praising him as a lawyer and a scholar. Mathew de Renzi's tomb from the 1630s in Athlone made the inscription central, recording de Renzi's accomplishments as a traveller, linguist and man of affairs. His only failing as a true Renaissance man was his lack of military experience, but this was compensated for by giving him a dubious genealogy, extending back to a fifteenth-century leader of Albanian resistance to the Turks. The now-lost Montgomery tomb at Greyabbey, County Down, had a similar inscription extolling the importance of travel, learning, administrative skills and military experience.[46]

The increased use of the epitaph was also a response to the settlers' need to explain and rationalise their new-found position as landowners, despite their humble origins. The epitaph provided an opportunity for some to set out their more prestigious connections in England or Scotland. The epitaph on the Chichester tomb at Carrickfergus, County Antrim, for instance, recorded the fact that Sir Arthur was a grandson of the Earl of Bath. More dubious was the inscription on the Bowen tomb at Ballyadam in Leix, which proclaimed:

> whose great descent was first from royal kings,
> whose never dying virtues live; for why
> whose fame eternalised he can never die.

The exact genealogical connection with 'royal kings' was not specified.[47] The problem of establishing a new lineage was not simply one of biology, but also of justification of the new-found position. Some used conquest as a justification. The 1617 memorial to John Wakely of Ballyburley, one of the settlers in the plantation of Offaly and captain of a troop of horse and foot, provides such a justification. John is represented holding a lance and wearing a cavalry sword, and to the right are the family arms surrounded by the trophies of war, including two plumed Irish helmets. Underneath is the decapitated head of a native Irishman. John's rights in Offaly were to be seen as the spoils of war.[48]

Over time this explanation was to fade from prominence. While most figures on early seventeenth-century tombs wore armour, in the latter half of the century they invariably wore civilian clothes.[49] By the 1630s it was not by right of conquest that most settlers claimed their status, but because it was ordained by God. John Hatten of Knockbally in Fermanagh referred in his 1632 will to 'the worldly state whereof it has pleased God to endow me', and by the late seventeenth century it was normal in Protestant wills to refer to the estate as being lent by God or as being 'wherewith the Lord has blessed me'.[50] Thus it was necessary to demonstrate on the public monument the claim that God had endowed the deceased with their fortune. This was usually done by way of an epitaph, which recorded the main feature of the deceased's life and his/her finer points, almost always with a heraldic device. The 1623 Stafford Monument in Wexford proclaimed 'God's gift is our possession. God's mercy is our protection.' On the other side of the political divide the epitaph could record the sufferings of the deceased, as at Kilconnell friary, County Galway, where Mathias Barnwall's inscription noted that he had been 'transplanted into Connacht with others by order of the usurper Cromwell'.[51]

CHANGES IN BURIAL PRACTICES

This change in tomb architecture to give prominence to the written inscription paralleled a change in burial practices. The heraldic funeral, important in the early part of the seventeenth century as a demonstration of a family's status, fell into disuse, and the funeral became a much simpler affair, often held at night to escape the notice of the heralds. Thomas Dineley, who toured Ireland in the 1680s, commented:

> Funerals in any expensive way... are in these days thought vain, I have neither seen nor heard of but one in above twelve months travail in the kingdom of Ireland... Nobles and gentry of eminent

condition and offices are either secretly conveyed to their sepulture in the dark…or niggardly buried in the day time…without the attendance of any officer of Arms whose dependence formerly used to be upon the performance of funeral rites and exequies…the daily church robberies obliterate the memory of the defunct, covetous filching, pilfery…having most sacrilegiously pict out, erazed and stolen away for the metals sake most of the inscriptions, epitaphs, arms, pedigrees and history of families upon the goodly tombs of our worthy ancestors.[52]

Similarly, from the 1650s the number of funeral certificates registered in Ulster's Office fell significantly.[53] The language of heraldry was collapsing under the weight of the written word. On the Tasburgh tomb of 1711 in Ross Errily, County Galway, it was felt necessary not only to carve the arms of the family on the monument, but also to provide an inscription to explain them. This cannot have been a light decision, since according to a 1690 agreement for a tomb in St Nicholas's Cathedral, Galway, lettering was charged at three pence a letter.[54]

With the rise in the popularity and respectability of the inscription, tombs became significantly simpler and cheaper. Many people took advantage of this development to erect memorials that comprised only a name, date of death and some details of their family. In this way, those outside the great landed families could establish an appropriate lineage for themselves.[55] As funeral monuments became more common, some families took the opportunity to obtain prestigious burial places in disused tombs. Many families had risen in the social scale as a result of the political readjustments of the late sixteenth and early seventeenth centuries. The Burkes of Derrymaglaughny in County Galway, who were descended from a cousin of the first Earl of Clanricarde, took possession of a medieval Burke tomb in Claregalway, County Galway, in the 1650s and imposed their arms on it, giving the family the appearance of antiquity and status (Illus 10.13). With the move down the social scale, the symbolism used on monuments also became much simpler, often representing a trade or profession of the deceased. Pattern books seem to have been used in some cases, as two clerical tombs in the Franciscan friary at Claregalway have an identical chalice and host on them.

10.13 A fifteenth-century niche-tomb of the Burke family at Claregalway friary in County Galway. The arms were added in the 1650s to lend a spurious antiquity to a local branch of a quite different family.

FUNERAL MONUMENTS AS HISTORICAL EVIDENCE

The problem of describing the complex pattern of social change in early modern Ireland is made more difficult by the scarcity of written documents. One instance of such change was the way the descendants of the Anglo-Norman settlers altered their description of themselves from 'Anglo-Irish' to 'Old English'. Historians have ascribed this change to a wide variety of influences, ranging from the political alienation of that group from the Dublin administration, to the impact of the Counter-Reformation.[56] The evidence of the funeral monuments indicates that this transformation may have been more complex and more fundamental than these explanations suggest. The changing pattern of funeral monuments would seem to reflect a radical change in the way society was organised. The factors bringing about this change were more diffuse than simply religion or politics, and were more gradual than might be suspected. While the trend away from representations of saints on tombs and commendations of the soul to saints in wills had been dated to the middle of the sixteenth century, such representations and commendations can be found well into the seventeenth century. The 1629 tomb of the first Viscount Mayo in Ballintubber Abbey in County Mayo, or the 1608 tomb of Richard Shee in St Mary's Church in Kilkenny, are both late examples of the early sixteenth-century 'Apostle' tombs. Similarly, in 1622 Nicholas Archdean of Kilkenny was happy to commit his soul to God, the Blessed Virgin Mary and all the holy company of heaven, as his fifteenth-century predecessors had done.[57] This serves as a reminder that the pace of change differed from region to region and often from individual to individual. The visual evidence of the funeral monuments, which document over time both the secular and sacred concerns of contemporaries, is a valuable measure of changing political, social and religious values, which can only be ignored at the peril of the historian.

11

Marie Davis

CHILD-REARING IN IRELAND, 1700–1830: AN EXPLORATION

Recent decades have seen a growing interest in the history of childhood in Britain, Europe and America. Sparked off by the seminal work of Philippe Aries[1] in 1960, there has been a surge in the publication of both academic books and articles on the subject, as well as works of more general interest.[2] Until recently, however, there has not been a comparable interest in this area of social history in Ireland.[3] The bulk of previous research relating to Irish children concentrated mainly on the educational aspects of their upbringing.[4] Some histories of privately endowed schools were written, as were a number of histories of the philanthropic bodies that founded schools for the poor.[5] The educational arrangements made by Catholic families for their children in the time of the Penal Laws and by the Huguenots and Quakers were also documented.[6]

By combining historical and art historical sources it is possible to present a more complete picture of eighteenth-century childhood than may be obtained by using textual sources alone. This essay explores various themes that concerned parents during the eighteenth century, using both visual and textual sources as appropriate.

HEALTH AND WELL-BEING

Evidence that many eighteenth-century Irish parents loved their children and were concerned for their welfare is to be found not only in letters and diaries, but in the many happy family portraits of parents with their children. The group portrait of Richard Lovell Edgeworth, his third wife Elizabeth and ten of his twenty-one children, portrayed by Adam Buck in 1787 (Illus 11.1) illustrates the obvious affection to be found within this family circle, and reinforces the

11.1 *The Edgeworth Family* 1787, Adam
Buck (1759–1833), Watercolour

This group portrait of Richard Lovell
Edgeworth with his third wife and ten
of his twenty-one children depicts a
warm family group, full of obvious
affection.

Private collection

expressions of solicitude for his children that were so frequently found in Richard Lovell
Edgeworth's correspondence. Maria, the famous novelist, sits opposite her father in the portrait, and behind his wife stands Honora, his daughter by his second marriage, who died of
consumption in 1790, aged fifteen, and of whose death her father wrote with great sadness.[7]
Several other children in the Edgeworth family also died of consumption.

Disease, especially smallpox, was an ever-present source of anxiety for parents, and one
they would rarely have wished to illustrate. One account of smallpox is provided by Henry
Flower (*c* 1717–52), elder son of Colonel William Flower, MP (later Baron CastleDurrow) of
Durrow, County Kilkenny, who developed the disease while at school in Kilkenny in 1728.[8]
The school accounts for the period list expenditure on board, food, wine and clothing, but several items relate specifically to medical expenses incurred during the boy's illness. A doctor
and apothecary were paid £2.5.0 and £6.9.6 respectively, and payments to servants who cared
for Henry were also listed.

Even before safe inoculation using the cowpox strain was developed by Edward Jenner in
the 1790s, some parents, anxious to save their children from death or disfigurement, allowed
their children to be inoculated with a mild strain of human smallpox. Writing in 1770, Anne,
a daughter of Sir Samuel Cooke MP, Lord Mayor of Dublin and wife of Walter Weldon, MP of
Sportland and Rahinderry, Queen's County, recorded details of her three children's inocula-
tions on 26 January.[9] Until 11 February the three children are recorded as recovering, but on
that date a more cheerful note is evident when the diary entry reads: 'Children poorly. They
eat meat this day ye first time.' By 24 February the children had obviously recovered, as they
were well enough to dine at their grandmother's house.

WET-NURSING PRACTICES

A common concern of parents, rich and poor alike, was the quality of wet-nursing. While written documentary material relating to wet-nursing in Ireland exists, no Irish illustration of this
subject has been found. The custom of employing wet-nurses was a long established one within
the upper classes. Since infant mortality was high, wives were expected to produce a child
each year in order to ensure succession; breastfeeding was frowned upon by husbands because
it provided a certain degree of contraception. Wealthy mothers regarded breastfeeding as both

170

injurious to the figure and a social inconvenience. It was common practice for wealthy parents to employ healthy mothers from the tenantry or nursing mothers living nearby to nurse their well-born babies. Occasionally the wet-nurse would live with the family, but it was more common for the child to be sent out to her home. Often the natural mother saw little of her offspring until the child had reached the age of three, and consequently she was generally unaware of the day-to-day conditions in which her child was brought up. Whether the wet-nurse was attentive or neglectful of her charges would not have been immediately obvious to an infrequently visiting mother.

During the course of the eighteenth century, doctors, philosophers and educationalists advanced new ideas about child care and education that reversed earlier practices. These new ideas were directed towards wealthy parents, and denounced the custom of employing wet-nurses for the first few years of children's lives. They seem to have had some success, for by the end of the nineteenth century the practice of employing wet-nurses was in decline.

EDUCATION AND SCHOOLING

Education is one of the best documented aspects of children's upbringing in the eighteenth century, both visually and in printed sources. The decision of an artist like James Malton (*c*1764–1803) to include an impressive eighteenth-century Dublin building, the Hibernian Marine School (Illus 11.2), in a riverscape, has left us with a valuable visual record of a school demolished during the twentieth century that would otherwise have been known only from documentary sources. Choosing a school for their children was a major concern for parents. School registers reveal the composition of their intake, and books and pamphlets written by the founders of philanthropic schools reveal the noble aims that led to their construction. Parliamentary concern resulted in a plethora of commissions, reports and government documents. From a visual point of view, the sources for schooling include architectural plans and elevations, satirical drawings and genre paintings.

11.2 *The Marine School, Dublin, looking up the River Liffey* 1796, James Malton (*c*1764–1803), Watercolour

The Marine School building became a storage depot in the nineteenth century and was finally demolished some years ago, but Malton's engraving records its impressive appearance soon after its construction.

National Gallery of Ireland (no 2704)

Some education took place in the home, and certain enlightened parents avidly read the works of the French philosopher Jean Jacques Rousseau, and were influenced by him. The wide appeal of the Edgeworths' *Practical Education* of 1798 may be gauged to a certain extent by a satirical illustration of a schoolroom interior by Caroline Hamilton (1777–1861), depicting an exhausted teacher and two bored girls sitting around a table on which lies a pile of educational treatises, among them *Practical Education* (Illus 11.3). On a similar educational theme, the same artist depicted a crying infant being forced by its determined parents to read and count instead of being allowed to play with its toy horse (Illus 11.4).

Some well-off Irish families sent their children to the best English public schools. A family tradition of attendance at a particular English public school usually influenced the choice of the educational establishment. The English school registers of the period are littered with the names of Irish families.

The impact of religious and ethnic minorities on the education and upbringing of children in Ireland is evident in the Quaker and Huguenot schools that were established in the late seventeenth and early eighteenth centuries. Quaker schools appeared in many areas, including Dublin, Mountmellick, County Laois, and Waterford; the Huguenots set up schools in Portarlington, County Laois, and Dublin. Concerned to maintain their identity, and with a view to carrying on their own cultural traditions, the strongly independent views of the Quakers and the intensely felt nationalism of the Huguenots were reflected in various aspects of their educational establishments. The Quaker preference was for boarding schools where children could, as in the home, be more easily inculcated with good manners and self-discipline. Most pupils in these schools were fee-paying, but the children of poor Quaker families were educated free. During the eighteenth century a change in the pattern of Quaker education became evident. Pupils from all religious denominations were now accepted into their schools, and privately owned Quaker schools such as Ballitore, County Kildare, were founded (Illus 11.5). This simple building reflects the modest lifestyle of the Quakers and is in sharp contrast to the grandiose Hibernian Marine School (Illus 11.2). By the early eighteenth century, Quaker merchants in Ireland had become more affluent and had begun to follow the practice of the landed classes of sending their sons to be educated at Quaker boarding schools in England.[10]

As refugees, the Huguenots hoped for an eventual return to France, and the initial aim of their Irish schools was to educate their young as native French. This encouraged some wealthy Irish parents from all over the country to send their children to the Portarlington schools, thereby giving them the opportunity to become fluent French speakers.

172

At the other end of the social scale, the eighteenth century saw the rise of the hedge-schools. Their existence is well documented in government reports, commissions, contemporary novels and the personal testimony of former pupils. Despite sporadic prosecution of hedge-schoolmasters, the poorer Catholic parents supported these schools morally and financially, preferring to pay the nominal fee required rather than send their children to the free Charter schools controlled by the Established Church.

The physical environment of the schools seemed to bear little relation to the standard of education received. Sir Thomas Wyse, a former hedge-school pupil, commented on the excellence of these schools and wrote: 'The lower class proportionally to their position are better educated than the upper.'[11] In 1779 the Huguenot artist Gabriel Beranger, while on a countrywide tour recording Irish antiquities, observed one enterprising schoolmaster utilising the roofless Ballintubber Abbey, County Mayo, where: 'I found a schoolmaster in the abbey with a parcel of children, his desk a large monument and the children sat on stones arranged.'[12] The setting of the roofless Ballintubber Abbey as a meeting place for a hedge-school reflects the determination of poor Catholic parents to circumvent the penal legislation and obtain an education for their children by any available means.

A step up from the hedge-schools were the small rural schools held indoors, one of which is illustrated by Nathaniel Grogan in *The Village Schoolmaster*, painted in the late eighteenth century (Illus 11.6). Here the artist depicts the practice of beating pupils with a furze branch, which otherwise would only be known through written descriptions, such as that by William Carleton in his *Traits and Stories of the Irish Peasantry*.[13] This is a good example of the visual and the literary coming together to illuminate a particular incident.

A valuable visual record of the interior of John Synge's experimental school for poor children of the Synge estate at Glanmore, Roundwood, County Wicklow, was painted by Maria Taylor

11.5 *Quaker School, Ballitore, County Kildare*, Thomas Urey Young (*fl* 203 2031880–88), Watercolour

This private Quaker boarding school was open to children of all denominations; the simple, though extensive, building contrasts with Dublin's impressive Marine School (Illus 11.2). National Gallery of Ireland (no 6288)

Above

11.6 *The Village Schoolmaster,* Nathaniel Grogan (c1740–1807), Aquatint

A disobedient or recalcitrant pupil is beaten with a furze branch, in an incident similar to those described in William Carleton's *Traits and Stories of the Irish Peasantry*: visual confirmation of a literary report.

British Museum

11.7 *Interior of John Synge's School at Roundwood, County Wicklow* c1820, Maria Spilsbury (Taylor) (1777–1823), Watercolour

In considerable contrast to Illus 11.6, pupils of various ages go about their tasks peacefully in a well-run experimental school (for the children of the Synge estate).

Private collection

in about 1820 (Illus 11.7). This watercolour not only records the work of this early nineteenth-century educationalist, but it also constitutes an important source of information for the social historian. Synge was a pupil and follower of the Swiss educationalist Pestalozzi, and the Roundwood non-denominational school was the first school based on Pestalozzian principles to be opened in the British Isles. Maria Taylor painted many groups of children, and the recording of minute detail is one of her characteristics.[14] It is likely that she was a frequent visitor to Roundwood school for she lived with the Tighe family at nearby Rosanna, County Wicklow, after 1795, as governess,[15] and she painted group portraits of both the Tighe and Synge families. *The Roundwood School* is likely to be an authentic record of the schoolroom interior and its activities, and several aspects of the Pestalozzian system have been identified.[16] The use of Pestalozzian tables in the centre and left foregrounds, and the boy in the background copying blackboard diagrams of form, provide evidence of the nature of the education being carried on in Synge's school.

Among the best documented eighteenth-century educational movements are the Charity schools, which flourished mainly between 1700 and 1730, and the Charter schools, founded in 1733 and phased out following government investigations in the years immediately prior to the establishment of the national education system in 1831. The Charity schools, founded by private individuals, were based on the concept of workhouse schools, devised by the English philosopher John Locke, in which poor children would be taught the basic elements of education and trained in a manual craft skill, such as spinning or weaving. A drawing of an early established Charity school for girls, founded by Mary Mercer in 1726, appears as an illustration on Brooking's Map of Dublin of 1728 (Illus 11.8). Private benefactors, clergymen and improving landlords, including Lord Perceval in County Cork, and the Earl of Abercorn in Strabane, County Tyrone, helped to establish Charity schools. Their motives were more than philanthropic, as they were fully aware of the benefits that would accrue to their property through having Protestant-educated and law-abiding tenants on their estates. In 1711 the Reverend Edward Nicholson of Cumin, near Sligo, founded, and subsequently maintained there, a Charity school for twenty-four boys. His two pamphlets, *A Method of Charity Schools*[17] and *Supplement to a Method of Charity Schools*,[18] intended as a guide to possible benefactors, provide much information about his motivation and the detailed running of the school. The following quotations are indicative of his philosophy:

> Instruction of the young … prevents their being only thieves … saves us from being robbed puts them in the way of a livelihood.[19]

> Where a Nation neglects setting a public fund for educating poor children … it is the duty of every good Christian to maintain same at his own expense.[20]

In his pamphlets Nicholson detailed his methods of administration, the cost of the children's maintenance, the school curriculum, and suggested future forms of employment for his pupils. He also devoted considerable attention to the question of providing children's uniforms, and was particularly concerned about cost and economy of cut. He reckoned on clothing a twelve-year-old boy for 7s. 3d a year, emphasising that 'The coat must have no gathering or pleats in the side, but cut straight down'.[21] One particularly interesting aspect of this cleric's educational philosophy was his concern to attract Catholic children into Protestant schools.

11.8 Mary Mercer's school for girls

This was an early Charity school for girls, founded by Mary Mercer in 1726; only two years later it was thought worthy of illustration on a map of Dublin.

Detail from Brooking's Map of Dublin, 1728

Pietas Corcagiensis, published in 1721, is a contemporary account of the founding of a Charity school for fifty boys and fifty girls, the Green-Coat Hospital in Cork city, in 1715 by the Reverend Henry Maule, rector of St Anne's, Shandon. This publication details the trustees' intentions, the names of benefactors, the curriculum offered, the moral training given to the pupils, and the daily dietary provisions. A 1719 engraving of the hospital included in *Pietas* shows the façade as it was in 1719, with two lead statuettes of Charity children on the gate piers. *Pietas* records: '…the Trustees ordered two charity boxes to be fixed up in the school, at the foot of two charity children dressed in their proper habits.'[22] The 'proper habits' are later listed in the Hospital's minutes book as being '…clothed in green and yellow, coats and capps [sic] of green, the lining of waistcoats and stockings of yellow'. Unlike the school itself, these statuettes still survive, and are now in storage in St Anne's Church, Shandon; they are a rare and valuable visual source for the costume historian (Illus 11.9 & 11.10). The preceding description of the 'proper habits' in the Hospital's minutes book can therefore be seen to tally with the statuettes.

The Charter schools founded in 1733 aimed to convert the poor Catholic children to the Established Church, an ambition voiced some years earlier by the archbishop of Armagh, Hugh Boulter (1672–1742), in a sermon at Tuam on 30 June 1730:

> …and if there were more Charity schools erected in this kingdom under proper Regulations, the youth would be more effectively brought up in the Christian knowledge than they are otherwise ever likely to be.

Boulter believed that the establishment of a countrywide system of schools would be infinitely preferable to the previous arrangement whereby the Charity schools depended for their existence on haphazard individual endowments; a proper school system might be the solution to civilising the native Irish and providing recruits to the Protestant faith. A royal charter for the founding of these schools was granted in 1733 under the title of 'The Incorporated Society in Dublin for Promoting English Protestant Schools in Ireland', and it had the distinction of receiving the first parliamentary grant made available for elementary education in the British Isles.

While the expressed intention of the Incorporated Society was the conversion of Catholic children, its commissioners did seek to provide them with a basic education, manual skill and subsequent apprenticeship. However, despite the detailed organisational structure created to oversee the running of the Charter schools, they failed in their objectives. Maladministration, inefficient supervision and committee members' apathy led to widespread abuses within the system, and the unfortunate pupils were the victims. Independent inspections and damning reports by the philanthropist John Howard in 1783, by the inspector of prisons, Sir Jeremiah Fitzpatrick in 1787, and by the Quaker John Stevens in 1818, as well as commissions of enquiry in 1788 and 1809–12, were all disregarded by parliament. Action was only finally taken following another adverse report of an 1825 commission. Financial support was withdrawn from the Incorporated Society and the schools were phased out over a period of six years. The surviving visual evidence includes both the internal layout and an elevation of a Charter School in the proposed ground plans contained in John Aheron's *General Treatise on Architecture*, published in Dublin in 1754 (Illus 11.11). The simple external appearance of Aheron's schools indicates the financial problems felt by the governors of the Charter schools following the fall in benefactions.

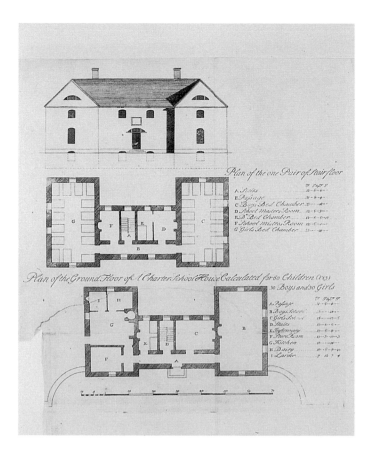

CLOTHING

The dress worn by Irish children is clearly a subject for which art historical sources are valuable, yet here too, documentary sources play their part in elucidating the subject. The provision of clothing was an integral part of Charity and Charter school philosophy, not only as a necessity, but as a means of identifying the recipients of charity. Masters and mistresses were in some instances instructed as follows:

> …that where children are clothed they cause them to wear their cloths [sic] every day, so that the Trustees and Benefactors may the better know them and mark their behaviour abroad.[23]

Most of the governing bodies drew up meticulous regulations regarding inmates' clothing, even if, as was later the case in the Charter schools, the prescribed clothing was seldom supplied. Clothes were regarded as a privilege by donors and were frequently taken back if recipients misbehaved. The almost invariable choice of blue as the colour of Charity children's uniforms in Ireland, as in England, was intentional. Firstly, as a means of identification, and secondly, it was intended to remind wearers of their humble station, as blue was the colour traditionally worn by servants and apprentices. Blue was also the cheapest available dye.

Parades of uniformed Charity children were a feature at public occasions in England during the eighteenth and nineteenth centuries, as the public liked to see the objects of their charity. Contemporary newspapers refer to similar parades in Ireland, where meagre details of dress are given, as in a report in the *Freeman's Journal* of a state procession held in Dublin in November 1765 to commemorate the birthday of King William III: '…the orphan children of soldiers… made a handsome appearance in their new cloathing [sic] of orange cockades and ribbons.'[24]

11.12 Detail from *Reverend Blake Kirwan Preaching on behalf of the Female Orphan House* 1806, Hugh Douglas Hamilton (1739–1808), Mezzotint

The group of girls behind the preacher are wearing the uniform stiff white cap and cuffs of the Dublin Female Orphan House, contrasting both with the fashionable clothes of the congregation and with the rags of the child on the right.

Private collection

11.13 Blue-Coat school uniform, *c*1675

Boys at the Blue-Coat school and King's Hospital in Dublin wore a blue frieze coat over yellow serge petticoats and yellow stockings, as shown here.

From Leslie Whiteside, *History of King's Hospital* (1980)

11.14 Detail of engraving of Ulster linen industry workers, William Hincks (*fl*1773–97)

A mother and child from a prosperous Ulster artisan family: the boy is well clad in a heavy green buttoned coat, breeches and shoes.

Private collection

11.15 *Blind Beggar Woman and Child*
1807, George Grattan, Oil on canvas
The dress of both mother and child appears to be carefully observed; note that the child is barefoot, while her mother is wearing shoes.
Royal Dublin Society

During the 1760s the lord lieutenant several times reviewed children from the Dublin Foundling Hospital who had been marched to Dublin Castle wearing their 'Windsor Uniform', an outfit consisting of blue suits and blue dresses with red collars and cuffs. The art of the period can enhance our knowledge of such public occasions, as in the 1806 mezzotint of H D Hamilton's painting *Reverend Blake Kirwan Preaching on behalf of the Female Orphan House* (Illus 11.12). The Charity Sermon was a popular social occasion in eighteenth-century Dublin, and the fashionable congregation as well as the uniformed orphans can be seen in the mezzotint. The Dublin Female Orphan House (1791) was exemplary in detailing and providing adequate clothing for its charges. Some of the older girls seen here are wearing the regulation stiffened white cap, white cuffs and shawl.

Records of two of the Blue-Coat schools — King's Hospital, Dublin, established in 1675, and St Stephen's Hospital, Cork, established in 1695 — refer to their pupils' uniforms. The first account refers in considerable detail to the boys' regulation blue frieze coats, which were worn over yellow serge petticoats and yellow stockings. An artist's impression of this style of uniform is illustrated (Illus 11.13). The second account states that upon each St Stephen's Day the boys were to be provided with 'decent blue coats and caps...together with all other convenient clothing'.[25]

Much detail about the dress of children of diverse social classes can be drawn from the art of the period, although the number of visual sources that accurately depict the dress of poor children are few. More commonly, the children appear in genre paintings in the foreground of crowd scenes or as tiny figures in a landscape, placed there as a compositional device. An exception to this are the artisans' children who appear in the 1783 series of William Hincks' engravings of the Ulster linen industry (Illus 11.14). In four of the series, numbers I, IV, V and VI, children are included, and are drawn of sufficient size to enable details of their dress to be studied. In V, an infant is shown wearing a low-necked dress and frilled baby cap. Clothes of similar style are frequently depicted during this period being worn by upper class children. An artisan's child wearing this type of clothes would therefore seem to indicate a degree of family prosperity. Hincks is generally regarded as having a good eye for detail and accurate in his depiction of industrial machinery; so it may be assumed that his clothed figures represent the contemporary dress of this social class. One must, however, always be aware of the licence exercised by creators of artistic works. George Grattan's *Blind Beggar Woman and Child* (Illus 11.15) gives a clear indication of the barefoot child's dress, and is also a pertinent comment on the widespread practice of begging that was then rampant in Dublin and frequently remarked on by visitors to the city.[26]

Aristocratic portraits provide a similar sort of evidence for the dress of upper class children, while the evolution in the style of children's clothes that took place during the late eighteenth century can be charted in Irish family portraits of the period. These family group portraits also provide us with strong evidence of the changing parental attitudes towards children.

The writings of doctors and educationalists, particularly Rousseau in his *Émile* (1762), who urged that children should have more freedom of movement both in their clothes and in their daily lives, strongly influenced parents and led in the late eighteenth century to more relaxed relationships and to new looser-style clothes for boys and girls.

The formality of clothing seen in the mid eighteenth-century paintings of Philip Hussey, such as *An Interior with Members of a Family* (1750s), (Illus 11.16), progressively gives way to a more relaxed scenario, as depicted in Robert Hunter's double portrait of *Sir Robert Waller and his Son Robert* (c 1770s), (Illus 11.17). Here the child's pose is very much in the spirit of Hogarth's 'disruptive children', who were frequently included in that painter's scenes of weddings and christenings, always in mischievous mood. A warm family relationship is to be seen again in Martin Cregan's *Francis Johnson and his Nephews* (1827), (Illus 11.18), but in this picture a hint of the formality that was to occur in the Victorian era appears in the children's clothing; the older boy is wearing a high-necked shirt and jacket, while the younger wears a fitted dress and pantaloons of heavy material.

For the art historian focusing on these paintings from a primarily aesthetic or technical viewpoint, there may be much to be gained by considering also the historical content of the eighteenth-century enlightenment and the changing social values of the period in which they were painted. Use of documentary sources will enrich the art historian's understanding of the cultural content of their visual material, while historians will derive benefits from their use of art historical sources.

11.16 *An Interior with Members of a Family* 1750s, Philip Hussey (1713–83), Oil on canvas
A well-to-do group in all the elegant formality of their clothing and possessions: note the elaborate wallpaper and the splendid Oriental carpet.
National Gallery of Ireland (no 4304)

11.17 *Sir Robert Waller and his Son Robert* c1770s, Robert Hunter (*fl*1745–1803), Oil on canvas

A much less formal portrait than Illus 11.16, and the clothes are also less formal: the boy wears an open frilled shirt, while his breeches — and his father's coat and waistcoat — are somewhat creased by use.

National Gallery of Ireland (no 4191)

11.18 *Francis Johnson and his Nephews* 1827, Martin Cregan (1788–1870), Oil on canvas

This portrait shows a warmly relaxed family grouping, but with a touch of formality in the clothes: note the boy's high-necked shirt and jacket.

Ulster Museum

12

Mairead Dunlevy

DUBLIN IN THE EARLY NINETEENTH CENTURY: DOMESTIC EVIDENCE

The early nineteenth century was a period of major change for almost all aspects of life in Ireland. The campaign for Catholic Emancipation achieved success in 1829; the Board of National Education was established in 1831; and the pioneering work of the Ordnance Survey introduced a new awareness of Irish history, antiquities and place names, all reflecting the spirit of improvement that prevailed. That same spirit could be seen in the pronouncements on art education, in the establishment of libraries, and in the persistent spread of penny post offices — even before official permission was granted — throughout the country.

The general artistic mood of the period also espoused freedom, movement, passion, and what were termed 'beautiful irregularities'. The same mood was reflected in the home: curtains were draped in a 'romantic' or dramatic style; furniture was placed away from the walls in a new 'casual' manner, and gardens, even in urban areas, were fashioned in a style similar to the natural landscapes of Oriental gardens. Indeed, some Dublin gardeners would seem to have adopted the Oriental style so fully that one critic could jeer at 'their winding walks — such as no human foot-step (except a reeling drunkard's) could have traced, yet these in the eyes of the proprietors are perfect models of Chinese'.[1]

BUILDING STYLES

In Dublin, the presence of the nobility had been reduced following the Act of Union in 1801, and the influence of the commercial middle class became increasingly more powerful. This

Opposite

12.1 In 1809, Wedgwood's commercial travellers used ware such as this to teach Irish retailers in country towns to make their counter displays more commercially attractive.

National Museum of Ireland

shift in influence may be seen in the transformation of the Duke of Leinster's town house into the home of the Dublin Society in 1815. Lord Powerscourt's town house was bought for a stamp office in 1807, and the Earl of Aldborough's house was transformed into a school in 1813.[2] The emphasis in new building shifted from catering for the demands of the gentry to constructing hospitals or commercial developments — such as The Corn Exchange, built at Burgh Quay about 1815, the three bridges built across the River Liffey in 1816, and the harbours built at Howth and Dún Laoghaire.

Although the Wide Streets Commissioners, established in the eighteenth century, continued to exercise control over house styles and streetscapes, they did so under financial constraints, and were consequently less ambitious and less demanding than before. Nevertheless, for the new middle-class suburbs with their wide and airy streets, sometimes overlooking squares, they encouraged house styles in which the new approach to living space, light, hygiene and fresh air could be indulged. This was in contrast to the congestion in the Liberties area of the city — the old medieval centre. There the working-class population was increasing rapidly, the destitution of those involved in traditional craft industries caused severe hardship, and the death-rate was high, due to malnutrition and cholera. Distinct though these two classes were, they were both keenly aware of each other; the bars outside kitchen-level windows and on window shutters, as well as the bolts and chains on exterior doors, were indicative of the fear of those living in wealthy homes — and their mistrust of the undeveloped policing system at the time.

TECHNOLOGICAL DEVELOPMENTS

The excitement about new ideas in design was encouraged by technological change. Steam power was introduced for boats, engines and looms, and people spoke of the possibility of introducing a railway system. Involvement and interest in further technological developments is shown in experimentation with the telegraph,[3] and in applications for patenting inventions — such as that of David Cooke in 1828 for his 'submarine'[4] and of George Malam in 1824 for a method of instantaneously extinguishing all of the street lights.[5]

This new spirit also had its effects on the domestic scene. Sheffield plate was so improved in the late eighteenth century that it eventually superseded pewter — a material that had served as the 'poor man's silver' for centuries. Moreover, the development of Wedgwood's cream colour and pearl ware allowed those of the middle class who were unable to afford fine porcelain to use fine ceramics as everyday ware (Illus 12.1).

A major development of the late eighteenth and early nineteenth centuries was the improvement in lighting systems. New types of lighting gave greater all-over light and allowed more flexibility in the set times for eating and sleeping. Nevertheless, the candle remained the most convenient method of artificial light, whether held in an expensive candlestick of silver, cut glass or fine ceramic, or in a modest one of wood or japanned tin, or simply a broken cup (Illus 12.2). More light was supplied by increasing the number of candles, by the use of candelabra (Illus 12.3) or chandeliers, by placing candlesticks in front of a mirror, or with torcheres, which raised the candles to shoulder height.[6] In 1783 Ami Argand from Geneva showed that a light equal to that of ten candles could be obtained by burning a circular wick in an oil-lamp. This revolutionary development was welcomed by the wealthy, and indeed oil-lamps became so popular that one Dublin supplier had a cistern capable of holding two thousand gallons of oil for lamps.[7]

IRELAND: ART INTO HISTORY

Above

12.2 Irish hospitality in the days of George IV (around 1815): note the source of light on the mantelpiece, and the doily under the wine-glass. The plain fireplace is typical of Dublin design.

Right

12.3 An elaborate table candelabrum, probably made in Waterford about 1790. The glass was cut to reflect the flickering candlelight.

National Museum of Ireland

12.4 'Dancing the quadrille': note the high light level made possible by gaslight in the 1820s. The increased intensity of light meant that the colour of women's clothing and of furnishings became stronger.
Detail from a Dublin cartoon, National Library of Ireland

12.5 *The Provost's House, Trinity College, Dublin*, James Malton (*c* 1764–1803), Ink and watercolour on paper, 1794
This shows a watercart passing the Provost's House in Dublin. Only the wealthy could expect clean supplies of domestic water on tap. The poor and many of the middle classes used wells or bought their water from carriers.
British Museum, London

There was even more excitement about the invention of gas lighting, and in the second decade of the nineteenth century in particular there were heated discussions on a proposal for lighting the principal streets and public buildings of Dublin by gas. There were allegations about the deliberate running-down of the oil-lamp system, and it was claimed that dirty oil was used to justify the new scheme. The corrupt intent of some of the Commissioners for Paving, Cleansing and Lighting was alleged, and there were threats of unemployment among Irish sailors working in the sperm whale fisheries, which produced lamp-oil. There was public concern about the cost of the project and it was contended that the money could be spent on relieving the hardship of the starving population in the Liberties.[8] Considering the state of development of the technology for gas lighting at the time, there may have been justification for some of the public concern, which claimed that 'the noxious vapour and deleterious effects produced by it [had already affected] the health and comforts of the inhabitants, besides the water in many of the streets, through which it is conducted, has been rendered so impure as to be unfit for use'.[9] Despite these protests, by the 1820s various gas-light companies were established in Dublin and many public buildings had installed this new lighting system. The bright overall light provided by gas (Illus 12.4) meant that colour became more important than before, for example in women's clothing, in the furnishing of rooms, and in the light levels of many pictures painted at the time.

Another major advance was the supply of piped water to homes and public fountains in poorer areas. Previously, piped water was available only to the wealthy — the supply of water to poorer homes often came from nearby wells or from regular deliveries by water-carriers (Illus 12.5). An Act of the Irish parliament of 25 March 1777 allowed Dublin Corporation to provide 'leaden branches' from several water mains to homes in return for annual fees.[10] Regular further legislation on this matter shows that there was difficulty in getting citizens to pay for water and that they objected to the 'frequent breaking up of the pavement of the streets of that City for repairing the pipe Water Works thereof'. From about 1816 the old timber mains were replaced with metal whenever the opportunity arose and when the city purse could afford it. The demands of industry, the fear of disease and a new attitude to personal hygiene forced this change. This supply of running water meant that people were able to change from the established custom of drinking beer, forced by poor-quality water, to that which was considered more refined — tea.

CLOTHING

The new approach to health could also be seen in dress (Illus 12.6 & 12.7). From the late eighteenth century the inhabitants of Dublin reduced the quantity of underclothing worn (Illus 12.8), and many stopped wearing periwigs. Both species were then so scantily dressed that men boasted about their 'elasticated' and skin-tight breeches, and women, dressed in flimsy muslin, depended on the warmth of their paisley shawls. This change of attitude extended even into the bedroom. For centuries people had dressed for bed in socks, nightcaps and gowns, and then, after they climbed up the bedsteps into the bed, they were protected from draughts with heavy lined curtains. Such measures created problems with heat and humidity. The feathers and down used in the pillows, bolsters and mattresses were not always treated properly, and some developed a strong, unpleasant smell (Illus 12.9). Moreover, the feathers,

12.6 *Portrait of Sir Edward S Lees* 1823, Thomas Clement Thompson (*c*1780–1857), Oil on canvas

About 1817, many gentlemen began to wear trousers. Unlike the poorer classes, however, they wore them tight, and usually of a drab colour.

General Post Office, Dublin

12.7 *Portrait of Lady Lees* 1823, Thomas Clement Thompson (*c*1780–1857), Oil on canvas

The companion portrait to Illus 12.6. The simulated slashing and the motifs on Lady Lees' red velvet gown were believed to reflect the fashions of the sixteenth century. Such revival trends were prevalent in times of insecurity and famine, as in the early 1820s, although Lady Lees is dressed in the finest velvet, silk, silk chiffon and jewellery.

General Post Office, Dublin

and the straw of the palliass or lower mattress, were affected by the warmth retained within the curtains and by the chamber-pot kept under the bed (Illus 12.10). Apart from the problem of odour, the general warmth and humidity encouraged bed lice to multiply. One solution to this problem, which was accepted by some 'eccentrics' and imposed on some servants, was the use of brass or metal beds. Another was to leave the curtains unpulled and the windows open, thus allowing a free passage of air.

HOUSES AND FURNISHINGS

Although the window is not left open in James Barry's painting *Iachimo Emerging from the Chest in Imogen's Bedchamber* (Illus 12.11), the new moon and what appears to be a square candle-holder placed most unusually in front of the window give the impression of light, of freedom and of the open air. This novel idea of the importance of having air in the bedroom was sufficiently widespread that people took an interest in stories such as that of Dr Lyne of Berehaven, County Cork, of whom it was said that in the 1750s he would not allow any of the windows of his home to be glazed. Friends boasted that for fifty years he slept in a bedroom with four open windows, and that neither he nor his family had a day's illness. This situation changed after he died from smallpox at the age of eighty-five — for the family glazed the windows and then got colds regularly![11] James Barry's portrayal suggests that Imogen was a health-conscious lady, and because of that she was daringly modern. He illustrates her modernity further by the black basalt bowl and the *rosso antico* vase on the mantelpiece — new ceramic wares, in simple classical styles, made fashionable by Wedgwood. These, as well as the book lying on the embroidery frame, suggest that while this young lady was educated and industrious, she was also more inclined to be a fashionable dreamy romantic.

If we ignore the theatrical props, such as Renaissance-style washhand-basin and jug, the angels at the bed-head, the bed-post, and Iachimo's theatrical dress and gaze, we can study the room itself. As Imogen has not pulled the bed curtains, the painted walls are visible. The ornate fireplace and the heavy damask curtains with the deep fringes are typical of a public room — such as a diningroom — and are not those of a bedroom, but the muslin covering on the dressing table and on the simple frame of the mirror was not unusual. The sewing-basket was copied at that time in more robust materials such as tinned plate and silver.

The sense of freedom, space and modernity depicted by Barry was not merely artistic convention. It carried over into all aspects of early nineteenth-century life, but especially into domestic life, which was also affected by the technical changes in water supply and lighting. On analysis of advertisements in contemporary newspapers, it would seem that the desirable urban residence of the early nineteenth century had at least one dining parlour, a spacious front drawingroom, a library or study, and at least three bed chambers, apart from servants' rooms. There would also have been a kitchen, pantry, scullery, wine-vault, coal-vault, stable, coach-house, hay-loft and lock-up yard. The principal rooms would usually have contained 'fashionable grates and marble chimney-pieces' (Illus 12.12).[12]

House furnishings depended to a large extent on the whims of the owner, and although people were exhorted to support Irish manufacturers in order to relieve the destitution of local trade and craftworkers, many seem to have preferred imported goods (Illus 12.13). To satisfy this demand, fine furniture was made locally in the foreign styles that were then so

12.9 The arrest of Lord Edward Fitzgerald, the patriot, in 1798. He had taken refuge in a feather-dealer's home — hence the comfortable bed.
National Library of Ireland

12.10 *A Room in Richmond Prison, Dublin* 1844, Henry O'Neill (1798–1880), Watercolour
Note the wallpaper and the holland blinds on the window. Also the curtained bed (warm but unhygienic).
National Museum of Ireland

12.11 *Iachimo Emerging from the Chest in Imogen's Bedchamber* c 1788, James Barry (1741–1806)

Barry's painting shows a room with plenty of moonlight and air. The notion that fresh air was desirable in a bedchamber was novel at the time.

Royal Dublin Society

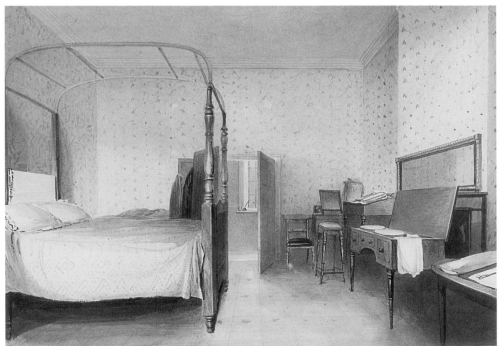

fashionable elsewhere — 'French'[13] and 'London' styles being two such examples that appear in advertisements. Local manufacturers of carpets and wallpapers, specialists who painted floors (Illus 12.14) and floorcloths,[14] and manufacturers of curtain and upholstery fabrics also satisfied their customers by following the designs of their foreign competitors. Despite this, it would seem that the financial success of the native producer remained limited. Although the Dublin Society gave premiums for carpet designs in the 1770s and the Irish carpet manufacturers boasted that their Dublin, Limerick and Cork carpets could be fitted, because of their various widths and sizes, on any stairs or in any size of room, yet these same firms gave particular emphasis in their advertisements to their holdings of imported Wilton, Brussels, Kidderminster, Venetian, Moorfields, Turkey and Scotch carpets.

Similarly, fashionable eighteenth-century Chinese, English and French wallpapers survive in a number of Irish homes (Illus 12.15).[15] They would have influenced the style of locally produced wallpapers, but in the early nineteenth century the Dublin Society tried to encourage originality in this field by offering premiums 'for the best invention in Pattern Drawing, either in foliages or Flowers, by an established Artist, each claimant to produce six full Patterns proper for Paper hanging'.[16]

Many specialists were available for the furnishing of homes. The most important was the upholsterer. As the specialist in home furnishing, he employed journeymen cabinet-makers to make and mend furniture, and to reupholster and cover furniture, on his premises. He also organised the making-up and fitting of curtains for windows and beds, the laying down of carpets, and he employed glass grinders and looking-glass frame-makers.[17] He was also the house and furniture auctioneer, the furniture removals man and, apparently, the person called in to do the 'spring cleaning'. Isaac Morgan & Sons of Mary Street charged Robert Brennan Esq of Eccles Street for:

9th January 1832
To taking up Carpets of 2 Parlours and 1 Drawing Room also the stair carpeting, Cleaning etc   4s.6d

16th January
To Beating and Cleaning Do. and for a Woman's time in repairing do.   5s.0d
To laying down and nailing the Carpets of Do. Rooms moving the furniture in and out   4s.0d
To Cleaning the Kitchen Chimney   1s.0d
To Do. 22 Windows @ 3d each   5s.6d
To 8 Days Scouring and Cleaning the House   10s.0d[18]

Another specialist was the house-painter. Although the brighter light produced by the Argand oil-lamp and the even greater all-over light produced by gas forced a change in colour schemes, this changeover was probably slow, and the high cost of certain paints would have militated towards the survival of traditional colours. Consequently there would seem to have been a consensus that kitchens (Illus 12.16) should be whitewashed, and the traditional chocolate brown be used for the woodwork on the kitchen level, with a dark green or lead colour on outhouses.[19] It was customary also that ceilings should be painted white and that many surfaces be stained and grained to replicate woods, particularly oak, mahogany, elm, ash and zebrawood.

Opposite top
12.12 A pleasantly relaxed scene in a fashionable home, early nineteenth century: note the attractive marble chimneypiece and the elaborate fire-grates.
National Library of Ireland

Opposite bottom, left to right
12.13 The Royal Arcade, Dublin, 1821: a shopping centre that concentrated on Irish-made goods. But it seems many purchasers preferred imported goods.

12.14 *A Room in Richmond Prison, Dublin* 1844, Henry O'Neill (1798–1880), Watercolour
This painting shows the fashion for painted floors (cheaper than carpets, though colder) that was prevalent at the time. Note also the undraped bed and the handsome washstand.
National Museum of Ireland

Ah! sure a pair was never seen so justly

Lord Bacon

G.H.^{in¹} The PIG Faced Lady of Manchester Square

This extraordinary Female is about 18 years of age — of High rank & great fortune.
Her body & limbs are of the most perfect & Beautiful Shape, but. her head &
Face resembles that of a Pig — she eats her Victuals out of a Silver Trough in the same
manner as Pigs do. & when spoken to she can only answer by Grunting !! her cheif
amusement is the Piano on which she plays most delightfully —

Left

12.15 'The pig-faced lady.' In the
background of this curious picture we
can see curtains held with a cloak-pin,
wallpaper with a border and a patterned carpet.

Private collection

Above

12.16 *A Kitchen Interior*, John Mulvany
(1766–1838), Oil on panel

A finely detailed painting showing a
typical flagged kitchen with shuttered
windows, plainly furnished, with a
variety of cooking implements clearly
displayed.

National Gallery of Ireland (no 1277)

Connoisseurs of the time believed that room colours should 'echo their uses. The colour of a library ought to be comparatively severe; that of a dining-room grave; and that of a drawing-room gay', that bedrooms should be in light colours and staircases in cool tones, free from contrasts. Moreover, it was said that the colour of the furniture in a room ought to influence the general colour used.[20] It is difficult to know whether Irish people accepted that advice — inventories of the period refer to bedrooms of green, yellow, chintz and even red. Mary Leadbetter visited a house in Wicklow where there would seem to have been a most unsophisticated approach to interior design, as the walls were 'adorned with paper of different colours cut small, pieces of looking glass etc'.[21]

Many, however, gave consideration to the overall decoration. When decorating the Council Chamber in the State Apartments in Dublin Castle, for example, the order was given that the wallpaper or paint colour should match the new carpet, and that the new oilcloth on the staircase should dictate the colour of the walls there.[22] The 'grave' colour, which J C Loudon recommended for diningrooms, seems often to have been interpreted as crimson. That certainly applied in the home of Thomas Pim of William Street, as in 1809 Margaret Boyle Harvey praised his diningroom because it was 'hung with crimson — and every article of furniture mahogany. In the recesses are mahogany cases, from the ceiling to the surbase, with glass doors lined with green silk, in one they keep books; in the other China they use every day — a very good contrivance and gives the room instead a good and elegant appearance'.[23]

Another room that shows the wealth of the occupant is Thomas Moore's study in his cottage in Sloperton (Illus 12.17). Moore is shown working at a drum table. The Irish harp and the early square piano nearby are indicative of Moore's interests. The shape of the ceiling, the simple fireplace and the direction of light through the window, suggest that the room is an attic. The flat appearance of the floor-covering and the fact that it was in a room that was used frequently may mean that this was of painted canvas or Scotch carpet. Comfort is suggested by the heavy curtains, which are draped over cloak pins, and the fact that the walls are painted with what was then an expensive colour.

In contrast, the presumably inexpensive paint colour 'drab' was the appropriate finish for the walls of a widow's room — that of Mrs Henry Grattan (Illus 12.18). The other symbols of her status are the portrait of her late husband and a simple flowerpiece. The formality of the portrait, however, is shown in the strong colour of the upholstery of the chair and stool, and the fact that the covers which would have protected them from everyday use were removed. The artist, Maria Spilsbury, shows Mrs Grattan still wearing her black mourning veil, but her dress seems to be of a style worn in the second period of mourning, thus dating the portrait to about 1822.

Harmony applied in items other than paint. J C Loudon ruled that 'the colours of the carpet should [not] be so brilliant as to destroy the effect of those of the paper, nor the contrary; and that the curtains should always be of a colour suitable to both. It is not necessary that they should be of the same colour, but that they should be of colours that harmonise or, in other words, look well together'.[24] Morine, chintz and muslin window curtains and draperies were popular: references to grey holland blinds occur regularly, as do moreen curtains in crimson or blue with fringe and silk lace trimming, held on gilt, brass or other poles, with rings and brass-end ornaments.[25]

12.17 *Thomas Moore in his Study at Sloperton Cottage*, English School, Oil on panel

The comfort and luxury of a gentleman's study: the songwriter Thomas Moore (1779–1852) at work in his home at Sloperton, England. The extensive library, the elegant furniture and the costly musical instruments all show that the owner is a man of wealth and culture.

National Gallery of Ireland (no 4312)

12.18 *Portrait of Mrs Henry Grattan*,
widow of the patriot Henry Grattan,
Maria Spilsbury (Taylor)
(1777–1823), Oil on canvas

One might have expected to find
Irish-made articles on display in such
a home, rather than the imported
glass vase that adorns the table.

National Gallery of Ireland (no 567)

12.19 *Portrait of a gentleman* 1801,
Johannes P Horstok (1745–1825), Oil
on canvas

The elaborate display of armour and
valuable objects suggests that the gentleman was a collector.

National Gallery of Ireland (no 650)

The variety of house furniture is suggested by auction notices: the sale in the Rev Godwin Swift's house in Dorset Street in April 1817 included mahogany parlour chairs, a large set of Northumberland tables, sideboards, breakfast tables, drawingroom chairs and sofas, pier and other glasses, pier cabinets, Indian cabinets, Wilton carpets, clocks in mahogany cases, hall and stair cases, (glass) bells for light, kitchen furniture and housekeepers' presses.[26] The furniture used could be modern, secondhand or antique: the latter two being bought either at auction or from an upholder (Illus 12.19). Ironmongers could sell items as diverse as brass and bronzed tea kettles and stands, 'best hardened tea and coffee pots', Argentine plate forks, spoons, ladles, candlesticks, japanned ware, door mats and rugs.[27] Ceramics and glass ranged from beer and wine glasses to lustres, salts, pans, jugs (Illus 12.20) and crocks, as well as table and tea services and ornamental ware (Illus 12.21). Indeed the variety required for table service is shown in the auction of the bishop of Cloyne's effects in 6 Merrion Street, which included steak dishes, an epergne, a tea urn, coffee urn, coffee jug, salvers, coasters, sauce boats (Illus 12.22), soup and sauce ladles, gravy, table and dessert spoons, a fish trowel, as well as lined damask, table 'lay-over' and napkins.[28]

Left

12.20 A handsome Donovan jug showing a Dublin Bay sailing scene with an early steam packet. Objects like this would never have been cheap.

George Stacpoole collection

Below

12.22 A gravy pot (or argyle) by Charles Harris, Dublin, 1811. The use of objects like this for regular dining presupposed an army of servants to clean and polish.

National Museum of Ireland

Above

12.21 Fit to grace any gentle lady's table: a Minton teapot, *c*1805–10, pattern number 268, sold by Donovan of Dublin and still in pristine condition.

National Museum of Ireland

4 " 9

C Mrs Ann McLoby
Housekeeper 1802/1737 P

4

2

16 Mary Faire
Laundry Maid R

12.23 A 'selection' of servants from Harriet Le Fanu's sketchbook of 1804: a housekeeper, two kitchen maids, a laundry maid, scullery maid, and probably a cook. The male servants included the coachman, postilion, gardener and labourers.

National Museum of Ireland

SERVANTS AND HOUSEKEEPING

Family homes on this scale required domestic servants. A scrapbook in which Harriet Le Fanu recorded her family, friends and servants shows the number of domestic servants employed by a comfortable family in Dublin about 1804 (Illus 12.23). Of the female staff there were a housekeeper, two kitchen maids, a laundry maid, scullery maid, and Matty (sic) McGeary, a woman who could have been the cook. The male servants illustrated include a coach man and postilion, gardener and labourers. The inclusion of two blackamoor butlers is surprising, although Sir Jonah Barrington, the memoirist and politician, does refer to their employment in Ireland at the end of the eighteenth century.

The prosperity that allowed a greater number of the population to consider themselves as middle class gave rise to a further separation between the 'family' and those they considered as inferiors. This applied not just to the impoverished in the streets, but to their own domestic servants. By the early nineteenth century the attitude to domestic servants had changed from the banter of Jonathan Swift's day to an authoritarian control. This control had grown to such a degree that by 1792 *The Cork Gazette* warned employers not to give discharges to incompetent servants, and it was said that even those who had devoted their lives to a family were left to beg in the streets when their working days were over.[29] Mr and Mrs S C Hall were shocked at how badly Irish servants were paid and how 'improperly' they were lodged in a country where food was fairly readily available. They questioned why food was locked up and servants given what was termed 'breakfast money' or an allowance to supply themselves with bread and food. They acknowledged though that Irish servants had good appetites![30]

The Dublin Society Report of 1827 on a scheme for the improvement and encouragement of servants, and the establishment in Belfast in 1836 of a Society 'for the Encouragement and Reward of Good Conduct in Female Servants' shows that there was concern amongst some people with regard to the treatment of servants. That 'encouragement', however, took the form of offering to award a servant four guineas after four years of faithful service if during that time the servant remained sober, honest, and of good moral conduct.[31]

Technical advances in the early nineteenth century improved the standard of living of the wealthy, but in some cases they increased the workload of domestic servants. The availability of running water for instance meant that the laundry could now be done at home, and so there was enthusiastic digging of drains so as to provide new-style laundries. Newly invented mangles for wringing clothes were also purchased. On the other hand, Count Rumford produced designs for enclosing the fireplace so as to maximise the use of heat and reduce the strain on the cook. Although his suggestions were controversial and few went as far as he recommended in supplying a separate plate for each kettle and stewpan on the range, his suggestion obviously influenced some of the change that eventually took place.[32]

Although this was a period when a new appreciation was developing of the Celtic past, little of it was visible in the homes of Dublin's middle class, which were little different from those of their friends in London.

13

Alistair Rowan

IRISH VICTORIAN CHURCHES: DENOMINATIONAL DISTINCTIONS

In the Ford Lectures delivered in the University of Oxford in 1978, F S L Lyons put forward the argument that in nineteenth-century Ireland four distinct cultures existed which remained separate from one another and contributed substantially to the anarchy that manifested itself in the Fenian disturbances of the 1860s, in the Easter Rising of 1916, the Irish Civil War and its aftermath, right down to the present day.[1] If we follow Lyons' view, culture is not seen as a unifying force in a fragmented society, a bulwark against anarchy, but quite the contrary. In Ireland, where several distinct cultures existed in Victorian life, their diversity became a force that worked against the evolution of a united Ireland, and in doing so acted as an agent of anarchy.

The first of the four cultures that Lyons identified in Irish society at the beginning of Queen Victoria's reign was the ancient Gaelic world — suppressed but never annihilated, numerically preponderant yet economically insignificant, and in religion Catholic. The second group was Anglo-Irish society — landed and perhaps also titled, used to the exercise of political power (though by 1837 that power had been somewhat limited), at home in the British Empire, though consciously not English, and in religion mainly of the Anglican confession of the Church of Ireland. The third culture was represented by the Protestant middle classes and working population of Ulster — by blood largely Scottish, right-thinking, energetic, puritanical, and in religion Nonconformist Methodist or Presbyterian. Finally, there was the culture of the English, which served to point up divisions, to set people at odds with each other, and to afflict Irish society. This was noted for its imported legislation, ready-made ideas or industrial artefacts, a culture running on the wheels of commerce and assisted by a rapidly expanding Irish railway system.

In the determination of these cultural preferences, religion played a large part. In spite of attempts to build a united society bound together by a common culture, each of these groups remained distinctive in its church-going habits, and indeed became increasingly polarised in Victorian Ireland. Each denomination evolved an architectural style expressive of its own affiliations and identity. This essay looks at Irish church building in the light of Lyons' thesis and suggests in broad terms an architectural pattern that may provide a visual and stylistic complement to his views.

NINETEENTH-CENTURY IRISH CHURCH ARCHITECTURE

Ireland, perhaps more than any other country in Europe, is a land of nineteenth-century churches. In 1787 there were 1001 Anglican churches in the country. By 1864 that number had increased by 578, and more than three-quarters of the older churches had been rebuilt. The nineteenth century, therefore, added something in the order of thirteen hundred Church of Ireland churches to the Irish countryside. The Presbyterians in 1834 counted 452 churches, a number that nearly doubled as a result of the divisions that followed the Disruption in Scotland in 1843. At least half the original total were built after 1800, so we may estimate that some six hundred or more Presbyterian churches were built in the nineteenth century. The Catholic Church has very few buildings that date from before 1790, but today its 1381 parishes boast some 3850 churches. In all, there are some 5750 churches in Ireland, almost all of which are nineteenth-century in origin. This is a remarkable number of new buildings: some fifty-seven every year, or more than one newly built church for every week in an entire century!

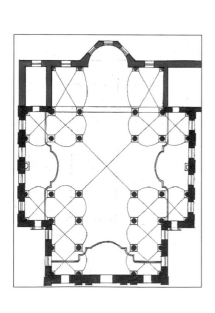

When a poor country such as Ireland supports a building programme of this scale, the architectural fare will inevitably tend to be wholesome rather than rich, and may descend at times to the 'buttermilk and potatoes' level — the staple diet of over three-quarters of the population in Victorian Ireland.

That architecture, and architectural style, can carry denominational connotations may be demonstrated by a Scottish entry in the 1855 *Visitation of Seats and Arms* compiled by Sir Bernard Burke, Ulster King of Arms. The Presbyterian parish church of Leckropt in Stirlingshire — a boxy Gothic Revival church built by James Stirling of Keir with pinnacled tower and perpendicular traceried windows — is described by Burke as 'one of the earliest ornamented among the Presbyterian erections in Scotland, and probably nothing less than the weight of the old laird's upright character could have persuaded the people and their clergy that they could permit towers, parapets and Gothic windows in their churches without becoming rank Papists'. In early nineteenth-century Scotland, Gothic is certainly Catholic or Episcopalian, and Scottish Presbyterians, for the most part, keep to the straight and narrow path of Late Georgian classicism in their church designs.

Burke's indulgent amusement at Presbyterian stylistic prejudice springs almost certainly from the fact that in his native Ireland, Gothic stood not for Catholicism but for the Anglo-Irish establishment, an elite society, hardly more than 10 per cent of the population, which supported the Church of Ireland. In Ireland, where Catholic and Presbyterian suffered similar exclusions under the Penal Laws, the two denominations could share an architectural style, for both built classical temples in conscious contrast to the established churches' Gothic towers. This difference can be seen about the turn of the century by contrasting the interiors of John Roberts' 'great church', now the Catholic cathedral at Waterford, begun in 1794, with Francis Johnston's rebuilt Chapel Royal at Dublin Castle — an essay in revived florid and spiky Gothic style, Rickman-like before its time, begun in 1807. The design by John Roberts is interesting in that while its idiom is identical to the enriched mid-Georgian classicism that characterised Church of Ireland buildings in the eighteenth century, its plan is continental in its origins — an elaborate centralised design on a Greek cross, where arms are set out by a series of giant Corinthian columns (Illus 13.1). A church on the scale of Waterford Cathedral, almost thirty metres square (Illus 13.2), may underscore the point that the black and white notions so often put forward about the lack of religious toleration during the Protestant ascendancy are sometimes overdrawn. Evidently, by 1794 a wealthy society had developed amongst the Catholic merchants of Waterford, which was able to afford a church of this grandeur and size.

Francis Johnston's Chapel Royal breaks new ground in a different way (Illus 13.3). It is not its plan that is new, but its highly developed and rich Gothic architecture, for it was the first neo-Gothic church within the city of Dublin (Illus 13.4). The next two establishment Protestant churches in the city — St George's, Hardwick Place, also by Johnston, and St Stephen's in Mount Street, by John Bowden — are indeed classical designs, but they are the last of their type. In this respect the Chapel Royal is the herald of a new age, ushered in almost accidentally as a direct consequence of political developments in Ireland.

Opposite bottom, left to right

13.1 Plan of Waterford Cathedral, John Roberts, 1794
The plan for this Catholic cathedral appears to be related to continental models, the design being based on a Greek cross, whose arms are set out by giant Corinthian columns.

13.2 Interior of Waterford Cathedral, John Roberts, 1794
The scale of the cathedral interior is evidence of the prosperity of the Catholic merchant class even under the Penal Laws (which restricted Catholic participation in the professions and much else).
National Library of Ireland (Lawrence Collection)

13.3 Chapel Royal, Dublin Castle,
Francis Johnston, 1807

A fine and highly elaborate example
of the Perpendicular style of Gothic
preferred by the (Anglo-Irish)
Church of Ireland in the early years
of the nineteenth century.

13.4 Interior of Chapel Royal, Dublin
Castle

Johnston's rich interior uses Gothic
detail in an essentially decorative
rather than a structural way, with
plaster vaulting, quasi-classical figura-
tive sculpture and Georgian balconies,
which would have had no place in an
authentic medieval church.

Irish Architectural Archive

REBUILDING PROGRAMMES

Of all the legislation enacted in Westminster to control the building industry in nineteenth-century Ireland, none had more effect on the appearance of the country than the Act of Union of 1800. The appearance of the country was in no way a concern of the London administration, yet the Union had architectural consequences of an unprecedented nature. In the first place, it gave compensation money to families who had lost political patronage through the suppression of the Irish parliament, and this money was widely spent prodigally in the modernisation and rebuilding of seats throughout Ireland over the following twenty years. John Nash, along with his pupils George and James Pain, and the Irish firm of Sir Richard and William Vitruvius Morrison, were the architects to profit most by this house-building boom, as the text and engraved plates of J P Neale's *Views of Gentlemen's Seats of Great Britain and Ireland* makes abundantly clear. For those who missed out on country house commissions, the Church of Ireland's rebuilding programme in the same period provided alternative opportunities. In terms of the fabric of Anglican churches around 1800, the rebuilding programme can hardly have been justified. The Church of Ireland had inherited the church property from the medieval period and had the responsibility to maintain and modernise it. It had undertaken this to some degree during the seventeenth and eighteenth centuries, yet after 1801 it embarked on an extensive rebuilding policy, for which the main impetus can only have been the political one of asserting that, though political control might have passed to Westminster, the Anglo-Irish were still an undisputed social ascendancy. This fact is proclaimed by a succession of tiny Gothic buildings dotted throughout the Irish landscape, all with only the most minimal pretensions to style beyond some primitive Gothic details. The majority were built between 1810 and 1833 with grant aid from the Board of First Fruits, to which the British government had voted over one million pounds by 1821. There is something toylike about these Board of First Fruit churches — plain boxy halls with dinky three-storey towers set at one end, and perhaps a series of stepped buttresses to decorate the sides and gable end. The library of the Representative Church Body of the Church of Ireland preserves six volumes of survey plans of these little structures, all from the ecclesiastical division, for which the architect James Pain was responsible. These simple outline drawings are a record of what Pain found, though in some cases where the

 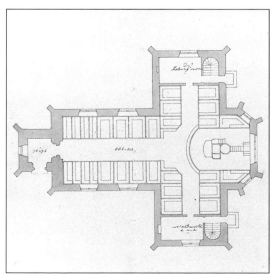

13.5 Newmarket Church, diocese of Cloyne, south elevation, Drawn by James Pain

One of hundreds of Church of Ireland churches built or rebuilt in the first quarter of the nineteenth century; an unusually elaborate example with ambitious Gothic detail.

Church of Ireland Representative Body Library, Dublin

13.6 Plan of Newmarket Church, diocese of Cloyne, Drawn by James Pain

James Pain was the supervising architect for the Church of Ireland in this area, but not all the churches he surveyed were designed by him. In this case, the elaborate design and detail suggest it may be Pain's own work.

Church of Ireland Representative Body Library, Dublin

13.7 Kilcooly Church, diocese of Cashel, Drawn by James Pain

This is a more modest and typical example of a rural Protestant church, of which hundreds may still be seen dotted around the countryside.

Church of Ireland Representative Body Library, Dublin

13.8 Plan of Kilcooly Church, diocese of Cashel, Drawn by James Pain

Church of Ireland Representative Body Library, Dublin

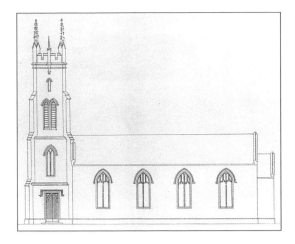
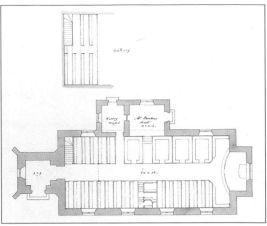

architecture is more developed and the elevations are more decorative, it seems likely that Pain was recording his own design. Newmarket Church, in the diocese of Cloyne (Illus 13.5 & 13.6) is an unusually elaborate design with ambitious Gothic detail; Kilcooly church in the diocese of Cashel (Illus 13.7 & 13.8) is more modest and more typical. In a country where more than 80 per cent of the rural population was housed in one or two-roomed thatched cottages, and where to have a slate roof over one's head was a grand thing, the symbolic value of the Board's churches must be obvious. In architecture, any general attempt at a developed Gothic style, at least until about 1830, is distinctively a feature of the Anglican Church of Ireland.

RURAL CHURCHES

The response of the urban populations, Catholic or Nonconformist, was to build classical temples. Before moving to the cities, however, it may be as well to put the country churches of the Church of Ireland into the context of the rival denominations. The problem for the Catholic and Presbyterian communities was the reverse of that which faced their Church of Ireland landlords. Both had to cope with large congregations and to erect much bigger churches with much less money. The Catholics were worst off. At first they could afford to build little more than large slated halls with plain walls, with perhaps, though not necessarily, some pointed windows and a stone cross on the gable ends. This was the basic Early Victorian Irish Catholic church, and for the entire Victorian period in Ireland, to put a cross on the gable of a church was to proclaim allegiance to Rome. The type is well characterised by the tiny gabled buildings shown in the background of the woodcut in Mr and Mrs S C Hall's *Ireland* of 1843, which depicts a primitive cart of the Irish peasantry (Illus 13.9). In the interiors of such early rural churches, a popular plan placed the altar in the centre of the long wall and arranged the congregation around it in a broad U-shape, with the altar set between two tall windows on either side. This pattern seems to have been copied from earlier eighteenth-century Presbyterian churches, where a pulpit replaced the altar, and the plan was often extended to include an arrangement of U-shaped galleries. Thus the two 'proscribed denominations' copied one from the other, and this unexpected correlation between Presbyterian and Catholic building in the Late Georgian period can be demonstrated further by the proliferation of T-planned churches throughout the Catholic parts of rural Ireland. The galleried T-plan church originated in seventeenth-century Scotland and recurs frequently in vernacular Presbyterian churches in Ulster throughout the Georgian period. Originally the staircases to the galleries were placed externally at the end of each arm, though by the early nineteenth century they tend to be incorporated within the building. Examples include the Presbyterian churches at Tassagh in County Armagh of 1784 and at Downpatrick about 1760, and the T-plan Catholic church at Grange in County Louth of 1762, now the oldest surviving Catholic church in the archdiocese of Armagh (Illus 13.10 & 13.11). J J McCarthy, the leading Catholic Gothic architect of the High Victorian period in Ireland, hated these old vernacular churches, and his favourite term of abuse, 'T-houses', seems clearly to acknowledge a Presbyterian meeting-house origin. The T-plan recurs with monotonous regularity in rural Catholic churches into the 1870s. Such a church may often have gained a polygonal sanctuary apse, which almost makes it cruciform, but its Nonconformist origin will be evident and it will always have, unlike its Presbyterian prototype, a cross to adorn its gables.

13.9 Engraving of a rural horse cart, with a Catholic church in the background.

The cross on the gable makes it clear that the simple building in the background here is a Catholic church. Apart from its pointed windows, it is otherwise little more than a large hall.

From Hall's *Ireland: Its Scenery and Character* (1843)

13.11 Plan of St James's Catholic Church at Grange, 1762

An example of an early Catholic plan of a long hall, with the congregation arranged in a U-shape around an altar at the centre of the long wall. Later converted to the popular T-plan shape.

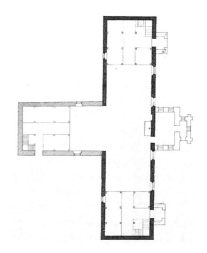

13.10 St James's Catholic Church at Grange, County Louth, 1762

The oldest surviving Catholic church in the diocese of Armagh, its design owes much to Scottish Presbyterian examples, though the cross on the gable marks it as Catholic.

Irish Architectural Archive

URBAN PRESBYTERIAN CHURCHES

By contrast to this, the urban setting was very different. Nonconformist temples are best studied in Belfast: the Presbyterians, though they suffered from discrimination, received a degree of government funding in the form of the Regium Donum that was granted annually to the church, the origins of which lie in the late seventeenth century. The Presbyterians in Ulster had an old tradition of church-building to draw upon. May Street Presbyterian church, designed by William Smith in 1829, with a broad façade culminating in an Ionic portico *in antis*, is one of the largest of the Late Georgian classical designs (Illus 13.12 and 13.13). Its side elevation gives a clear indication of the U-shaped gallery which, by that time, had become traditional in Presbyterian church plans, while the mouldings around the upper floor windows — without imposts — suggest that Smith had been looking at Sir John Soane's designs for the Belfast Academical Institution, begun in 1809. In Donegall Square the Methodist church, by the Dublin architect Isaac Farrell, was built as a complete Corinthian temple front of six giant columns with short flanking wings. There is, however, in the Nonconformist spirit something inimical to display or obvious enrichment, and so, though Presbyterians and Methodists accounted for some 650,000 of the population in 1846, their churches tend to be best characterised by such useful words as 'trim' and 'neat', much employed by the writers of gazetteers in Ulster. All Presbyterian structures are neat: only rarely do they scale the architectural heights. A solemn little stucco temple, such as the Presbyterian church of 1843 in Downshire Road in Newry, County Down, or its near relative — one might almost say replica — the Reformed Presbyterian church of 1860 at the opposite end of Ulster, at Raphoe in County Donegal (Illus 13.14), is the most that can be hoped for. Both have an Ionic portico *in antis*, with two free-standing columns framing a loggia entrance to the church. This is a common type, though the majority of classical Presbyterian churches do not run to quite such sculpturesque luxury, and a stuccoed classical box with channelled masonry on the ground floor and usually a U-shaped gallery carried on cast-iron columns inside is the norm.

The grandest Presbyterian churches, or those of greatest architectural interest, are usually exotic productions, imports from England or Scotland, like the two large plain churches put

13.12 May Street Presbyterian Church, Belfast, William Smith, 1829
One of the larger urban Presbyterian churches, with a broad façade and an impressive Ionic portico.

13.13 Interior of May Street Presbyterian Church, Belfast
The interior of the May Street church shows the U-shaped gallery, characteristic of Presbyterian designs, centred on a pulpit.
Photograph: Hugh Doran

IRELAND: ART INTO HISTORY

13.14 Former Reformed Presbyterian Church, Raphoe, County Donegal, 1860

A restrained elegance characterises this former Presbyterian church at Raphoe, with its fine Ionic portico.

Irish Architectural Archive

13.15 Findlater's (Presbyterian) Church, Parnell Square, Dublin, Andrew Heiton, 1862–4

A thoroughly typical later Presbyterian church in a High Victorian Gothic style, paid for by the Findlater family (grocers and wine-merchants). The site was purchased from the Catholic archbishop of Dublin, with whom the local Presbyterians had good relations at this time.

Irish Architectural Archive

up by the Fishmongers Company at Ballykelly and Banagher on their County Derry estates, which are reminiscent of the barnlike style of Inigo Jones's St Paul's Covent Garden. Both were designed by the company's London surveyor, Richard Suitor, in the mid 1820s. Much later is the weirdly attenuated Abbey Presbyterian church in Parnell Square, Dublin, designed by Scottish Gothic Revival architect Andrew Heiton of Perth, and built between 1862 and 1864 (Illus 13.15). The church was paid for by Dublin's wealthy Presbyterian grocers, Alex Findlater and Company. Such worthy behaviour on the part of commerce is all very Scottish, but an interesting side-light is thrown on interdenominational politics by the sale of the site — which encompassed the last two houses on the north side of the square — to the congregation by Cardinal Paul Cullen, in recognition of the fact that the Nonconformists on the north side of the city tended to vote for the cardinal's candidates in municipal elections. Abbey Church is of course Gothic, yet it is of an odd, debased character that is easily distinguished from the Church of Ireland's preferred style at this time. By the later nineteenth century all denominations in Ireland had embraced some form of Gothic, yet there are still clear distinctions of style; the Presbyterians on the whole preferring Late Perpendicular designs that allowed them to continue to build well-lit open halls, which could accommodate U-shaped galleries, only now within a Gothic skin. E P Gribbon, Samuel Patrick Close, and Robert Young of Young and McKenzie, architect of the General Assembly Halls in Belfast (Illus 13.16), are the leaders of this Late Perpendicular school.

13.16 Interior of the General Assembly Halls, Belfast, Young and McKenzie, 1900–05

Even when adopting Gothic models, Presbyterian designers like Robert Young preferred the Late Perpendicular, which could accommodate a well-lit hall with broad galleries.

National Library of Ireland (Lawrence Collection)

URBAN CATHOLIC CHURCHES

Inevitably the real battleground of church building in Irish cities is occupied by the Catholic Church. Here the story must begin in 1816 with the committee to build St Mary's Metropolitan Catholic Chapel in Dublin, now the Pro-Cathedral, in which Sir Richard Morrison seems to have played a decisive part. As a Protestant and head of the architectural profession in Ireland, Morrison was aided on the committee by the architect John Sweetman and by his one-time clerk, John B Keane, who was to become a major Catholic architect in his own right. Inevitably, post-Union politics ensured that St Mary's should not be sited on Dublin's triumphal thoroughfare, Sackville Street (now O'Connell Street). The cathedral site is therefore on a side street, with its main façade to Marlborough Street, busy with Morrisonian Greek detail, but a little cramped on its corner site (Illus 13.17). The side elevation and interior of the building are of greater quality. The large model that was made for the church still survives (Illus 13.18), and contains further evidence for the original design of the interior. The interior, which continues the Greek Doric of the façade, though the columns were to be rather uncomfortably wide in their spacing for such an order, seems to derive from continental models — perhaps the style of Chalgrin in Paris — rather than from English examples. Indeed for its date there would have been few British examples to offer as an appropriate model for a Catholic congregation. Morrison, or perhaps more probably Keane, proposed one original and rather elegant feature: the succession of clerestory lights, approximately to the pocket vaults of a Gothic design, pierced through the first row of coffers above the main entablature, which is shown in the model. This is an idea that may carry us back to the Abbé Laugier and the search for lightness in French classical design, though the notion was lost in the finished work, as in execution the cathedral became heavier and a dome replaced the clerestory lights. This elegant system of lighting was, however, adopted by Keane for the nave of Longford Cathedral in 1840, and by Patrick Byrne for St Audoen's Church in Dublin in 1841 (Illus 13.19).

The design of the Pro-Cathedral in Dublin acted rather as the Castle Chapel had done to establish the style for its successors. With two early exceptions, the Church of St Michael and St John, and St Peter's, Phibsborough, all the other Catholic churches in Dublin are classical: St Andrew's, Westland Row, by James Bolger, a Greek Doric design with a T-plan interior of 1832; St Francis Xavier, the Jesuit church in Gardiner Street, by J B Keane, built in the same year, though more consciously Roman in character, with a cruciform plan; John Leeson's

13.17 St Mary's Metropolitan Catholic Chapel (now Pro-Cathedral), Dublin (commenced 1816)

Dublin's Catholic Pro-Cathedral, set on a cramped site on a side-street, was planned some years before the remaining religious disabilities were removed by Catholic Emancipation (1829). The building was designed by a committee headed by Richard Morrison, himself a Protestant.

From a nineteenth-century water-colour, Irish Architectural Archive

13.18 Original model for St Mary's, Dublin (now Pro-Cathedral)

The original model for Dublin's Pro-Cathedral featured a series of clerestory lights, possibly proposed by John Keane, which would have lightened the design. In the finished building these were omitted.

Irish Architectural Archive

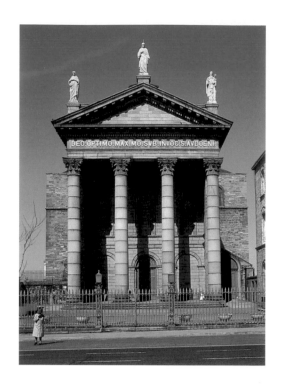

Left

13.21 Interior of St Mel's (Catholic) Cathedral, Longford

Here John Keane has carried into execution the series of clerestory lights proposed (but not realised) for the Pro-Cathedral in Dublin.

Irish Architectural Archive

Far left

13.19 St Audoen's Catholic Church, Dublin, Patrick Byrne, 1841–6

The imposing Roman portico of St Audoen's, completed in the 1890s in a late example of the preference for classical forms established (by the design of the Pro-Cathedral) as the norm for Catholic church design in the nineteenth century.

Left

13.20 St Mel's Cathedral, Longford, commenced 1840

The massive bulk of St Mel's Cathedral, astonishingly ambitious in its pastoral setting on the edge of a midlands town. Interrupted by the Famine, it took more than fifty years to complete the building, when the portico was finally added by George Ashlin.

Above

13.22 Interior of St Michael's (Catholic) Church, Gorey, County Wexford, A W N Pugin, 1839

One of the first of eighteen churches designed by Pugin in Ireland, St Michael's is based on Dunbrody Abbey and uses 'real' materials in its stone piers and exposed roof rafters.

Irish Architectural Archive

Right

13.23 Catholic church, Rathmines, Dublin, Patrick Byrne, 1850

This rich Roman interior, with its centralised cross-shaped plan and its saints set high in their niches, reflects the powerful influence of continental models on Catholic church building in Early Victorian Ireland.

National Library of Ireland (Lawrence Collection)

St Nicholas of Myra in Francis Street; Patrick Byrne's 'Adam and Eve', the Franciscan church, St Paul, Arran Quay, and Rathmines parish church of 1850. Keane's grandest design, though it was not to be completed in his own lifetime, is St Mel's Cathedral in Longford. This massive plain block building, which was begun in 1840, was interrupted during the Famine, then continued by John Bourke, who added the campanile from 1854, and was not completed until 1893, when its rather routine Ionic temple front was finished under the supervision of George C Ashlin (Illus 13.20). The metropolitan bulk of Longford Cathedral is astonishing in its pastoral setting on the edge of an Irish midlands town, and its interior is memorable too. Here Keane resurrected the Pro-Cathedral clerestory idea, but adapted the openings to the pattern of the segmental lights that Sir William Chambers had used much earlier in the chapel of Trinity College, Dublin. Their rhythmic succession, accentuating the beat of the columns in the segmental vault of the nave roof, does much to lighten the structure, both in terms of architectural pattern and of real illumination (Illus 13.21). It is churches such as these that led a correspondent in *The Dublin Penny Journal*, a short-lived weekly magazine published between 1832 and 1836, to observe that classicism had become the style of the Catholic Church in Ireland. He proposed two reasons for this: first, such a style distinguished the Catholic churches very clearly from the Established church, which the Roman clergy no doubt thought was of considerable value; and secondly, both the education that the clergy had received and the most appropriate architectural prototypes to hand were continental.

These observations were made just at the time when the young Augustus Welby Northmore Pugin (1812-52), a convert to Rome, had pronounced classical architecture to be pagan, and Gothic to be the only truly Christian style. His radical views are expressed succinctly in a letter that he sent from Rome in 1847:

> I have now seen Rome and what Italian architecture can do, and I do not hesitate to say that it is an imperative duty on every Catholic to defend true and Christian architecture with his whole energy. The modern churches here are frightful; St Peter's is far more ugly than I expected, and vilely constructed — a mass of imposition — bad taste of every kind seems to have run riot in this place… Were it not for the old Basilicas and the associations connected with the Early Christian antiquities, it would be unbearable. The Sistine Chapel is a melancholy room, the Last Judgement, a painfully muscular delineation of a glorious subject, the Scala Regia a humbug, the Vatican a hideous mass, and St Peter's is the greatest failure of all.

How would ideas of this character — delivered with the emphasis of educated diction, articulated in an English accent, and from the lips of a recent convert — have impressed the resident Irish hierarchy? Irish churchmanship is usually conservative, slow to absorb bright ideas from outside, and inevitably Pugin's career in Ireland — as in England — was fraught with difficulty and misunderstanding. As a young man of enormous talent, trained by his father, a draughtsman, Pugin first arrived in Ireland in 1830 to direct the building of St Peter's Chapel, Wexford, and the chapel of the Loreto Convent at Rathfarnham, County Dublin. In architectural terms he had some success. He built the Abbey Church of St Michael in Gorey, County Wexford, begun in 1839, which was one of his most authoritative designs (Illus 13.22). Here he worked in a Ruskinian way, letting the masons evolve elements of the structure themselves, and avoiding the miniaturist effects and over-enrichment that marred so many of his earlier designs. Pugin sought to give his design an identifiable local character.

There is a round-tower stair at the corner of the north transept and a convincing display of stepped Irish battlements on the tower over the crossing.

Between 1839 and 1845 Pugin was to embark on eighteen Irish commissions, fourteen of which were for churches or convent buildings. At Gorey, in County Wexford, he worked with the Wexford builder Richard Pierce, and it was through Pierce that his style gained a fragile hold in Wexford city, whose famous twin churches were erected to Pierce's design between 1851 and 1858. Apart from their obvious debt to Pugin — St Oswald's, Liverpool, in some sense inspired the designs — these churches of the Immaculate Conception and the Assumption are remarkable in that though they are hardly a mile apart, they are identical, and were built so by the express desire of the bishop 'to prevent jealousy and unpleasant comparisons amongst the townspeople'.

Pugin's collaborator at Rathfarnham, the Dublin architect Patrick Byrne, was less inclined to pay compliments to his young English colleague by imitating his style. In Byrne's office and in the Irish capital, classicism was still entrenched. Two churches by Byrne make this clear: St Audoen's in Thomas Street, designed in the very heart of the old city in 1841, and Rathmines Parish Church, begun in 1850 and on a good site in a growing and wealthy district, with a high Baroque dome whose silhouette presides triumphantly over the whole area. Here Pugin's view of the modern churches of the Eternal City is relevant, for St Audoen's and Rathmines Church are Roman Catholic structures that exult in their very Romanness. The richly sculpted Corinthian capitals, the flamboyantly gesticulating acroterion statues, the temple fronts, all are richly Roman, and so too are Byrne's interiors. Rathmines is reminiscent of Alessi's S Maria del Carignano, with four saints — St Charles Borromeo, St Francis Xavier, St Vincent de Paul and S Filippo Neri — set high in niches at the crossing piers (Illus 13.23). In yet another of his commissions, Byrne was to carry the classical battle into the Puginesque stronghold of Wexford itself, remodelling in 1856 the interior of the ancient Franciscan church there as a barrel-vaulted basilica. Pugin regarded this sort of architecture as 'the vilest trash'. In articles for *The Dublin Review* in 1841 and again in *An Apology for the Revival of Christian Architecture* in 1842, he made his opinion plain that the Irish clergy were 'deplorably apathetic and ignorant' and that Irish Catholic architects had no conception of the nature of the Gothic crusade on which he had embarked. Some might admire Pointed architecture, but they did not admire it on true principles, and considered 'Italian paganism equally handsome'.

JOSEPH WELLAND — AN INFLUENTIAL FIGURE

Perhaps the greatest irony of Pugin's Irish intervention is that the first body that seems to have been prepared to accept his ideas was the Ecclesiastical Commission of the Church of Ireland. In 1833 the government had set up a new commission, replacing the Board of First Fruits, to supervise the established church-building programme throughout the country. A board of four architects was appointed to approve designs, and after a reorganisation in 1843, its functioning became the responsibility of one man, Joseph Welland. As a Protestant church architect, Welland had impeccable qualifications. A relative of the bishop of Down, he had trained in Dublin in the office of John Bowden and had worked as an architect in the Tuam division of the old Board of First Fruits. It was therefore natural to him to build in a Gothic style, and clearly he would have approved of Pugin's ideas. A Welland church is characterised by a scrupulous regard for the building materials — stone, timber, glass and slate — and for their appropriate expression. Part of Pugin's crusade had been to establish the 'truthful' use of materials and the individual expression of the elements in a building, which constituted its whole design. Thus a chancel should be clearly expressed as separate from the nave of the church; a porch from the aisle to which it was attached; a sacristy from the chancel, and so on. Differences could be marked by a change in the height or the slope of the roof, by a step in the line of a wall, or by the conscious use of a buttress to mark a change of function inside the building. By a similar rationale, Pugin held that the interior of a church should exhibit openly the materials from which it was constructed. This can be seen in his Irish churches, as in the interior of St Michael's, Gorey (Illus 13.22 & 13.24), and in his two cathedrals at Killarney (Illus 13.25) and Enniscorthy. In their interiors, plain plaster is boldly juxtaposed with ashlar stone surrounds and areas of carved enrichment. Ceilings are usually panelled in timber in the most sacred areas, while elsewhere the system of roof rafters is left open to view and given visual enrichment by exposing and emphasising the trusses and braces by which it is supported. Triple lancets are used for east windows, with Vessica or trefoil lights, and double-chamfered arcades support the walls between the aisle and the nave. Welland took over all of these ideas. His richly archaeological design for St Swithin's, Magherafelt, County Derry (Illus 13.26), amply illustrates the extent to which the Pugin message had been absorbed by 1856 when it was designed. Though slightly modified and simplified in execution, notably in the spire, it is one of Welland's grandest churches. The individual parts of the building are clearly distinguished: the isles have double-chamfered arcades, and braced timber trusses and exposed rafters support the roof. Welland's little Church of Ireland parish churches — Killela, at Swatragh, County Derry, Tobermore in County Tyrone, Castlebellingham, County Louth, and St Mary's, Nenagh, County Tipperary (Illus 13.27), are classic examples.

13.24 Interior of the roof of St Michael's Church, Gorey, A W N Pugin, 1839

Pugin's roof designs highlight the structural features, with elaborate systems of purlins, braces and rafters left open to view. He believed a building should show rather than conceal its structure and building materials.

Irish Architectural Archive

13.25 St Mary's (Catholic) Cathedral, Killarney, A W N Pugin and J J McCarthy

Pugin's lofty and inspiring Gothic design at Killarney cathedral is in complete contrast to the massive horizontality of Keane's St Mel's Cathedral (Illus 13.20), commenced earlier in the same decade.

Irish Architectural Archive

13.26 St Swithin's Church, Magherafelt, County Derry, Joseph Welland, 1856

This drawing shows one of Welland's grandest and largest churches, with a richly developed Puginian interior.

Church of Ireland Representative Body Library, Dublin

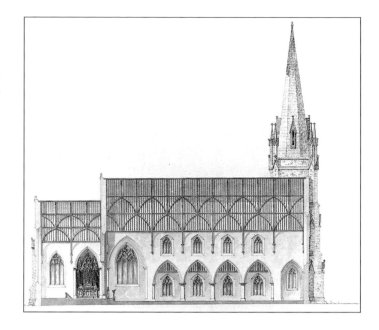

13.27 St Mary's, Nenagh, County Tipperary, Joseph Welland

The architect's drawing for this small Gothic church illustrates clearly its designer's intention to articulate the different parts of a building, one from another.

Church of Ireland Representative Body Library, Dublin

DUBLIN'S UNIVERSITY CHURCH

While Welland presided over the construction of little churches like Tobermore and Killela, the Catholic community in Dublin was embarking on a historic new venture. In 1850 the archbishops and bishops of Ireland, meeting at the National Synod at Thurles, took a decision to establish a Catholic University in Dublin, which was the logical outcome of their opposition to the recently established Queen's Colleges. One of the most energetic advocates of the Catholic University was Cardinal Paul Cullen, archbishop of Armagh and apostolic delegate to Ireland. Cullen, acting on his own initiative, invited John Henry Newman to come to Ireland as first rector of the new university. Two houses were acquired on the south side of St Stephen's Green, and in the back garden of the smaller property, number 87, Newman decided to erect a University Church.

Pugin's remarks about the solace he found in Rome in the few old basilicas and the associations connected with Early Christian antiquities are important, for it is these very associations that Newman, and his architect friend John Hungerford Pollen, brought under tribute in the University Church. The work on the church was begun in June 1855, and it opened for Easter 1856. It is arguable whether Newman's church is architecture or decoration. It certainly offers a vivid illustration of the hierarchy of architectural values in Victorian theory, for Newman describes his intention thus: 'My idea was to build a large barn and decorate it in the style of a basilica with Irish Marbles', and he invited Pollen — essentially a decorator — to come to Dublin as professor of fine arts in the Catholic University, to help him to decorate his barn. The University Church covers exactly the plan of the back garden of number 87. It is approached by a narrow passage down the side of the house and has a very individual Torcello-type porch, with two large Byzantine capitals on stumpy columns on either side of the door. The interior is memorable for the forest of columns that support the deep back gallery, and also for the mixture of Venetian and Roman Early Christian detail (Illus 13.28). The apse over the altar is a copy of the mosaic apse in San Clemente in Rome, while the baldacchino and choir balcony, on the east side of the altar, are copied from St Mark's, Venice.

In selecting these Early Christian models, Newman and Pollen behaved with some subtlety. Their choice of style is still Roman Catholic in the Dublin classical sense, and yet it cannot be open to a Puginian charge of paganism. Here is a style that is not Gothic, yet is patently Christian, and it even accords with the English avant-garde in basing its forms on the brick and

13.28 Interior of University Church, St Stephen's Green, Dublin
John Hungerford Pollen, 1855–6
Commissioned by John Henry Newman, first rector of the new Catholic University, the design reflects his interest in Roman Early Christian architecture, and particularly the church of San Clemente, the Roman house of the Irish Dominicans.
Irish Architectural Archive

IRELAND: ART INTO HISTORY

13.29 St Malachy's Church, Belfast, Thomas Jackson, 1842

This early example of neo-Gothic church architecture in Belfast, with its elaborate (and fake) plaster vault, is in complete contrast with Pugin's style as shown in St Michael's, Gorey, built three years earlier.

Irish Architectural Archive

marble architecture of Italy, to which young G E Street had so recently drawn attention. That San Clemente, whose apse is quoted in St Stephen's Green, is the house of the Irish Dominicans in Rome, may also have influenced Newman's choice of style. His church is not quite a sole example of its type. When the Dominicans came to rebuild their friary in Waterford in 1878, the English firm of Goldie and Child supplied them with an unusually hybrid and rather good design, redolent with Roman atmosphere, from the shallow classical façade — such as Vignola or Della Porta might have squashed into a Roman street — to its basilican interior, with a classical clerestory and exposed Italianate roof timbers. For its date, Goldie and Child's Dominican church in Waterford is something of a freak. It would be wrong to distinguish it as the last instance of a classical taste in Catholic Ireland, for many of the more ambitious churches that have been mentioned took a very long time to complete — Byrne's St Audeon's was not finished until 1888; the Franciscan church at City Quay, Cork, begun by the Pain brothers, only received its monumental Ionic portico in 1866, and Longford Cathedral was not finished until 1893. Nonetheless, by the early 1860s a Gothic Revival style had generally been accepted by all denominations.

DEVELOPMENTS IN CATHOLIC CHURCH ARCHITECTURE

The changeover in Catholic church circles is first to be noted where Pugin never set foot, in Ulster. Here in the 1830s and 1840s, a group of architects — James Kirkpatrick in Coleraine, Thomas Duff of Newry and Thomas Jackson of Belfast — popularised the rather playful forms of Perpendicular as interpreted by Late Georgian architects. In these Ulster Catholic churches, sham plaster vaults and big galleries, both of which were anathema to Pugin, appear prominently. Perhaps the most interesting is Jackson's Church of St Malachy in Belfast of 1842. Its exterior recalls the Regency idiom of John Nash, and its interior furnishes a comparatively late example of the once-popular plan with the altar on the long wall, copied from Presbyterian examples (Illus 13.29). Bearing in mind the comments of the anonymous author in *The Dublin Penny Journal* who suggested that Catholics built in a classical style to distinguish their churches from the Church of Ireland, it is possible that the congregation in St Malachy's and the other Catholic parishes who built Gothic in Ulster did so, at this early date, to distinguish their buildings from the Nonconformists, who made up the majority in Ulster and who regularly built in a classical style.

Gothic as a Catholic style in Dublin was established in the 1860s largely through the efforts of two men: James Joseph McCarthy and George Coppinger Ashlin. Ashlin was the pupil and Irish partner of Edward Welby Pugin, who had opened a Dublin office to superintend the completion of his father's Irish work. In 1860 Pugin and Ashlin were commissioned to design the large Augustinian church in Thomas Street, the funding of which proved so erratic that it was only to be opened fifteen years later, and was not completed until 1892 (Illus 13.30). *The Irish Builder* in a review of the finished design in July 1861 asserts that it was Ashlin alone who was entitled to the credit for the architectural firm's Irish projects, though aspects of the church, particularly its curved apse, gabled side elevations and chisel-shaped slate spire, which lends a distinctive outline to the entire city skyline, derived from Flemish examples, are characteristic of E W Pugin's own style. The interior is characteristic of Ashlin, with polished granite columns whose heavy vegetable capitals step regularly down the nave to a sanctuary filled with coloured light, from five tall two-light windows with rather flat four-centred arched heads.

George Ashlin was twenty-four when the Augustinian church was begun. When he was thirty he married his partner's sister, Mary Pugin, and through him the Puginesque aesthetic was continued to the end of the century. He came on the scene just in time to pick the plums that had been prepared for the Catholic classicist Patrick Byrne. In the late 1850s Byrne had at last turned to a rather tame Gothic style, only to die in 1862, when most of the jobs in his office passed to George Ashlin. Two notable examples in Dublin are Donnybrook Church of 1863 and St Joseph's, Glasthule, of 1867 (Illus 13.31). Both churches display, in some measure, the perennial problem for Catholic congregations of having to make too little go too far. They have busy fronts but rather plain attenuated sides, and in neither case was there ever the money to build the spires. Spires became rather important for the politics of church-building in the 1880s and 1890s, for they too had a symbolic value.

On 31 December 1870, under the provisions of Prime Minister William Gladstone's Irish Church Act, the Church of Ireland was disestablished, and with it went the Ecclesiastical

13.30 Augustinian church and monastery, Thomas Street, Dublin, Edward Pugin and George Ashlin, designed 1860

This imposing design illustrates the mature Gothic style firmly established in Catholic architecture by 1860. Edward Pugin opened a Dublin office to continue his father's work, with George Ashlin as his pupil and partner.

13.31 St Joseph's Church, Glasthule, Dublin, George Ashlin, 1867

George Ashlin, who married Edward Pugin's sister Mary, designed many Irish Catholic churches in the second half of the nineteenth century. Finance was often a problem, and the spires shown in this design in *The Irish Builder* were never built.

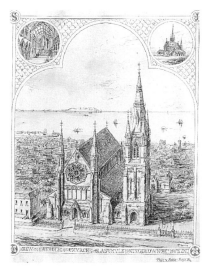

13.32 Church of the Sacred Heart, Omagh, County Tyrone, William Hague 1893

After the disestablishment of the Church of Ireland in 1869, Catholic church-builders felt able to compete on more equal terms, and Catholic churches like this one in Omagh are often found on dominating sites, expressing a conscious rivalry and a new triumphalism.

13.33 St Joseph's Catholic Church, Carrickmacross, County Monaghan, James McCarthy, 1862

J J McCarthy was the earliest among Irish Catholic architects to follow Pugin's example and a major protagonist of Victorian Gothic design in Ireland.

13.34 St McCartan's Cathedral, Monaghan, James Joseph McCarthy, begun 1862

Another fine McCarthy church in Monaghan, the cathedral was not finished until 1892, when the spire was completed by William Hague.

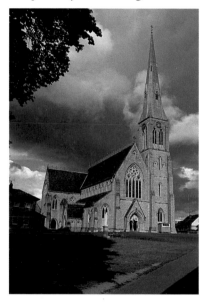

Commission. The Regium Donum of the Presbyterians was also discontinued, and at the same time the government endowment of the Roman Catholic college at Maynooth came to an end. The Anglo-Irish, bitterly opposed to these measures, lost face, while the Catholic Church gained new status. From the 1870s onwards a new consciousness, even a sense of triumphalism, attends the siting and design of Irish Catholic churches. Frequently they are set in a spirit of open confrontation beside their disestablished rival. In Ulster the principal Catholic churches in Derry, Letterkenny, Enniskillen, Omagh, Armagh, Cavan and Strabane, all conform to this rule. And in these exercises of ecclesiastical one-upmanship, the height of the spire — what the Italians call *campanilesimo* — is crucial. The Church of the Sacred Heart by William Hague, in Omagh, provides the neatest demonstration of this architectural rivalry (Illus 13.32). Begun in 1893, it is not quite on the highest part of the hill above the river, but it is Hague's church that dominates the town, stealing the thunder of J E Roger's St Columba's, built in the year after disestablishment, 1870. Hague's design envisages a wilful asymmetry in the height of his two spires, perhaps an Ulster echo of the noble asymmetry of Chartres, and in its location it is certainly rather successful.

The master builder of Catholic Gothic spires is James Joseph McCarthy. In 1849 McCarthy had been instrumental in founding the Irish Ecclesiological Society to promote proper Gothic design in Catholic churches. In 1851, when he was thirty-four, he took over the commission to design St Eugene's Cathedral in Derry, and in 1852 he began designs for St Saviour's Dominican Church in Dublin — the first ecclesiological church in the capital — which was persistently misattributed to A W N Pugin, a compliment to McCarthy's correct style. From these beginnings he developed a practice, which was to involve eighty-one commissions, including some of the most elegant Gothic designs in Ireland. The Puginesque character of McCarthy's mature work is evident in two of his churches from County Monaghan, St Joseph's, Carrickmacross, of 1862 (Illus 13.33), and the cathedral of St McCartan in Monaghan town (Illus 13.34), which was begun in the same year though not finished until 1892, when William Hague — the same architect as at Omagh — completed the spire. It was McCarthy also who took over and completed both the chapel of St Patrick's College, Maynooth, following in the wake of Pugin, and the Roman Catholic cathedral in Armagh — a huge, rather forbidding French Gothic design which challenged in its scale and hill-top site, the meagre Protestant cathedral across the valley, meanly restored by L N Cottingham in 1837.

New Church of Ireland Ventures

Disestablishment in 1869, or the threat of it in the 1860s, left the Church of Ireland uncertain of its future. Yet while Gladstone schemed and plotted in Westminster, the hierarchy in Dublin, almost it seems as an act of defiance, embarked on a show of strength. The two medieval cathedrals of the city — the late twelfth-century Christ Church and the early thirteenth-century St Patrick's — were in Protestant hands. In 1863 an extensive and regrettably thorough restoration of St Patrick's had begun through the dictatorial philanthropy of Benjamin Lee Guinness, third son of Dublin's famous brewer, an ecclesiastical commissioner and an architectural amateur whose distrust of the architectural profession led him to place the entire restoration solely in the hands of a local firm of builders, Murphy and Sons. Benjamin Guinness himself supervised the builders, and the cathedral was returned to the dean and chapter, bright and shining, with good new middle-pointed detail, at the end of 1865. As disestablishment began to be discussed, it was rumoured that the English government intended to give back one of the cathedrals to the Catholic Church and, as St Patrick's had just been restored, that seemed to threaten Christ Church. In response to this threat, the dean of Christ Church, on the very eve of disestablishment, commissioned George Edmund Street to prepare a scheme for the restoration of the cathedral and the building of a new synod hall. The stratagem worked, for Street was later employed to restore the whole cathedral, the costs being paid this time by the Roe family, famous Dublin distillers.

It is worth noting that Street was not an Irish architect and that his intervention in Ireland, like that of Pugin before him, may be taken to illustrate the fourth ingredient in the cultural anarchy of Victorian Ireland — the importation of alien attitudes and standards from over the water. Street has not been admired in Dublin for condemning the famous Late Gothic Long Choir of Christ Church so as to be able to rebuild his own notion of the original polygonal sanctuary, partly based on Westminster Abbey. Like Pugin, he perhaps felt the need to go native in Ireland, and as a result he added above the aisle walls a row of stepped Irish battlements, which the original building had never known. English attitudes and English architectural ideals were not to be as easily accommodated here.

A parallel to Street's predicament is supplied by the design of another Protestant church about this time, St Bartholomew's, Clyde Road, Dublin, built to designs of Thomas Wyatt in 1867 (Illus 13.35), just before disestablishment, and decorated later by Sir Thomas Deane. In English terms the interiors of Street and Wyatt's churches are characteristic of High Anglican tractarian designs, rich with polished marble and tile work, but otherwise in no way remarkable. Yet the work of these two English architects is different, distinctively non-native, and uncomfortable on Irish soil. The Church of Ireland is deeply suspicious of ritual, and profoundly low church in its artefacts and attitudes. Trollope's novel *Castle Richmond*, written in 1861, contains some vivid and illuminating sketches on Church of Ireland attitudes. It is a tale of the disinheritance of a landed family — the Fitzgeralds — and is set in County Kerry against the stark background of the Famine. At one stage in the misfortunes of the family, it appears that the Fitzgeralds will have to leave Ireland to settle on a drastically reduced income in a villa in St John's Wood. A maiden aunt, as embattled in her prejudices against the Oxford movement as Catholicism, and closely supported in her opinions by the rector of Drumbarrow and his wife, Mrs Townsend, goes to the Glebe House to break the news to her friends.

13.35 St Bartholomew's (Church of Ireland), Clyde Road, Dublin, Thomas Wyatt, 1867

This was one of the last Protestant churches erected before disestablishment. A famous dispute arose here in 1890, when a parishioner was allowed to place a cross behind the altar in memory of a relative: the first cross to appear so close to the communion table in an Irish Protestant church.

Irish Architectural Archive

'I trust you will be able to find someone there who will preach the Gospel to you,' said Mrs Townsend, in a tone that showed how serious were her misgivings on the subject.

'I will search for one at any rate,' said Aunt Letty. 'You need not be afraid that I shall be a back slider.'

'But they have crosses now over the communion tables in the churches in England,' said Mrs Townsend.

'I know it is very bad,' said Aunt Letty. 'But there will always be a remnant left. The Lord will not utterly desert us.'

Mrs Townsend and Aunt Letty had no doubt seen too many crosses on the gables of certain churches to feel confident about developments in the Church of England liturgy; and their spiritual heirs were still very much alive at the time when Street restored Christ Church and St Bartholomew's was decorated. In 1890, a Mr A G Wolseley presented an altar cross to St Bartholomew's in memory of his mother, and the select vestry agreed to its being erected behind the altar — it was not to be placed on the altar. This was the first cross in Ireland to appear in a Protestant church in such close proximity to the communion table, and immediately a storm of protest broke out. A group calling itself the Protestant Defense Association took the vicar and select vestry to the diocesan court, and when the court ruled in favour of the legality of the position of the cross, the association appealed to the General Synod. A group of outraged clergymen then published an address to the vicar, urging him 'with brotherly esteem' to adopt 'some way of restoring peace and goodwill'. The vestry continued its folly until, following a ruling with the synod, the altar cross was removed and set on a wrought-iron stand between the choir stalls, at a height so nicely calculated that from the centre of the nave of the church it seemed to float upon the altar itself. Only three congregations in Dublin maintained services of a character compatible with High Victorian Anglican churchmanship: St John's, Sandymount; All Saints, Grangegorman, and St Bartholomew's — and, of course, the two cathedrals, although St Patrick's always tended to be less high.

THE CELTIC REVIVAL STYLE

One other element affected denominational styles in the Victorian age. About 1865, Church of Ireland theologians became enchanted with an audacious, and in terms of current theology, not wholly absurd theory. This related to the nature of the early Irish Church and to Patrician Christianity, whose monuments had been the subject of archaeological research, carried out for the most part by the scions of landed families whose hobby was excavating the ruins of the Irish countryside. Of these antiquaries the most systematic was George Petrie, and when Daniel O'Connell died and the nation turned its attention to the design of a memorial suitable for the Liberator of Catholic Ireland, it was Petrie who suggested the assembly of a group of structures at the gates of Glasnevin Cemetery: a round tower, a stone-roofed oratory and a Celtic high cross. In the event, only the tower was erected, but the whole project focused new attention on the possibility of a Celtic Revival for Irish church design. The Protestant church was first in the field, supporting its stylistic pretensions with theological arguments of entertaining ingenuity. The key to these arguments was the Synod of Rathbreasail, held in 1111, through which a new diocesan structure had been imposed on the Irish Church, which at the same time adopted continental patterns of worship and administration. Through the influence of the energetic St Malachy, Irish monasticism was reorganised on the Roman pattern and, according to the Church of Ireland apologists, from that moment on the true ancient Church

13.36 St Eunan's Catholic Church, Raphoe, County Donegal, Timothy Hevey, 1874

An early example of the Celtic Revival style in a Catholic church, complete with round tower and high-pitched roof.

Irish Architectural Archive

13.37 Dunlewey Catholic Church, County Donegal, Timothy Hevey, 1877

This impressive Celtic Revival church, a development of Hevey's design at Raphoe, employs marble from Mount Errigal on its façade.

of Ireland ceased to be, turning itself in national terms into a schismatic body, owing ultramontane allegiance to Rome. Where in Victorian Ireland did the light of ancient Celtic Christianity still shine clear and pure? The answer was obvious — in the services and liturgy of the Church of Ireland, a church whose clergy, like the early Irish clergy, might be married, and who owed no allegiance to the bishop of Rome.

Thus it is that in the late 1860s the Church of Ireland began to build attractive little structures in a Celtic Revival style. Two of the first examples that are known, both designed in 1865, are St Patrick's, Ballyclog, County Tyrone, by William Welland, who had succeeded his father as architect to the Ecclesiastical Commissioners, and St Patrick's, Jordanstown, County Antrim, by William Henry Lynn. Lynn's church is the more archaeological of the two, with a skilful grouping of high-gabled single-cell units which build up the complex plan of the church, and a stumpy round tower as the belfry. Welland by contrast is rather free-wheeling in his approach to his models, but the intention to build an ancient Irish church is none the less clear. It is significant that, in his sermon on the dedication of Jordanstown church, the bishop of Connor chose the occasion as a suitable one on which to rehearse the national and theological arguments as to the appropriateness of the style.

The style caught on. Before long, three more churches followed: the parish church at Kilcock in County Kildare by J E Rogers, dating from 1868, St Eunan's, Raphoe (Illus 13.36), and the mountain-country church at Dunlewey, on the lower slopes of Errigal in County Donegal (Illus 13.37) — the last two being designed by a young Belfast architect, Timothy Hevey, in 1874 and 1877. The dedication of Dunlewey to the Sacred Heart establishes at once that the Catholic Church did not leave its Protestant rival long in unchallenged possession of the Celtic Revival style. Timothy Hevey was indeed an old pupil of George Ashlin, and as a frequent contributor of illustrations to *The Irish Builder,* was well placed to encourage the Celtic Revival, which soon became the common property of all denominations, surviving into the present century with distinguished examples such as Rudolph Maximillian Butler's Catholic church at Newport in County Mayo of 1916, and Ralph Byrne's Church of the Four Masters in Donegal town, designed in 1931.

This Celtic Revival is in a sense the last stylistic throw of the Anglican Church in Ireland, yet if we return to Lyons' thesis, we would do violence to the evidence if we suggested that a clearly denominational stylistic preference was as marked in 1890 as it was in 1820 or even at the mid century. The stylistic differences have become more a matter of subtle modulation than of the straightforward contradictions argued by Pugin in his famous book *Contrasts* (1836). No self-respecting nationalist of whatever denomination could tolerate for long the Anglican Church's claim to an exclusive right to the style of ancient Irish churches, and so our architectural picture is clouded over with common forms and common claims. But the divisions between the different Irish communities are still real, and architectural guidelines remain — size, the height of spires, the site, and the presence or absence of crosses.

INTRODUCTION (PP 8–12)

1. In exploring this idea, the editors have been influenced by the following works, among others: David Lowenthal, *The Past is a Foreign Country* (Cambridge 1985); Simon Schama, *The Embarrassment of Riches* (London 1987); R I Rotberg and T K Rabb (eds), *Art and History* (Cambridge 1988); Peter Paret, *Art as History* (Princeton 1988); David Freedberg and Jan de Vries, *Art in History: History in Art* (Santa Monica 1991); and Francis Haskell, *History and its Images* (New Haven and London 1993).

2. A B Grossart (ed), *Lismore Papers* (10 vols, London 1886–8), 1st ser, ii, p30; Nicholas Canny, *The Upstart Earl* (Cambridge 1982), pp87–91.

3. For example, Raymond Gillespie, 'Describing Dublin: Francis Place's visit, 1698–9' in Adele Dalsimer (ed), *Visualising Ireland: National Identity and the Pictorial Tradition* (Boston 1993), pp99–118.

4. For an essay on this theme, see Brian P Kennedy, 'Towards a manifesto for art and the sacred' in *Studies*, lxxxii (1993), pp311–22.

5. Raymond Gillespie, *The Sacred in the Secular: Religious Change in Catholic Ireland, 1500–1700* (Vermont 1993), pp7–8.

6. Bodleian Library, Oxford, Rawlinson Ms C439, f5.

7. For example, Brian P Kennedy, 'The traditional Irish thatched house: image and reality, 1793–1993' in Dalsimer, *Visualising Ireland*, pp165–79.

8. For a pioneering example of this, F R Bolton, *The Caroline Tradition of the Church of Ireland* (London 1958), pp204–50. A good model for this type of study is Nigel Yates, *Buildings, Faith and Worship* (Oxford 1991).

9. Keith Jeffery, 'The Great War in modern Irish memory' in T G Frazer, Keith Jeffery (eds), *Men, Women and War: Historical Studies, xviii* (Dublin 1993), pp144–52.

10. For examples of the materials available, A K Longfield, 'Some eighteenth-century Irish tombstones' in *Journal of the Royal Society of Antiquaries of Ireland*, lxxv (1945), pp76–84; lxxvi (1946), pp81–8; lxxvii (1947), pp1–4; lxxviii (1948), pp170–74.

11. Myrtle Hill, Vivienne Pollock, 'Images of the past: photographs as historical evidence' in *History Ireland*, ii, 1 (spring 1994), pp9–14.

12. T C Barnard, 'The political, material and mental culture of the Cork settlers, c1650–1700' in Patrick O'Flanagan, Cornelius Buttimer (eds), *Cork: History and Society* (Dublin 1993), pp322–33.

CHAPTER 1 (PP 15–25)

1. See Bamber Gascoigne, *How to Identify Prints* (London 1986); a useful guide to manual and mechanical processes of print-making, including aquatint.

2. E MacDowel Cosgrave, 'A contribution towards a catalogue of engravings of Dublin up to 1800…part II' in *Journal of the Royal Society of Antiquaries of Ireland*, xxxv (1905), p367, says that 'Malton struck off a few impressions from the etched plates before they were aquatinted, and coloured some of them by hand…

The copies meant for colouring were printed in sepia'. The opinion concerning the use of sepia is contradicted in *Scenery of Great Britain and Ireland in Aquatint and Lithography 1770–1860 from the Library of J R Abbey* (London 1952), p316, where it is suggested that 'All copies of the earlier issue were engraved in a dark sepia, quite unsuitable for colouring… It is … doubtful if copies [of the bound volume] were issued in colour until a period approaching 1820…'.

3. Malton's first prospectus announced four numbers of six views at one and a half guineas a number. A later prospectus announced that twenty-four out of thirty views taken would be published in six numbers of four views at a guinea a number; after the publication of the third number, in which a list of subscribers was to appear, the price was to be advanced to twenty-six shillings to all not on the list. E MacDowel Cosgrave, 'A contribution', p366.

4. The other extant watercolours are: *The Royal Exchange* in the Henry E Huntington Library and Art Gallery, San Marino, California; *The Provost's House* in the British Museum; *View from Capel Street* in the Victoria and Albert Museum; *Interior of the Long Room, Trinity College* in Trinity College Dublin. Other Dublin views unconnected with those engraved for the bound volume of 1799 survive.

5. These details are taken from the *Illustrated Summary Catalogue of Drawings, Watercolours and Miniatures [in the National Gallery of Ireland]*, compiled by Adrian Le Harivel (Dublin 1983), pp497–9.

6. Algernon Graves, *The Royal Academy of Arts, A Complete Dictionary of Contributors…* (8 vols, London 1905–6).

7. A selection of the plates from Niklaus Wilhelm von Heideloff's *Gallery of Fashion* (London 1794–1802), is reproduced in *Gallery of fashion…plates by Heideloff and Ackermann with an introduction by Sacheverell Sitwell [and] notes…by Doris Langley Moore* (London 1949).

CHAPTER 2 (PP 26–42)

1. Alfred P Smyth, *Celtic Leinster. Towards an Historical Geography of Early Irish Civilisation AD 500–1600* (Dublin 1982). Peacock's *Pattern* is an exception to this generalisation, having been analysed by W H Crawford, 'The Patron, or Festival of St Kevin at the Seven Churches, Glendalough, 1813' in *Ulster Folklife*, xxxi (1986), pp37–47.

2. J H Andrews, *Plantation Acres. An Historical Study of the Irish Land Surveyor and his Maps* (Belfast 1985), p166.

3. For example, see P J Duffy, 'Carleton, Kavanagh and the south Ulster landscape c1800–1950' in *Irish Geography*, xviii (1985), pp25–37; also 'Patrick Kavanagh's landscape' in *Éire–Ireland*, xxi (1986), pp105–19.

4. John Berger, *Ways of Seeing* (London 1972), p10; see also Hugh Prince, 'Landscape through painting' in *Geography*, lxix (1984), p15.

5. See Jay Appleton (ed), *The Aesthetics of Landscape* (Oxford 1980), p16.

6. See Kenneth Clark, *Landscape into Art* (London 1949), p34.

7. John Barrell, *The Dark Side of the Landscape* (Cambridge 1980); Ann Bermingham, *Landscape and Ideology. The English Rustic Tradition 1740–1860* (Los Angeles 1986).

8. Hugh Prince, 'Art and agrarian change 1710–1815' in Denis Cosgrove and Stephen Daniels (eds), *The Iconography of Landscape* (Cambridge 1988), pp98–118.

9. Kenneth Clark, *Landscape into Art*, p33–5, 77.

10. See David Lowenthal, 'Finding valued landscapes' in *Progress in Human Geography*, ii (1978), pp373–418; also Lowenthal and Hugh Prince, 'English landscape taste' in *Geographical Review*, lv (1965), pp186–222; also Prince, 'Real, imagined and abstract worlds of the past' in C Board, R J Chorley *et al* (eds), *Progress in Geography. International Reviews of Current Research*, iii (1971), pp1–86.

11. Important artists like Sir Joshua Reynolds, Thomas Gainsborough, J M W Turner and the Irishman James Barry, through their opinions and reputations, shaped the academic establishment; but how independent they were of patronage is a moot point. For background on the social context of art in the eighteenth century, see D H Solkin, 'The battle of the Ciceros: Richard Wilson and the politics of landscape in the age of John Wilkes' in Simon Pugh (ed), *Reading Landscape* (Manchester 1990), pp41–65.

12. Lowenthal and Prince, 'English landscape taste', p81; see also Bermingham, *Landscape and Ideology*, p13–14, on the relationship between popular landscape imagery and landscape garden design in the eighteenth century; also Tom Williamson and Liz Bellamy, *Property and Landscape* (London 1987), chapter 10, for aesthetic influences on planting in the countryside by the early nineteenth century.

13. For the backgrounds to artists working in Ireland, see Anne Crookshank and the Knight of Glin, *The Painters of Ireland* (London 1978); Bruce Arnold, *A Concise History of Irish Art* (New York 1977); Brian P Kennedy, *Irish Painting* (Dublin 1993).

14. Hugh Frazer, *Essay on Painting* (Dublin 1825), p28.

15. Ann Bermingham, *Landscape and Ideology*, p4.

16. *Illustrated Summary Catalogue of Drawings, Watercolours and Miniatures [in the National Gallery of Ireland]* compiled by Adrian Le Harivel (Dublin 1983); Rosalind Elmes, *Catalogue of Irish Topographical Prints and Original Drawings* (Dublin 1943). About 15 per cent of the placenames in Elmes' *Catalogue* could not be identified. Where illustrations have appeared in more than one publication, only one instance is recorded in Illus 2.2.

17. There was a clear pattern to tours in Ireland in the eighteenth and early nineteenth centuries, with a preference for Leinster, Munster and east Ulster. Trips generally began in Dublin, following the road to Carlow and branching towards Wexford, Waterford or Cork via Clonmel; or to Cashel and Limerick and Killarney; or Drogheda, Newry, Belfast and the Giant's Causeway. Visits to Connacht and west Ulster were comparatively rare. This assessment is based on an examination of the itineraries of approximately one hundred tours between 1750 and 1850, which is a sample of a much larger number contained in

Dr C J Woods' unpublished *Index of Tours in Ireland*, in progress, Royal Irish Academy. I am grateful to Dr Woods for allowing me to inspect his bibliography.

18. From Leitch Ritchie, 'Ireland Picturesque and Romantic' in *Heath's Picturesque Annual* (London 1837), p75.

19. *Illustrations of the Landscape and Coast Scenery of Ireland from Drawings by George Petrie, A Nicholl and H O'Neill* (Dublin 1843); for an account showing typical contemporary interests, see Michael Quane (ed), 'Tour in Ireland by John Harden in 1797' in *Journal of Cork Historical and Archaeological Society, 2nd ser, lviii* (1953) to lx (1955); also Pádraig Ó Maidin, 'Pococke's tour of south and south-west Ireland in 1758' in *Jn Cork Hist Arch Soc, 2nd ser, lxiii–lxv* (1958–60), which was mainly concerned with romantic scenery, antiquities and gentlemen's seats.

20. Stana Nenadic, 'Land, the landed and the relationship with England: literature and perception, 1760 to 1830', paper read at 5th Conference of Scottish and Irish Historians in St Andrews, June 1990; see also Peter Howard, 'Painters' preferred places' in *Journal of Historical Geography*, xi (1985), pp138–54; also Jane Zaring, 'The Romantic face of Wales' in *Annals of the Association of American Geographers*, lxvii (1977), pp397–418.

21. John Carr, *Tour of Ireland* (Dublin 1805), p140.

22. Sir William Wilde, *Memoir of Gabriel Beranger, and his Labours in the Cause of Irish Art and Antiquities from 1760 to 1780* (Dublin 1880) includes an account of tours by Beranger between 1773 and 1781.

23. Wilde, *Memoir of Gabriel Beranger*, p36.

24. Beranger's watercolour sketches, Royal Irish Academy, published in *Beranger's Views of Ireland*, edited by Peter Harbison (Dublin 1991).

25. Mr and Mrs S C Hall, *Ireland: Its Scenery and Character* (3 vols, London 1841–3), iii, p392. Most of the sketches are details of antiquities that are not included in Elmes' *Catalogue*. There were also twenty sketches for Wexford, twenty-one for Kilkenny and twenty-two for Tipperary.

26. Lady Chatterton, *Rambles in the South of Ireland During the Year 1838* (London 1839), p16.

27. *The Scenery and Antiquities of Ireland Illustrated from Drawings by W H Bartlett* (London nd).

28. Anne Plumptre, *Narrative of a Residence in Ireland During the Summer of 1814 and that of 1815* (London 1817), preface.

29. Chatterton, *Rambles in the South of Ireland,* p71.

30. Quoted in Michael Booth, 'The landscape of Melodrama' in *Landscape Research*, xv (1990), p9; see Ann Bermingham, 'Reading Constable' in Pugh, *Reading Landscape*, pp111–18 for background on artistic landscape and realism.

31. Stana Nenadic, 'Land, the landed and the relationship with England.'

32. Thomas Reid, *Travels in Ireland in the Year 1822* (London 1823), p215.

33. Angelique Day and Patrick McWilliams (eds), *Ordnance Survey Memoirs of Ireland; Parishes of Co Fermanagh 1, 1834–5* (Belfast 1990), p12.

34. T W Freeman, *Pre–Famine Ireland* (Manchester 1957), p18.

35. See P J Duffy 'Carleton, Kavanagh and the south Ulster landscape c1800–1950.'

36. See W H Crawford, 'The patron, or festival of St Kevin' for commentary on Peacock's painting.
37. See Crookshank and the Knight of Glin, *Painters of Ireland,* p194.
38. *Illustrations of the Landscape and Coast Scenery of Ireland from Drawings by G Petrie, A Nicholl and H O'Neill* (Dublin 1843). For a discussion of the use of thatched houses as picturesque elements in landscape art in Ireland, see Brian P Kennedy, 'The traditional Irish thatched house: image and reality 1793–1993' in Adele M Dalsimer (ed), *Visualising Ireland: National Identity and the Pictorial Tradition* (Boston 1993), pp165–79.
39. Kevin Whelan, 'Settlement and society in eighteenth century Ireland' in T B Barry (ed), *Settlement History in Ireland. A Review* (forthcoming).
40. Ritchie, 'Ireland picturesque and romantic', p75. This apparent absence of class divisions in society and landscape can be attributed either to lack of conspicuous investment in housing and dress by the better-off Catholic rural dwellers or the generalised view from the main road.
41. J H Andrews, 'Changes in the rural landscape of late 18th and early 19th century Ireland: an example from County Waterford' (unpublished paper), and Geographical Society of Ireland field excursion in Kildare/Westmeath by Andrews, 13 October 1990; see also Hugh Weir, *Houses of Clare* (Whitegate 1986).
42. Longleat House, Wiltshire, Mss maps, Bath Estate.
43. Alistair Rowan, *The Buildings of Ireland. North West Ulster* (London 1979), pp46–58.
44. See T Jones Hughes, 'The large farm in 19th century Ireland' in Alan Gailey and D Ó hÓgáin (eds), *Gold Under the Furze – Studies in Folk Tradition* (Dublin nd), p96.
45. Plumptre, *op cit,* p215.
46. Whelan, 'Settlement and society'. Whelan identifies five major regions, ranging from a cattle-grazing region with rudimentary settlement forms in the midlands, through the 'discreet, comfortable world of the strong farmer' in north and south Leinster, to the emerging industrial landscapes of the north-east.
47. George Barret (1728/32–1784) was one of the best known Irish landscape painters of the eighteenth century and an exponent of the Romantic school. James Arthur O'Connor (1792–1844) continued the tradition of leaving Ireland for England, though he was popular as a painter of houses in Ireland. See Thomas Bodkin, *Four Landscape Painters* (2nd edn, Dublin 1987), who describes the pressures on artists like Barret and O'Connor to make a living.
48. Arthur Young, *A Tour in Ireland, 1776–9,* ed A W Hutton (2 vols, London 1892), ii, p35.
49. Ann Bermingham, *Landscape and Ideology,* p84. 'I'm sure we could several times between Cashell and this [Holycross] reckon ten or twelve ruins of Castles Abbeys & Monasteries in our view': from 'Tour in Ireland by John Harden in 1797' in *Journal of Cork Historical and Archaeological Society*, 2nd ser, lviii (1953), p30; Harden was a notable Irish traveller and landscape artist of the late eighteenth century, with fashionable antiquarian and picturesque interests.
50. Chatterton, *Rambles in the South of Ireland,* pp3–4.
51. Edward Malins and The Knight of Glin, *Lost Demesnes. Irish Landscape Gardening 1660–1845* (London 1976) is written on the basis of paintings and drawings of these landscape elements.
52. An assessment of the development of parks in Ireland between the seventeenth and the nineteenth centuries, currently being undertaken by Terence Reeves-Smith, underscores their significance in the Irish landscape: he estimates that there were about 850,000 acres in parks in Ireland in the early nineteenth century or 10 per cent of the total land area of the island. T Reeves-Smith, 'The evolution of Irish demesnes from the seventeenth to the twentieth centuries', paper read to the Dublin Historic Settlement Group, 13 March 1991, University College Dublin.
53. See David Large, 'The wealth of the greater Irish landowners 1750–1815' in *Irish Historical Studies*, xv (1966–7), p29, though A P W Malcomson's *John Foster — The Politics of the Anglo-Irish Ascendancy* (Oxford 1978) would tend to qualify this with reference to the nature of estates' title and leasing arrangements.
54. Bermingham, *Landscape and Ideology,* pp13–14.
55. Andrews, *Plantation Acres*, pp156–7.
56. A P W Malcomson, ' Absenteeism in 18th century Ireland' in *Irish Economic and Social History*, i (1974), pp15–35; PJ Duffy, 'The evolution of estate properties in south Ulster 1600–1900' in W J Smyth and K Whelan (eds), *Common Ground* (Cork 1986), pp84–109.
57. The National Gallery, London, in Prince, 'Art and agrarian change', p104, and Berger, *Ways of Seeing*, p106.
58. Printed in Malins and Knight of Glin, *Lost Demesnes*, p56.
59. John Hutchinson, 'Intrusions and representations: the landscape of Wicklow' in *GPA Irish Arts Review Yearbook 1989–90*, pp91–9, has pointed to the importance of the opening of Wicklow in the 1790s, and Connemara in the mid nineteenth century, for artistic accessibili ty. Hutchinson also examines the stylised approach to the depiction of the Wicklow mountain landscape in the eighteenth and early nineteenth centuries.
60. John Sproule (ed), *The Resources and Manufacturing Industry of Ireland* [incorporating a catalogue of the Dublin Exhibition], (Dublin 1854), p446.
61. See Andrews, *Plantation Acres,* chapter 6.
62. Isaac Weld, *Illustrations of the Scenery of Killarney and the Surrounding Country* (London 1812), pii.

Chapter 3 (pp43–60)

1. J R R Adams, 'Popular art in Belfast, 1824–1836' in *Ulster Folklife*, xxix (1983), pp43–6.
2. Lindsay Proudfoot, 'Landlord motivation and urban improvement on the Duke of Devonshire's Irish estates, *c*1792–1832' in *Irish Economic and Social History*, xviii (1991), pp 16–17.
3. *First Report of the Commissioners Appointed to Inquire into the Municipal Corporations in Ireland*, appendix part 1 [27], HC 1835, xxvii, p66 [All references to page numbers in Parliamentary Papers are to the printed pagination]; Samuel Lewis, *A Topographical Dictionary of Ireland* (2 vols, London 1837), i, p565.
4. W E Vaughan and A J Fitzpatrick, *Irish Historical Statistics: Population, 1821–1971* (Dublin 1978), p34.
5. *First Report of Commissioners of Inquiry into the State of the Irish Fisheries*, 1836, appendix [77], HC 1837, xxii, p15.
6. *Report on the Irish Fisheries 1836*, HC 1837, xxii, pxi.
7. *Report on the Irish Fisheries 1836*, HC 1837, xxii, p170.
8. *Municipal Corporations (Ireland) Report*, appendix I, HC 1835, xxvii, p66.
9. John Mannion, 'The Waterford merchants and the Irish-Newfoundland provisions trade, 1770–1820' in L M Cullen and Paul Butel (eds), *Négoce et Industrie en France et en Irlande aux xviiie et xixe Siécles* (Paris 1980), pp27–44; *Pigot's National Commercial Directory of Ireland* (Dublin 1824), pp316–17.
10. Anthony Marmion, *The Ancient and Modern History of the Maritime Ports of Ireland* (London 1855), p556.
11. L M Cullen, *Life in Ireland* (London 1968), p88.
12. *Pigot's National Commercial Directory of Ireland*, p316.
13. M Roberts, 'Women and work in sixteenth-century English towns' in P J Corfield and Derek Keene (eds), *Work in Towns 850–1850* (Leicester 1990), pp93–4.
14. *Copies of the Schedules of Tolls and Customs at Fairs and Markets in the Several Counties of Ireland*, HC 1830 (264), xxvi, pp187–8.
15. *Municipal Corporations (Ireland) Report*, appendix I [27], HC 1835, xxviii, p611.
16. *Report of the Commissioners Appointed to Inquire into the State of the Fairs and Markets in Ireland*, pt ii: *Minutes of evidence* [1910], HC 1854–5, xix, p257.
17. H D Inglis, *A Tour Throughout Ireland in the Spring, Summer and Autumn of 1834* (2 vols, London 1835), i, p63.
18. *Poor Inquiry (Ireland): Supplement to Appendix D, containing baronial examinations relative to earnings of labourers, cottier tenants, employment of women and children, expenditure…*, [36], HC 1836, xxxi, p252.
19. *Poor Inquiry (Ireland): Appendix E containing baronial examinations relative to food, cottages and cabins, clothing and furniture, pawnbroking and savings banks, drinking…*, [37], HC 1836, xxxii, p31.
20. *Poor Inquiry (Ireland): Supplement to Appendix D*, HC 1836, xxxi, p252.
21. *Report on the Irish Fisheries 1836*, HC 1837, xxii, pp164, 165, 167, 170, 174.
22. *Report on the Irish Fisheries*, HC 1837, xxii, pp 201, 207.
23. *Report on the Irish Fisheries*, HC 1837, xxii, pp 324, 326.
24. *Report on the Irish Fisheries*, HC 1837, xxii, p197.
25. *Report on the Irish Fisheries*, HC 1837, xxii, p206.
26. *Report on the Irish Fisheries*, HC 1837, xxii, p18.
27. *Report on the Irish Fisheries*, HC 1837, xxii, p206.
28. *Report on the Irish Fisheries*, HC 1837, xxii, p199.
29. Published by Thames & Hudson (London 1984), p123.
30. J C Coleman, 'The craft of coopering' in *Journal of the Cork Historical and Archaeological Society*, 2nd ser, xlix (1944), pp79–89.
31. A T Lucas, 'A block-wheel car from Co. Tipperary' in *Journal of the Royal Society of Antiquaries of Ireland*, lxxxii (1952), pp135–44; and 'Block-wheel car from Slievenamon, Co. Tipperary', *JRSAI*, lxxxiii (1953), p100.
32. W H Crawford, 'The patron, or festival of St Kevin at the Seven Churches, Glendalough, County Wicklow 1813' in *Ulster Folklife*, xxxi (1986), p43.
33. Mrs M J O'Connell, *Charles Bianconi: A Biography 1786–1875* (London 1878), illustrations facing pp47 and 116, as well as the title page.
34. *Poor Inquiry (Ireland): Appendix F*, [38] HC 1836, xxxiii, p354.
35. *Poor Inquiry (Ireland): Supplement to Appendix D*, HC 1836, xxxi, p352.
36. L M Cullen, *An Economic History of Ireland since 1660* (London 1972), pp105–8.
37. These few comments on women's dress should be read as annotations on the pioneer survey by Mairead Dunlevy, *Dress in Ireland* (London 1989), especially pp84–6, 104, 109–13, 135–42 and many of the illustrations.
38. *The Parliamentary Gazetteer of Ireland* (3 vols, London 1844), iii, p483.
39. *Poor Inquiry (Ireland): Appendix E*, HC 1836, xxxii, p91.
40. P E M Caffrey, 'Sampson Towgood Roche, miniaturist' in *Irish Arts Review*, iii, 4 (winter 1986), pp14–20; *The Irish Ancestor*, v, 1 (1973), front cover and plates 1–4.

Chapter 4 (pp61–74)

1. Kevin Whelan, 'Introduction' to Henry Blake, *Letters from the Irish Highlands of Connemara* (Reprint Clifden 1993), pp3–5. (Original ed London 1825.)
2. Henry Blake, *Letters from the Irish Highlands of Connemara* (London 1825), p251.
3. Thomas Robert Malthus, *Essay on the Principles of Population* (London 1798), p96.
4. Gearóid Ó Tuathaigh, *Ireland before the Famine 1798–1848* (Dublin 1972), p157.
5. R F Foster, *Modern Ireland* (London 1988), p334.
6. Mr and Mrs S C Hall, *Ireland: Its Scenery and Character* (3 vols, London 1841–3), ii, p409.
7. National Library of Ireland, Ms 10201. Margaret Stokes' letters to Osborne (21 May 1900) and Purser (24 May 1900).
8. National Gallery of Ireland, Ms 106, Margaret Stokes' incomplete biography of Burton (*c*1900).
9. Ann M Stewart, *Royal Hibernian Academy of Arts, List of Exhibitors and Their Works* (3 vols, Dublin 1985–7), i, p102.
10. Paul Caffrey, 'Samuel Lover's achievement as a painter' in *Irish Arts Review*, iii, 1 (spring 1986), pp51–55.
11. J MacFarlane, 'Sir Frederic William Burton RHA (1816–1900): his life and work', BA thesis, Trinity College, Dublin, 1976.
12. National Gallery of Ireland, Ms 106.
13. William Stokes, *The Life and Labours in Art and Archaeology of George Petrie* (London 1868).
14. W G Strickland, *Dictionary of Irish Artists* (2 vols, Dublin and London 1913), i, pp130–31.
15. Augusta Gregory, 'Sir Frederic Burton' in *The Leader*, i, 15 (1900), p231.
16. T W Moody (ed), *Thomas Davis 1814–45* (Dublin 1945).
17. Ó Tuathaigh, *Ireland Before the Famine*, pp186–8.
18. Cyril Barrett, 'Irish nationalism and art 1800–1921' in *Studies*, lxiv (1975), pp405–6.
19. Stokes, *The Life of George Petrie*, p132.
20. National Gallery of Ireland, Ms 106.
21. Both pictures were burned in a fire at the 'Pantechnicon' in Motcomb St, London.
22. George Petrie, *Irish Penny Journal*, i, 14 (1840). Cover front page.
23. Augusta Gregory, 'Sir Frederic Burton', p232.
24. Algernon Graves, *The Royal Academy of Arts. A Complete Dictionary of Contributors…* (8 vols, London 1905–6).

25. W M Thackeray, *The Irish Sketch Book* (2 vols, London 1843), i, p30.
26. Royal Irish Art Union, *Annual Report* (Dublin 1839–40).
27. Stokes, *The Life of George Petrie*, p375.
28. Mr and Mrs S C Hall, *Ireland: Its Scenery and Character*, ii, pp409–10.
29. I am grateful to John de Courcy Ireland for this information.
30. Stewart Blacker, *Irish Art and Artists* (Dublin 1845), p18.
31. Oskar Fischel, *Raphael* (2 vols, London 1948), plates 58–67, 11, p77.
32. Richard Ormond and John Turpin, *Daniel Maclise 1806–1870* (London 1972), pp67–8.
33. Fischel, *Raphael*, plate 261, p271.
34. Stokes, *The Life of George Petrie*, p132.
35. Stokes, *The Life of George Petrie*, p61.
36. H A D Miles and D B Brown, *Sir David Wilkie* (Raleigh, North Carolina Museum of Art, 1987), pp242–3.
37. Marcia Pointon, *Mulready* (London 1985), pp132–5.
38. Richard Ormond, *Sir Edwin Landseer* (London 1982), p148.
39. Arthur Young, *A Tour in Ireland*, ed Constantia Maxwell (Cambridge 1925), p187.
40. Stokes, *The Life of George Petrie*, p 62.
41. Anne O'Dowd, *Common Clothes and Clothing 1860–1930* (Dublin 1990), p8.
42. Brid Mahon, *Irish Dress* (Dublin 1974), pp152–4.
43. Hely Dutton, *A Statistical and Agricultural Survey of the County of Galway* (Dublin 1824), pp355–8.
44. Mairead Dunlevy, *Dress in Ireland* (London 1989), p135.
45. A C Haddon and C B Brown, 'The ethnography of the Aran Islands' in *Proceedings of the Royal Irish Academy*, ii (1891–3), pp768–830.
46. John M Synge, *The Aran Islands* (London 1911), p17.
47. Anne O'Dowd, *Common Clothes and Clothing 1860–1930*, p7.
48. A T Lucas, 'Footwear in Ireland' in *Journal of the Louth Archaeological Society*, xiii (1956), pp 374–6. Megan McManus, *Crafted in Ireland* (Ulster Folk and Transport Museum Exhibition Catalogue 1986), pp67–8.
49. Séamas MacPhilib, 'Gléasadh Buachaillí i Sciortaí' in *Sinsear*, iv (1982–3), p134.
50. Synge, *The Aran Islands*, p19.
51. O'Dowd, *Common Clothes and Clothing 1860–1930*, p9.
52. Dunlevy, *Dress in Ireland*, p168.
53. Richard Scott, *The Galway Hooker* (Dublin 1985).
54. Haddon and Brown, 'The ethnography of the Aran Islands.'
55. Paul O Sullivan (ed), *The Aran Islands 1900* (Dublin 1977), pp133–8.
56. E Estyn Evans, *Irish Folk Ways* (London 1957), p289.
57. Seán Ó Súilleabháin, 'Adhlachadh leanbhaí' in *Journal of the Royal Society of Antiquarians of Ireland*, lxix (1939), pp208–15.
58. Synge, *The Aran Islands*, p53.
59. Seán Ó Súilleabháin, *Wakes and Amusements* (Dublin 1967), pp130–45.
60. Gearóid Ó Crualaoich, 'The ritual of the Irish merry wake' in *Cosmos*, vi (1990), pp145–58.
61. Evans, *Irish Folk Ways*, p251.
62. O'Sullivan (ed), *The Aran Islands 1900*, pp108–11.
63. Synge, *The Aran Islands*, p17.
64. Evans, *Irish Folk Ways*, pp87–8.
65. Evans, *Irish Folk Ways*, p67.
66. I am grateful to Dr Anne O'Dowd, Folklife Division, The National Museum of Ireland, for this information.
67. O'Sullivan (ed), *The Aran Islands 1900*, p125.
68. Evans, *Irish Folk Ways*, p268.
69. John O'Sullivan, 'St Brigid's Crosses, Folklife' in *Journal of Ethnological Studies*, xi (1973), pp60–61.
70. Lady Augusta Gregory, *Seventy Years 1852–1922* (London 1974), p144.
71. *Ibid* p143.
72. William Shaw, *The Knights of England* (2 vols, London 1906), ii, p376.
73. William Vine, 'The fine arts in Ireland' in *The Connoisseur*, xxxiv, 134 (1912), pp97–8.
74. Augusta Gregory, 'Sir Frederic Burton', p232.
75. Martin Haverty, *A Report of the Excursion of the Ethnological Section of the British Association from Dublin to the Western Islands of Aran in September 1857* (Dublin 1859).

Chapter 5 (pp75–88)

1. John O'Rourke, *The History of the Great Irish Famine of 1847* (Dublin 1875).
2. R Dudley Edwards and T D Williams (eds), *The Great Famine: Studies in Irish History 1845–52* (Dublin 1956).
3. Cecil Woodham-Smith, *The Great Hunger* (London 1962).
4. Joel Mokyr, *Why Ireland Starved: A Quantitative History of the Irish Economy, 1800–1850* (London 1983).
5. Mary E Daly, *The Famine in Ireland* (Dublin 1986).
6. Cormac Ó Grada, *The Great Irish Famine* (London 1989).
7. S H Cousens, 'Regional death rates in Ireland during the Great Famine from 1846 to 1851' in *Population Studies*, xiv, 1 (1960), pp55–74; 'Regional variation in mortality during the Great Irish Famine' in *Proceedings of the Royal Irish Academy*, lxiii (1963), sect c, pp127–49; P M A Bourke, 'The extent of the potato crop in Ireland at the time of the Famine' in *Journal of the Statistical and Social Inquiry Society of Ireland*, xx, 3 (1959–60), pp1–35; J S Donnelly Jnr has contributed several essays on the Famine, including 'Famine and Government response' in W E Vaughan (ed), *A New History of Ireland, v, Ireland Under the Union I, 1800–1870* (Oxford 1989), pp272–285; 'The administration of relief' in *A New History of Ireland v, Ireland Under the Union I 1800–1870*, pp294–306 & pp316–31; 'A famine in Irish politics' in *A New History of Ireland, v, Ireland Under the Union I, 1800–1870*, pp357–71; Margaret Crawford, 'Dearth diet and disease in Ireland 1850: a case study of nutritional deficiency' in *Medical History*, xxviii, 2 (1984), pp151–61; 'Scurvy in Ireland during the Great Famine' in *Journal of the Society for the Social History of Medicine*, i, 3 (1988), pp281–300; 'Subsistence crises and famines in Ireland: a nutritionist's view' in Margaret Crawford (ed), *Famine: The Irish Experience 900–1900: Subsistence Crises and Famines in Ireland* (Edinburgh 1989), pp198–219.
8. The Irish medical journals, such as *The Dublin Medical Press* and the *Dublin Journal of Medical Science*, contain numerous and detailed reports of sickness and death, commenting on the prevalence of disease and starvation throughout the country during the years 1846 to 1849.
9. My thanks are due to the staff of the Reference Section of the Belfast Public Library who gave me access to the relevant volumes of *The Illustrated London News*. Their co-operation was invaluable.
10. Leonard De Vries, *Panorama 1842–1855. The World of the Early Victorians as seen through the eyes of The Illustrated London News* (London 1967), p10.
11. Quoted in De Vries, *Panorama 1842–1855*, p9.
12. *De Vries, Panorama 1842–1855*, p11.
13. W G Strickland, *Dictionary of Irish Artists* (2 vols, Dublin and London 1913), ii, pp88–89; Frances Gillespie, Kim-Mai Mooney and Wanda Ryan, *Fifty Irish Drawings and Watercolours* (Dublin 1986), p27.
14. *The Illustrated London News*, x (1847), pp100–101.
15. Raymond Lister, *Prints and Printmaking. A Dictionary and Handbook of the Art in Nineteenth-Century Britain* (London 1984), p334.
16. *The Illustrated London News*, viii (1846), p240.
17. This engraving of the city of Dublin was presented along with a folder to subscribers of *The Illustrated London News*, viii (1846), frontispiece supplement.
18. W G Strickland, *Dictionary of Irish artists*, i, p351.
19. *The Illustrated London News*, ix (1846), p293.
20. *The Illustrated London News*, ix (1846), p293.
21. *The Illustrated London News*, xv (1849), p444.
22. *The Illustrated London News*, x (1847), p44.
23. *Transactions of the Central Relief Committee of the Society of Friends during the Famine in Ireland 1846 and 1847* (Dublin 1852).
24. *The Illustrated London News*, x (1847), p100.
25. *The Illustrated London News*, xv (1849), p406.
26. Daniel Donovan, 'Observations on the peculiar diseases to which the famine of the last year gave origin, and on the morbid effects of insufficient nourishment' in *Dublin Medical Press*, xix (1848), p67.
27. Joseph Lalor, 'Observations on the late epidemic fever' in *Dublin Journal of Medical Science*, v (1848), pp21–2.
28. *Transactions of the Central Relief Committee of the Society of Friends during the Famine in Ireland 1846 and 1847*, p163.
29. Thomas Armstrong, *My Life in Connaught* (London 1906), p13.
30. J S Donnelly Jnr, 'Landlord and tenant' in W E Vaughan (ed), *A New History of Ireland, v*, p336.
31. From Sir W F Butler, *Sir William Butler: An Autobiography* (2nd edn, London 1913), p12. A footnote to this reference in *A New History of Ireland*, v, p337, points out that because Kennedy had worked to keep substantial numbers of the destitute from receiving Poor Law relief at the time of the crisis, his subsequent remarks may well be transference of guilt.
32. *The Illustrated London News*, xv (1849), p405.
33. Extracted from J S Donnelly Jnr, 'Landlord and tenant' in *A New History of Ireland*, v, p338.
34. *The Illustrated London News*, xv (1849), p394.
35. *The Illustrated London News*, xv (1849), p394.
36. *The Illustrated London News*, x (1847), p44.
37. *The Illustrated London News*, x (1847), p117.
38. Mokyr, *Why Ireland Starved*, pp264–5.
39. *Transactions of the Central Relief Committee of the Society of Friends during the Famine in Ireland 1846 and 1847*, p172.
40. *The Illustrated London News*, x (1847), pp116–17.
41. *The Illustrated London News*, xv (1849), p404.
42. *The Illustrated London News*, x (1847), p117.
43. T K Rabb and Jonathan Brown, 'The evidence of art' in R I Rotberg and T K Rabb (eds), *Art and History* (Cambridge 1988), p5.
44. Lorenz Eitner, *Géricault's Raft of the Medusa* (London 1973), p35.
45. E H Gombrich, ' "The mask and the face": the perception of physiognomic likeness' in E H Gombrich, Julian Hochberg, Max Black, *Art, Perception, and Reality* (Baltimore 1972), p17.
46. L P Curtis, *Apes and Angels: The Irishman in Victorian Caricature* (Newtown Abbot 1971), pp83–4.
47. Julian Hochberg, 'The representation of things and people' in Gombrich, Hochberg, Black, *Art, Perception, and Reality*, p69.
48. Gombrich, 'The mask and the face', p1.
49. Rabb and Brown, 'The evidence of art', p5.

Chapter 6 (pp91–102)

1. For background and a treatment of O'Connell and ballads see GD Zimmermann, *Songs of Irish Rebellion: Political Street Ballads and Rebel Songs 1780–1900* (Geneva 1967); for the supply of handkerchiefs for the Clare election with O'Connell's portrait see Fergus O'Ferrall, *Catholic Emancipation: Daniel O'Connell and the Birth of Irish Democracy 1820–30* (Dublin 1985), p191; see also Daniel Maclise's picture, *Snap-Apple Night* (1833, private collection), which shows a woman in the foreground wearing a shawl with a large portrait of O'Connell.
2. See James N McCord, 'The image in England: the cartoons of HB' in M R O'Connell (ed), *Daniel O'Connell, Political Pioneer* (Dublin 1991), pp57–71, and Miles L Chappel and James N McCord, 'John Doyle, Daniel O'Connell "The Great Liberator", and Rubens: the appropriate and appropriation in political caricature' in *Southeastern College Art Conference Review*, xi, 2 (spring 1987), pp127–34.
3. Anne Crookshank and the Knight of Glin, *Irish Portraits 1660–1860* (Dublin 1969), p20.
4. Michael MacDonagh, *Daniel O'Connell and the Story of Catholic Emancipation* (Dublin 1929), pp51–2; the quoted remark in MacDonagh mistakes 1810 for 1813, when the portrait appeared.
5. See note in M R O'Connell (ed), *The Correspondence of Daniel O'Connell* (8 vols, Dublin 1972–80), [hereafter cited as *O'Connell Corr*], iii, p173, that John Comerford executed a miniature of O'Connell about 1800; see W G Strickland, *A Dictionary of Irish Artists* (2 vols, Dublin and London 1913), i, p200.
6. Oliver MacDonagh, *The Hereditary Bondsman: Daniel O'Connell 1775–1829* (London 1988), p117.
7. *O'Connell Corr*, ii, Letter 968, p398.
8. *O'Connell Corr*, iii, Letters 1229, 1240, p173, p183.
9. See O'Ferrall, *Catholic Emancipation*, p104 and *O'Connell Corr*, iii, Letter 1240, p183.
10. Crookshank and the Knight of Glin, *Irish Portraits 1660–1860*, p72.
11. For Haydon's observation see Chappel and McCord, 'John Doyle', p131.
12. Geraldine F Grogan, *The Noblest Agitator: Daniel O'Connell and the German Catholic Movement 1830–50* (Dublin 1991), p29.
13. See poster reproduced in Fergus O'Ferrall, *Daniel O'Connell* (Dublin 1981), p63.
14. D J O'Donoghue (ed), *Essays Literary and Historical by Thomas Davis* (Dundalk 1914), pp112–15.
15. Quoted by John Turpin in his survey article 'Irish history painting' in *GPA Irish Arts Review Yearbook 1989–90*, pp233–47; on Barry see W L Pressly, *The Life and Art of James Barry* (New Haven and London 1981), and the important

article, Luke Gibbons, 'A shadowy narrator: history, art and romantic nationalism in Ireland, 1750–1850' in Ciaran Brady (ed), *Ideology and the Historians: Historical Studies, xvii* (Dublin 1989), pp99–127.

16. See Jeanne Sheehy, *The Rediscovery of Ireland's Past: The Celtic Revival 1830–1930* (London 1980).
17. *O'Connell Corr*, vi, Letter 2593, p219.
18. *O'Connell Corr*, viii, Letter 3206, pp20–21.
19. See Catalogue for sale by James Adam and Sons, Dublin, 17 May 1990; Lot purchased by the National Museum of Ireland.
20. See Sheehy, *Rediscovery of Ireland's Past*, pp23, 36; for 'Repeal cap' see John Turpin, *John Hogan: Irish Neoclassical Sculptor in Rome 1800–1858* (Dublin 1982), p82.
21. Charles Gavan Duffy, *Young Ireland: A Fragment of Irish History 1840–45* (2 vols, London 1896), ii, p60.
22. *The Nation*, 19 June 1847; *The Pilot*, 9 June 1847.
23. *O'Connell Corr*, vii, Letter 3078a, p261.
24. Turpin, *John Hogan*, p40; the details about Hogan are drawn from this excellent study of Hogan's career and works, see pp65–6, 81–2, 144–5, 148–9; for an earlier portrait bust of Daniel O'Connell, executed in 1828, by Peter Turnerelli (1774–1839), see Noel Kissane, *The Irish Face* (Dublin 1986), pp38–9.
25. Donal McCartney, 'The changing image of O'Connell' in K B Nowlan and M R O'Connell (eds), *Daniel O'Connell: Portrait of a Radical* (Belfast 1984), pp10–31.
26. There is a reproduction of the membership card 'The Volunteers of 1782 Revived' in Sheehy, *Rediscovery of Ireland's Past*, p28.
27. *O'Connell Corr*, viii, Letter 3435, p245.
28. See Homan Potterton, *The O'Connell Monument* (Ballycotton 1973), which treats the principal monument to O'Connell in Dublin to detailed examination.

Chapter 7 (pp103–117)

1. See especially G L Mosse, *The Nationalisation of the Masses: Political Symbolism and Mass Movements in Germany from the Napoleonic Wars Through the Third Reich* (New York 1975); 'Mass politics and the political liturgy of nationalism' in Eugene Kamenka (ed), *Nationalism: The Nature and Evolution of an Idea* (London 1976), pp38–54; and 'Caesarism, circuses and monuments' in G L Mosse, *Masses and Man: Nationalist and Fascist Perceptions of Reality* (New York 1980), pp104–18. Also, Eric Hobsbawm and Terence Ranger (eds), *The Invention of Tradition* (Cambridge 1983); Lynn Hunt, *Politics, Culture and Class in the French Revolution* (Berkeley 1984); Maurice Agulhon, *Marianne Into Battle: Republican Imagery and Symbolism in France, 1789–1880* (Cambridge 1981); Charles Rearick, *Pleasures of the Belle Epoque: Entertainment & Festivity in Turn-of-the-Century France* (New Haven and London 1985); James Epstein, 'Understanding the cap of liberty: symbolic practice and social conflict in early nineteenth-century England' in *Past and Present*, 122 (1989), pp75–118; and Paul Pickering, 'Class without words: symbolic communication in the chartist movement' in *Past and Present*, 112 (1986), pp144–62.
2. There were about twenty major statues in London in the year of Victoria's accession; in the year of her death there were over two hundred. The rate of statue-building in British provincial cities after 1850, particularly in the industrial midlands and north, was probably equal to that of London. See Arthur Byron, *London Statues: A Guide to London's Outdoor Statues and Sculpture* (London 1981), and David Cannadine, 'The context, performance and meaning of ritual: the British monarchy and the "Invention of Tradition", c1820–1977' in Hobsbawm and Ranger, *Invention of Tradition*, p164, Table 4. Also, Benedict Read, *Victorian Sculpture* (New Haven and London 1982), especially pp82–120; Marvin Trachtenberg, *The Statue of Liberty* (London 1976); Maurice Agulhon, 'La statuomanie et l'histoire' in *Ethnologie Française*, iii–iv (1978), pp145–72; Albert Boime, *Hollow Icons: The Politics of Sculpture in Nineteenth Century France* (Kent, Ohio and London 1987); and William Cohen, 'Symbols of power: statues in nineteenth-century provincial France' in *Comparative Studies in Society and History*, xxxi (1989), pp491–513.
3. 'On the role of symbolism in political thought' in *Political Science Quarterly*, lxxxii (1967), p194. Also, Benedict Anderson, *Imagined Communities: Reflections on the Origin and Spread of Nationalism* (London 1983); James E Young, 'The biography of a memorial icon: Nathan Rapoport's Warsaw Ghetto monument' in *Representations*, xxvi (spring 1989), pp69–106; Benedict Anderson, 'Cartoons and monuments: the evolution of political communication under the New Order' in D Jackson and Lucien Pye (eds), *Political Power and Communication in Indonesia* (Berkeley, California 1978); and Robin Jeffrey, 'What the statues tell: the politics of choosing symbols in Trivandrum' in *Pacific Affairs*, liii (1980), pp484–502.
4. James Young, 'Biography of a memorial icon', p71. Also, Boime, *Hollow Icons*, pp13–14.
5. See David I Kertzer, *Ritual, Politics and Power* (New Haven and London 1988), chs 6–8; L Jakubowska, 'Political drama in Poland: the use of national symbols' in *Anthropology Today*, vi (Aug 1990), pp10–13; and David Kowalewski, 'The protest uses of symbolic politics: the mobilization functions of protester symbolic resources' in *Social Science Quarterly*, lxi (1980), pp95–113.
6. Cyril Barrett, 'Irish nationalism and art, 1800–1921' in *Studies*, lxiv (1975), pp396, 398 and *passim*. Also John Turpin, 'Oliver Sheppard's 1798 memorials' in *Irish Arts Review Yearbook, 1990–91* (1991), pp71–80; Ken Inglis, 'Father Mathew's statue: the making of a monument in Cork' in Oliver MacDonagh and W F Mandle (eds), *Ireland and Irish-Australia: Studies in Cultural and Political History* (London 1986), pp119–36; Timothy J O'Keefe, 'The art and politics of the Parnell monument' in *Éire-Ireland*, xix (1984), pp6–25; and Homan Potterton, *The O'Connell Monument* (Ballycotton 1973); Jeanne Sheehy, *The Rediscovery of Ireland's Past: The Celtic Revival, 1830–1930* (London 1980), and Belinda Loftus, *Mirrors: William III and Mother Ireland* (Dundrum 1990). Read, *Victorian Sculpture, passim*.
7. *The Nation*, 27 May 1843, p523.
8. See Potterton, *O'Connell Monument*; The O'Connell Centenary Committee, *The O'Connell Centenary Record, 1875* (Dublin 1878), pp1–2; *The Monuments of Dublin: A Poem by M C G* (Dublin 1865); and 'Monuments' in *Dublin Builder*, iv, 71, 1 Dec 1862, pp300–1.
9. John Morisy, *A Wreath for the O'Brien Statue* (Dublin 1871), p26.
10. On the suspension of monument-building during the Land War, see *Leinster Leader*, 7 June 1890; *The Nation*, 24 Mar 1888.
11. Potterton, *O'Connell Monument*, *passim*.
12. *The Nation*, 24 Mar 1888. For a similar decay in the state of national monuments see 'The preservation of the memorials of the dead in Ireland' in *Royal Historical and Archaeological Association of Ireland*, iv [c1888, nd]; *The Nation*, 17 Nov 1888.
13. Report of a speech by J J O'Gorman, *The People* [Wexford], 6 Aug 1898, Supplement, p3.
14. Report of a speech by John Field at Kilcock, Co Kildare, *The Nation*, 11 May 1898.
15. Speech to the '98 Centennial Association, *The Nation*, 22 Feb 1898.
16. One of the most active of them was the National Monuments Committee, which, as its name implied, specialised in putting up memorials to worthy dead. On the IRB and its monument-building activities see Leon O'Broin, *Revolutionary Underground: The Story of the Irish Republican Brotherhood, 1858–1924* (Dublin 1976), ch 3.
17. The '98 centenary awaits full-scale analysis, but aspects of it are treated in Timothy J O'Keefe, 'The 1898 efforts to celebrate the United Irishmen: the '98 centennial' in *Éire-Ireland*, xxiii (1988), pp51–73; W F Mandle, *The Gaelic Athletic Association and Irish Nationalist Politics, 1884–1924* (London and Dublin 1987), ch 4, and O'Broin, *Revolutionary Underground*, ch 6. See also, National Library of Ireland [hereafter cited as NLI], Irish News-Cuttings Compiled by the Chief Secretary's Office, lvi–lvi, 'The '98 Centenary' and NLI Ms 5181.
18. See, for example, the objectives of the centenary movement as expressed in a public circular of Feb 1897, *Daily Independent*, 26 Feb 1897. Also, National Archives, Dublin, State Paper Office, CBS File 17, 025/S and general newspaper coverage of the event, week of 16–20 Aug 1898.
19. Speech of Sir Thomas Edmondes, *The People* [Wexford], 2 Nov 1898.
20. *Sinn Féin*, 8 Dec 1906, p1, report of a debate in the Dublin South-East branch of Sinn Féin, and 'Statues and statue-raising', *Sinn Féin*, 15 Dec 1906, p3. Also see 'A study in proportion', *Sinn Féin*, 3 Aug 1907, p4, and 'The Parnell monument atrocity', *Sinn Féin*, 15 Feb 1908, p4.
21. *The Irishman*, 29 July 1882, p72.
22. Statements of Henry Dixon, vice-president of the '98 Centenary Committee, *The '98 Centenary Record* in the *Weekly Independent*, 17 Mar 1898, p9. See also speeches of William Delaney, *Leinster Leader*, 1 Sept 1900, p7; Richard Jones at Rotunda, *Daily Independent*, 21 June 1898; J M Johnson, *Dundalk Democrat*, 16 July 1898; Maude Gonne speaking to John O'Leary, 28 Jan 1897, NLI, Ms 8002/34.
23. Speech of W J Ryan to Kildare nationalists, 1 Oct 1899, *Leinster Leader*, 7 Oct 1899, p5.
24. *United Irishman*, 4 Nov 1899.
25. *Sinn Féin*, 8 Dec 1906, p1. See also Morisy, *O'Brien Statue*, p27.
26. *Weekly Independent*, 30 July 1898, p1.
27. Morisy, *O'Brien Statue*, p28; *The Nation*, 19 Aug 1898.
28. *New Ross Standard*, 4 Aug 1905.
29. *Daily Independent*, 23 June 1897.
30. *The Nation*, 17 June 1876, pp3, 8.
31. See, for example, descriptions of Manchester Martyrs demonstrations in County Wexford and Cork city, *Freeman's Journal*, 30 Nov 1908, 9 Sept and 24 Nov 1909. See also *Dundalk Democrat*, 9 Mar 1901; *Freeman's Journal*, 5 Apr 1915; *Leinster Leader*, 8 Sept 1917.
32. *Freeman's Journal*, 2 Aug 1915.
33. National Archives, State Paper Office, CBS File 24, 177/S.
34. Inspector John Mallon to the under secretary, 24 Sept 1897, National Archives, State Paper Office, CBS File 14, 521/S; *Daily Independent*, 18 Jan 1898, '98 Centenary Committee'.
35. *The Irishman*, 19 Aug 1882, p114; *Freeman's Journal*, 23 June 1897.
36. In a similar gesture of defiance, Bandon nationalists erected their '98 monument on the town's bridge. The bridge was allegedly a no-go area for Catholics until the mid nineteenth century. *Cork County Eagle*, 24 Aug 1901.
37. 'The nature of mass demonstrations' in *New Society*, 23 May 1968, p755.
38. *The Daily Nation*, 16 Aug 1898; '*The '98 Centenary Record*', p7 in the *Weekly Independent*, 28 May 1898, and *Ibid* 20 Aug 1898.
39. *New Ross Standard*, 4 Aug 1905; *Weekly Freeman*, 11 June 1898.
40. *Leinster Leader*, 1 Sept 1900; *The People* [Wexford], 2 Nov 1898; *New Ross Standard*, 28 June 1907.
41. *The Times*, 14 Dec 1903; *New Ross Standard*, 2 June 1905.
42. The Parnell stone came from the family quarries in County Wicklow; the New Ross stone was taken from the town's Three Bullet Gate, the scene of fierce fighting during the rebellion. *Weekly Independent*, 14 Oct 1899; *The People* [Wexford], 14 Dec 1898.
43. *The People* [Wexford], 19 May 1900. On the Monasterevin monument, see speech of J P Dunne, *Leinster Leader*, 7 July 1900, p7. On the Wexford cross, speech of Sir Thomas Edmondes, *The People* [Wexford], 2 Nov 1898, p8.
44. Advertisement for Wightman and Co, Belfast, *Shan Van Vocht*, Oct–Nov 1898. Also, NLI Mss 5181, p225 and 17,644. Within days of the unveiling of Enniscorthy's '98 monument, Eason's in Dublin offered photographic postcards of the ceremony. *The Echo* [Enniscorthy], 6 June 1908.
45. Edna Longley provides many perceptive observations on the links between political and religious ceremonies in Ireland in 'The Rising, the Somme and modern Irish memory' in Máirín Ní Dhonnchadha and Theo Dorgan (eds), *Revising the Rising* (Derry 1991), pp29–49. On mission crosses, see John Sharp, *Reapers of the Harvest: The Redemptorists in Ireland, 1843–1898* (Dublin 1989), pp25–8 and Kevin A Laheen, 'Parish mission crosses' in *O'Dwyer Cheshire Home Annual Journal*, 1989. I am grateful to Prof Emmet Larkin for the latter reference.
46. James Loughlin, 'Constructing the political spectacle: Parnell, the press and national leadership, 1879–86' in D George Boyce and Alan O'Day (eds), *Parnell in Perspective* (London 1991), esp. pp226–7. See also K T Hoppen, *Elections, Politics, and Society in Ireland, 1832–1885* (Oxford 1984), pp423–35.
47. *Irish News/Belfast Morning News*, 11 Aug 1898; *Freeman's Journal*, 16 Aug 1898.
48. The account of the ceremonies that follows is drawn from descriptions that appeared in the 16 August editions of the *Freeman's Journal*, the *Daily Independent* and the *Daily Nation*. There are other accounts of the ceremonies in

National Archives, State Paper Office, CBS Files, 16,952/S, 17,007/S, 17,025/S. Drawings of the celebrations appeared in the *Weekly Freeman* and *Weekly Independent*, 21 Aug 1898. *The Black and White* magazine (Sept 1898) published photographs of street scenes.

49. *Daily Independent*, 16 Aug 1898.

50. Kate Maxwell to John Redmond, 28 July 1898, NLI Ms 15,236/10; *Shan Van Vocht*, Sept 1898, p162.

51. See E Estyn Evans, *Irish Folk Ways* (London 1957), pp292–3; Pauric Travers, 'Our Fenian dead: Glasnevin Cemetery and the Genesis of the republican funeral' in James Kelly and Uáitéar MacGearailt (eds), *Dublin and Dubliners: Essays in the History and Literature of Dublin City* (Dublin 1990), pp52–72.

52. See NLI, Irish Newscuttings, xliii, 'Manchester Martyrs, 1891–1912', and Travers, 'Our Fenian dead'. By contrast, when constitutional nationalists dedicated foundation stones of monuments, they did so with much less attention to funereal symbolism. See coverage of the O'Connell and Parnell dedication ceremonies, *Freeman's Journal*, 9 Aug 1864; *The Irishman*, 13 Aug 1864; Potterton, *O'Connell Monument*, pp2–3; *Daily Nation*, *Freeman's Journal*, and *Daily Independent* for 9 Oct 1899, and O'Keefe, 'Parnell monument', pp6–7.

53. Breandán Ó hEithir, *The Begrudger's Guide to Irish Politics* (Dublin 1986), p152. See also Oliver MacDonagh, *States of Mind: A Study of Anglo-Irish Conflict, 1780–1980* (London 1983), p101.

54. Nina Witoszek, *The Theatre of Recollection: A Cultural Study of the Modern Dramatic Traditions of Ireland and Poland* (Stockholm 1988), p39 and *passim*. See also her 'Ireland: a funerary culture?' in *Studies*, lxxvi (1987), pp206–15.

55. See Loftus *Mirrors*, pp 59–64; and Sheehy, *Rediscovery of Ireland's Past*, *passim*.

56. *Weekly Independent*, 30 July 1898.

57. William Bulfin, 'Rambles in Éirinn' in *Sinn Féin*, 11 Aug 1906, p4.

58. See, for example, John Gooch, 'Attitudes to war in late Victorian and Edwardian England' in Brian Bond and Ian Roy (eds), *War and Society* (New York 1975), pp88–102; Anne Summers, 'Militarism in Britain before the Great War' in *History Workshop*, ii (1976), pp104–23; G Best, 'Militarism and the Victorian public school' in Brian Simon and Ian Bradley (eds), *The Victorian Public School* (Dublin 1975); Robert H MacDonald, 'Reproducing the middle-class boy: from purity to patriotism in the Boys' Magazines, 1892–1914' in *Journal of Contemporary History*, xxiv (1989), pp519–39; W J Reader, *At Duty's Call: a Study in Obsolete Patriotism* (Manchester 1988); John M MacKenzie, *Propaganda and Empire: The Manipulation of British Public Opinion, 1880–1960* (Manchester 1985); and Seamus Deane, 'Wherever Green is Read' in Ní Dhonnchadha and Dorgan (eds), *Revising the Rising*, pp94–6.

59. Stephen J Brown, *Ireland in Fiction* (Dublin 1919) and *A Guide to Books on Ireland* (Dublin 1912).

60. The exceptions were Oliver Sheppard's '98 statues in Wexford (1905) and Enniscorthy (1908).

61. 'Statues and statue-raising' in *Sinn Féin*, 15 Dec 1906, p3; Maud Gonne MacBride, *Servant of the Queen: Reminiscences* (London 1974), pp282–3; *Dundalk Democrat*, 23 Sept 1899, 23 Feb 1901 and 14 Sept 1901.

62. *The Irish Builder and Engineer*, 20 July 1918 as cited in Jane Leonard, 'Lest we forget' in David Fitzpatrick (ed), *Ireland and the First World War* (Dublin 1988), p59.

63. Maud Gonne MacBride, *Servant of the Queen*, p282.

64. Sheehy, *Rediscovery of Ireland's Past*, p92.

65. In fact, the majority of '98 monuments bore inscriptions of patriotic poetry in English only, the favourite being lines from John Kells Ingram's 'Memory of the Dead', which appeared originally in *The Nation* in 1843. A few of the memorials that went up after 1900 showed the growing influence of the Gaelic League and carried inscriptions in Irish and English.

66. D George Boyce, *Nationalism in Ireland* (2nd edn, London and New York 1991), ch 8.

CHAPTER 8 (PP118–131)

1. Obituary, *The Leader*, xci, 1, 28 July 1945, pp14–15.

2. *The Irish Times*, 11 July 1945, p3.

3. *The Irish Press*, 11 July 1945, p1.

4. *The Leader*, 28 July 1945, pp14–15.

5. C P Curran, 'Albert Power RHA' in *Father Matthew Record*, August 1945.

6. Kitty Clive, 'Albert Power RHA' in *The Leader*, lxxxv, 15, 7 Nov 1942, pp290–92.

7. These reports are available in the National Library of Ireland, the National College of Art and Design, Thomas Street, Dublin, and the library of the Victoria and Albert Museum, London.

8. Report in *Wolfe Tone Weekly*, i, 36, 7 May 1938, p5.

9. For an account of the Dublin Metropolitan School of Art, see John Turpin, 'The Metropolitan School of Art 1890–1923' in *Dublin Historical Record*, xxxvii, 2 (1984), pp59–78; xxxviii, 2 (1985), pp42–52; xxxviii, 3 (1985), pp86–102.

10. Clive, 'Albert Power.'

11. National Gallery of Ireland, Orpen Mss. The letter is undated but it is likely to have been written sometime between 1908 and 1914.

12. This is quoted in Allan Wade, *A Bibliography of the Writings of W B Yeats* (London 1951), p627.

13. *Irish Builder and Engineer*, 13 Apr 1918, p186 and *Freeman's Journal*, 1 Apr 1918, p2.

14. 'Topical touches' in *Irish Builder*, lxi, 9, 3 May 1919, p205.

15. Sinn Féin was founded by Arthur Griffith in 1905, and was reorganised in the spring of 1917 when Éamon de Valera became president. Cathal Brugha and Michael Collins built the movement on a nationwide basis on a platform of Irish independence and a withdrawal from Westminister. The election of 1918 was a sweeping victory for Sinn Féin and its members. The first Dáil Éireann was formed on 19 January 1919.

16. Terence MacSwiney was a member of Sinn Féin, representing Cork in the first Dáil Éireann. He was elected Lord Mayor of Cork in March 1920, but was arrested the following August under the Defense of the Realm Act. He embarked on a hunger strike in Brixton jail, which captured international attention, and died after fasting for seventy-four days.

17. For an account of this commission I am indebted to James Power, son of the sculptor. See also Curran, 'Albert Power, RHA', p3.

18. *Freeman's Journal*, 26 Oct 1920, p6.

19. *The Irish Times*, 13 Aug 1928, p5.

20. *The Irish Times*, 13 Aug 1928, p5.

21. *All Hallows' Annual* (1922), p16.

22. See 'The importation of worked stone and marble' in *The Irish Builder*, xxi, 11, 25 May 1929, pp459–61.

23. 'Im sheashamh ag an altóir' in *Irisleabhair Gearrbhaile* (spring 1931).

24. Albert Power gave a lecture on his work in November 1935.

25. Clive, 'Albert Power.' See also Sighle Bhreathnach-Lynch, 'The Pádraic O'Conaire commission' in *Irish Arts Review Yearbook 1993*, pp244–9.

26. Clive, 'Albert Power.'

27. *Leitrim Observer*, 18 May 1940, p3.

28. Recollections of John Mulhern, native of Kiltyclogher, County Leitrim.

29. Letter, *The Irish Times*, 26 Jan 1939.

30. Interview with Rory Brugha, son of Cathal Brugha, 21 Feb 1989. He maintains that the culprit was Seán Russell, an IRA man on the run, who was entirely sympathetic to Kathleen Brugha's views. Some years later the plaque was found in the home of the late Austin Stack's widow, a friend of Mrs Brugha.

31. The meeting of the sub-committee was held on 9 Nov 1944. I am indebted to the late Donnacha O'Súilleabháin of Conradh na Gaeilge for this information.

32. *The Irish Times*, 11 July 1945, p3.

CHAPTER 9 (PP132–152)

1. See F S L Lyons, *Ireland Since the Famine* (London 1973); John A Murphy, *Ireland in the Twentieth Century* (Dublin 1975); Ronan Fanning, *Independent Ireland* (Dublin 1983); Roy Foster, *Modern Ireland 1600–1972* (London 1988); Joseph Lee, *Ireland 1912–1985* (Cambridge 1989).

2. Belinda Loftus, *Mirrors: Orange and Green* (Dundrum 1994), pp84–6.

3. Janet E and Gareth W Dunleavy, *Douglas Hyde: A Maker of Modern Ireland* (Berkeley, California 1991), p184; and Douglas Hyde, 'The necessity of de-anglicizing Ireland', a paper delivered before the Irish National Literary Society, Dublin, 25 Nov 1892, in Sir Charles Gavin Duffy, Dr George Sigerson and Dr Douglas Hyde, *The Revival of Irish Literature* (London 1894).

4. Trinity College, Dublin, Ms 8003/9, Correspondence of Thomas MacGreevy.

5. Eoin MacNeill, 'The Irish nation and Irish culture' in *Ireland-American Review*, i (1938), pp77–8.

6. *Census of Population 1926, x, General Report* (Dublin 1934), p64.

7. *Irish Statistical Survey 1955* (Dublin 1956), p32.

8. *Census of Population of Ireland 1946 and 1951, General Report* (Dublin 1958), p193.

9. *Census of Population 1946, 1951*, pp195–7.

10. *Census of Population 1946, 1951*, p176.

11. David Scott, 'Posting Images' in *Irish Arts Review Yearbook 1990–1991* (1991), pp188–95: a useful examination of the art and semiotics of Irish postage stamps.

12. The author is grateful to Michael Giffney, stamp dealer, for this information.

13. Michael Johnston, 'The Thin Green Line', RTE Radio 1, 21 Jan 1991.

14. John Bowman, *De Valera and the Ulster Question 1917–73* (Oxford 1982), p13.

15. Bowman, *De Valera*, p8.

16. Robert Fisk, *In Time of War: Ireland, Ulster and the Price of Neutrality 1939–45* (London 1983), p91.

17. Joseph P O'Grady, 'The Irish Free State passport and the question of citizenship 1921–4' in *Irish Historical Studies*, xxvi (1988–9), pp396–405.

18. Public Record Office, London, Mint 220/824, Deputy Master Robert Johnson, Royal Mint to Irish Dept of Finance, 1 May 1923. The author is grateful to Colm Gallagher, Dept of Finance, Dublin, for providing transcripts of the letters on this file. See Colm Gallagher, 'The Great Seal of Ireland' in *Seirbhís Phoiblí*, xiv, 3 (April 1994), pp17–27.

19. PRO London, Mint 220/824, Johnson to Irish Dept of Finance, 27 Jan 1924.

20. PRO London, Mint 220/824, Johnson to Phillips, 18 Jan 1928.

21. W B Yeats, 'What we did or tried to do', introduction to *The Coinage of Saorstát Éireann* (Dublin 1928), p5.

22. *Parliamentary Debates: Seanad Éireann*, 6, col 501.

23. Leon Ó Broin, *Just Like Yesterday* (Dublin 1986), p93.

24. *Parliamentary Debates: Dáil Éireann*, 125, col 1723.

25. *Parliamentary Debates: Dáil Éireann*, 125, cols 1723–4.

26. See Brian P Kennedy, 'The traditional Irish thatched house: image and reality, 1793–1993' in Adele Dalsimer (ed), *Visualizing Ireland: National Identity and the Pictorial Tradition* (Boston 1993), pp164–79.

27. Author's interview with Dr George Furlong, 29 May 1984.

28. Nicholas Sheaff, 'The Shamrock Building', *Irish Arts Review*, i, 1 (spring 1984), p27.

29. See Frank McDonald, 'From the rubble of the Rising' in *The Irish Times*, 27 Apr 1991; Maura Shaffrey, 'Sackville Street/O'Connell Street' in *The GPA Irish Arts Review Yearbook 1988*, pp 144–56; Michael Bannon (ed), *The Emergence of Irish Planning 1880–1920* (Dublin 1985), and *Planning – The Irish Experience, 1920–1988* (Dublin 1989).

30. Brian P Kennedy, *Dreams and Responsibilities: The State and the Arts in Independent Ireland* (Dublin 1990), pp38–9.

31. Michael Laurence Clarke, 'The Geneva Window' in *The Stained Glass of Harry Clarke* (exhibition catalogue, The Fine Art Society, London 1988).

32. Brian Fallon, 'Geneva Window goes to America' in *The Irish Times*, 24 May 1988.

33. *Parliamentary Debates: Dáil Éireann*, 107, col 118.

34. Peter Figgis, 'Remembering Art O'Murnaghan' in *Irish Arts Review*, ii, 4 (winter 1985), pp41–4.

35. Benedict Kiely, 'Father Senan O F M Cap: The Corpulent Capuchin of Capel Street', in Brian P Kennedy (ed), *Art is My Life: A Tribute to James White* (Dublin 1991), pp120–26.

36. 'The Cost of An Gúm', *Irish Independent*, 24 Jan 1966 [a translation of an article 'Costas an Ghúim', which appeared in *Comhar*, Nov 1965].

37. See Thomas Ryan *et al*, *Seán Keating and the ESB* (Dublin 1985), and Brian Kennedy, 'Irish landscape painting in a political setting 1922–48' in Myrtle Hill and Sarah Barber (eds), *Aspects of Irish Studies* (Belfast 1990), pp47–54.

38. *Thomas Davis: Selections from his Prose and Poetry*, with an introduction by T W Rolleston (Dublin 1889). The centenary of Davis's death saw the publication of a number of books celebrating

his contribution to cultural nationalism: see *Thomas Davis: Essays and Poems*, with an introduction by Éamon de Valera (Dublin 1945), and M J McManus (ed), *Thomas Davis and Young Ireland* (Dublin 1945).
39. Fr Timothy Corcoran S J, 'How English may be taught without anglicising' in *The Irish Monthly*, June 1923, p272.
40. James Devane, 'Is an Irish Culture Possible?', *Ireland To-Day*, Sept 1936, pp21–32.
41. See Kenneth McConkey, 'Paintings of the Irish Renascence' in *Irish Arts Review*, iii, 3 (autumn 1986), pp19–21.
42. McConkey, 'Paintings', p 19. Quoted from a speech delivered at the Banquet of the Irish Academy of Letters, 17 Aug 1937. See A Norman Jeffares, *A Commentary on the Collected Poems of W B Yeats* (London 1968), p482.
43. *The Catholic Bulletin*, xxv, 4, Apr 1935, p273.
44. Fr Timothy Corcoran S J, 'The integral teaching of history' in *The Irish Monthly*, Jan 1929, pp9–12
45. Alfred O'Rahilly, 'The teaching of history', *Studies*, xii (1923), p260.
46. Fr Stephen Brown S J, *The Central Catholic Library: The First Ten Years of an Irish Enterprise* (Dublin 1932), p31.
47. Fr P J Gannon S J, 'Literature and Censorship', *The Irish Monthly*, lxv, no 769, July 1937, p439.
48. Terence de Vere White, 'The Personality of Jack B Yeats' in Roger McHugh (ed), *Jack B Yeats: A Centenary Gathering* (Dublin 1971), pp42–3.
49. Seán Ó Faoláin, 'Autoantiamericanism' in *The Bell*, xvi, 6 Mar 1951, p22.
50. Seán Ó Faoláin, 'The Dangers of Censorship' in *Ireland To-Day*, Nov 1936, pp57–63.

Chapter 10 (pp155–168)

1. E S Shuckburgh (ed), *Two Biographies of William Bedell* (Cambridge 1902), p203.
2. For example, Charles Jackson (ed), *The Autobiography of Mrs Alice Thornton* (Durham 1875), pp19–28; H E Malden (ed), 'Richard Broughton's Devereux papers' in *Camden Miscellany, xiii* (London 1924), pp6–11; Historical Manuscripts Commission, *Report on the Laing Mss* (2 vols, London 1914), i, pp132–5. For Gaelic Irish examples, W M Hennessey (ed), *The Annals of Loch Ce* (2 vols, London 1871), *sub anno* 1636; John O'Donovan (ed), *Annála Ríoghachta Éirinn* (7 vols, Dublin 1851), *sub anno* 1608.
3. Richard Caulfield (ed), 'Wills and inventories, Cork' in *Gentleman's Magazine* (1861), p532; A B Grossart (ed), *Lismore papers* (10 vols, London 1886–8), 1st ser, pp30, 31; National Archives, Dublin, RC 10/9, p425; RC 5/15, p263; RC 5/21, p345.
4. Caulfield, 'Wills and inventories' in *Gentleman's Magazine* (1862), p31 (1861), p257; National Archives, RC 10/1, p285; RC 10/3, p535.
5. James Mitchell, 'Mayor Lynch of Galway: a review of the tradition' in *Journal of the Galway Archaeological and Historical Society,* xxxii (1966–71), pp45–51.
6. *Journal of the Association for the Preservation of the Memorials to the Dead* [hereafter cited as *Mems Dead*] iv (1898–1900), p188; viii (1910–12), p97; iii (1895–7), p47; ii (1892–4), pp33, 38, 210.
7. J M Clark, *The Dance of Death* (Glasgow 1950), p95. For a medieval representation of this, Robert Cochrane, 'Abbey Knockmoy, County Galway: notes on the building and "frescoes" ' in *Journal of the Royal Society of Antiquaries of Ireland,* xxxiv (1903–4), p251.
8. H M Roe, 'Cadaver effigial monuments in Ireland' in *Journal of the Royal Society of Antiquaries of Ireland,* xcix (1969), pp1–19; *Mems Dead,* iv (1898–1900), pp276–9; Finbar McCormick, 'The symbols of death and the tomb of John Forster in Tydavnet, County Monaghan' in *Clogher Record,* xi, 2 (1983), pp273–86.
9. National Archives, RC 5/8, p505; RC 5/12, pp207, 390.
10. E P Shirley (ed), 'Extracts from the journal of Thomas Dineley' in *Journal of the Royal Society of Antiquaries of Ireland*, viii (1864–6), pp445–6; John Bradley, 'The medieval tombs of St Canice's Cathedral' in Adrian Empey (ed), *A Worthy Foundation: the Cathedral Church of St Canice, Kilkenny* (Dublin 1985), pp51-2; *Mems Dead,* iii (1895–7), p336; E C Rae, 'Irish sepulchral monuments of the later Middle Ages' in *Journal of the Royal Society of Antiquaries of Ireland*, c (1970), p21; National Archives, RC 5/28, p471.
11. Described in *Mems Dead*, vi (1904–6), pp47–63; Grossart, *Lismore Papers*, Ist ser, i, p167, 179, 247–8.
12. Described in *Mems Dead,* vi (1904–6), pp69–71; Grossart, *Lismore Papers*, 1st ser, iii, p35.
13. N P Canny, *The Upstart Earl* (Cambridge 1982), pp12, 13, 43.
14. National Library of Ireland, Ms 11,060/7. I am grateful to Tom Connors for pointing out this reference to me.
15. National Archives, RC 10/7, p12.
16. National Archives, RC 10/2, pp389–90.
17. Colm Lennon, *The Lords of Dublin in the Age of Reformation* (Dublin 1989), p134; M J Talbot, *The Monuments of St Mary's Cathedral* (Limerick 1976), p7.
18. Heather King, 'Seventeenth-century effigial sculpture in the north Meath area' in Etienne Rynne (ed), *Figures from the Past* (Dublin 1987), pp283–307.
19. E C Rae, 'The Rice monument in Waterford Cathedral' in *Proceedings of the Royal Irish Academy*, lxix (1970), sect c, p4.
20. John Hunt, *Irish Medieval Figure Sculpture* (2 vols, Dublin 1974), i. pp108–11.
21. Denis Murphy (ed), *Triumphalia Chronologia Monasterii Sanctae Crucis* (Dublin 1891), p52.
22. A M Freeman (ed), *The Annals of Connacht* (Dublin 1944), *sub annis* 1537, 1543; Hennessey, *Annals of Loch Ce, sub annis* 1527, 1585, 1636. Hunt, *Irish Medieval Figure Sculpture,* ii, plates 189, 248–9, 250–52; for wills see H F Berry (ed), *Register of Wills and Inventories of the Diocese of Dublin* (Dublin 1898).
23. Charles McNeill, A J Otway-Ruthven (eds), *Dowdall Deeds* (Dublin 1960), p215.
24. National Archives, RC 10/1, pp353–4; RC 5/5, p773.
25. Katharine Simms, *From Kings to Warlords* (Woodbridge 1987), esp chs7–10.
26. For an analysis of the Kildare lineage society, Laurence McCorristine, *The Revolt of Silken Thomas* (Dublin 1987), pp21–35.
27. Hunt, *Irish Medieval Figure Sculpture,* i, pp105–8; Rae, 'Irish sepulchral monuments', p4.
28. H M Roe, 'Instruments of the Passion: notes towards a survey of their illustration and distribution in Ireland' in *Old Kilkenny Review,* 2nd ser, ii, 5 (1982), pp527–34.
29. J J Buckley, *Some Irish Altar Plate* (Dublin 1943), pp28, 38.
30. For example, National Archives, RC 5/8, p71.
31. James Jocelyn, 'The Renaissance tombs at Lusk and Newtown Trim' in *Journal of the Royal Society of Antiquaries of Ireland*, ciii (1973), pp153–66.
32. Margaret Murphy, 'The high cost of dying: an analysis of *pro anima* bequests in medieval Dublin' in W J Sheils and Diana Wood (eds), *The Church and Wealth: Studies in Church History, xxiv* (Oxford 1987), pp111–22; National Archives, RC 5/8, pp32, 160.
33. John Lodge, *The Peerage of Ireland*, ed Mervyn Archdall (7 vols, Dublin 1789), iii, p82.
34. Edmund Hogan, *Distinguished Irishmen of the Sixteenth Century* (London 1894), p419; P J Duffy, 'Farney in 1634: an examination of Thomas Raven's survey of the Essex estate' in *Clogher Record,* xi, 2 (1983), pp 245–56.
35. Heather King, 'Irish wayside and churchyard crosses, 1600–1700' in *Post-Medieval Archaeology,* xix (1985), pp13–33.
36. Connor Ryan, 'Religion and state in seventeenth-century Ireland' in *Archivium Hibernicum* xxxiii (1975), pp122–31.
37. Elizabeth Hickey, 'Monument to Sir Thomas Cusack' in *Ríocht na Midhe,* iv, 5 (1971), pp75–91.
38. For a corpus of these see Rolf Loeber, 'Sculptured monuments to the dead in early seventeenth-century Ireland' in *Proceedings of the Royal Irish Academy*, lxxxi (1981), sect c, pp267–93; *Mems Dead,* vii (1907–9), pp 302–3.
39. Jocelyn, 'Rennaissance tombs', pp159–60; *Mems Dead,* vi (1904–6), pp92–6; Homan Potterton, *Irish Church Monuments* (Belfast 1975), p19; William Carrigan, *The History and Antiquities of the Diocese of Ossory* (4 vols, Dublin 1850), iv, pp150–51.
40. Edmund Curtis, 'Extracts out of heralds books in Trinity College, Dublin' in *Journal of the Royal Society of Antiquaries of Ireland*, lxii (1932), pp41–2; Terence MacCarthy, 'Ulster Office, 1552–1800', MA thesis, Queen's University, Belfast, 1983.
41. John Bossy, 'The Counter-Reformation and the people of Catholic Ireland' in T D Williams (ed), *Historical Studies, viii* (Dublin 1971), pp155–69.
42. H M Roe, 'Illustrations of the Holy Trinity in Ireland, 13th to 17th centuries' in *Journal of the Royal Society of Antiquaries of Ireland*, cix (1979), p102, fig 35. The origin of the carving may be the panel illustrated in fig 34a. Only the two end panels of the French tomb survive; the sides at present mounted with it do not belong to the tomb. For its destruction in 1653 see Trinity College, Dublin, Ms 886, f43.
43. Raymond Gillespie, 'Funerals and society in seventeenth-century Ireland' in *Journal of the Royal Society of Antiquaries of Ireland,* cxv (1985), pp86–91.
44. F E Ball (ed), 'Extracts from the journal of Thomas Dineley' in *Journal of the Royal Society of Antiquaries of Ireland*, xliii (1913), pp283–4; Loeber, 'Sculptured monuments', appendix 2.
45. For an interesting case of an inscription in Irish, that of Rory McMahon of Kilcock, County Meath, in 1576, see *Mems Dead,* vii (1907–9), pp154–5.
46. *Mems Dead,* vi (1904–6), p95; v (1901–3), pp180–82; N W English, 'The Sir Mathew de Renzi memorial in Athlone' in *Journal of the Old Athlone Society,* ii, 5 (1978)), pp1–4; Hickey, 'Monument to Sir Thomas Cusack', pp87–88.
47. *Mems dead,* ii (1892–4), pp536–40; iii (1895–7), pp195–6.
48. Elizabeth Hickey, 'The Wakleys of Navan and Ballyburly' in *Ríocht na Midhe,* v, 4 (1971), pp3–5.
49. King, 'Seventeenth-century effigial sculpture', pp284–6. For an architectural parallel in the move from fortification to more domestic buildings, Dudley Waterman, 'Moyry, Charlemont, Castleraw and Richill: fortification to architecture in north of Ireland, 1570–1700' in *Ulster Journal of Archaeology,* 3rd ser, xxiii (1960), pp97–123. Such architectural changes are consistent with the passage from a lineage to a 'civil' society.
50. National Archives, RC 5/6, p49; National Archives, Prerogative court will book, 1644–84.
51. *Mems Dead,* i (1890–92), p180; viii (1910–12), p173; v (1901–3), pp 281–2.
52. E P Shirley (ed), 'Extracts from the journal of Thomas Dineley' in *Journal of the Royal Society of Antiquaries of Ireland,* v (1858–9), pp31–2.
53. McCarthy, 'Ulster Office', p168.
54. *Mems Dead,* ii (1892–4), p502; iii (1895–7), p326; National Library of Ireland, Ms 2745, f 11v.
55. One effect of this was that individuals became more sensitive to what was inscribed in the tombs of others. For one dispute see *Records of the General Synod of Ulster* (3 vols, Belfast 1890), i, p136.
56. Aidan Clarke, 'Colonial identity in early seventeenth-century Ireland' in T W Moody (ed), *Nationality and the Pursuit of National Independence: Historical Studies, xi* (Belfast 1978), pp57–9, 71; Ciaran Brady, 'Conservative subversives: the community of the Pale and the Dublin administration' in P J Corish (ed), *Rebels, Radicals and Establishments: Historical Studies,* xv (Belfast 1985), pp29–30.
57. National Archives, RC 5/4 p349; RC 5/5, pp763, 805.

Chapter 11 (pp169–183)

1. Philippe Aries, *Centuries of Childhood* (Paris 1960, English edn, London 1962). Much of his work has now been superseded. It is controversial, especially his view that parents were not upset by the death of their children. See Adrian Wilson, 'The infancy of the history of childhood' in *History and Theory*, xix (1980), pp132–53.
2. Lawrence Stone, *The Family, Sex and Marriage in England, 1500–1800* (London 1977); Ralph Houlbrooke, *The English Family 1450–1750* (London 1984); Ivy Pinchbeck and Margaret Hewitt, *Children in English Society* (2 vols, London 1969–73); Linda Pollock, *A Lasting Relationship. Parents and Children over Three Centuries* (London 1987); Linda Pollock, *Forgotten Children: Parent-Child Relations from 1500 to 1900* (Cambridge 1983); Lloyd de Mause, *The Evolution of Childhood* (London 1976); J H Plumb, 'The new world of children in eighteenth-century England' in *Past and Present*, 67 (1975), pp64–93; Valerie Fildes, *Wet Nursing. A History from Antiquity to the Present* (Oxford 1988).
3. The recent spate of work on women's history, for example, Margaret MacCurtain and Mary O'Dowd (eds), *Women in Early Modern Ireland* (Dublin 1991), and the foundation of two

Irishwomen's history groups, suggests that interest in matters of domestic social history is rapidly increasing.

4. Joseph Robins, *The Lost Children: A Study of Charity Children in Ireland 1700–1900* (Dublin 1980); P J Dowling, *A History of Irish Education* (Cork 1971); D H Akenson, *The Irish Educational Experiment* (London 1970); J J Auchmuty, *Irish Education, A Historical Survey* (London and Dublin 1937).

5. Leslie Whiteside, *History of King's Hospital* (Dublin 1980); Helen Clayton, 'Societies formed to educate the poor in Ireland in the eighteenth and nineteenth centuries', M Litt thesis, Trinity College, Dublin, 1981; Kenneth Milne, 'Irish Charter Schools' in *Irish Journal of Education*, viii, 1 (1974), pp3–29.

6. Thomas Corcoran, *State Policy in Irish Education 1536–1816 Exemplified in Documents* (Dublin and London 1916); *Education Systems in Ireland from the Close of the Middle Ages: Selected Texts with Introduction by T Corcoran* (Dublin 1928); *Some Lists of Catholic Lay Teachers and their Illegal Schools in the Later Penal Times with Historical Commentary, Maps and Illustrations* (Dublin 1932); Michael Quane, 'Aspects of education in Ireland 1695–1795' in *Journal of the Cork Historical and Archaeological Society*, 2nd ser, lxxiii (1968), pp120–35; 'Castledermot Charter School' in *Journal of the Kildare Archaeological Society*, xiii (1963), pp463–87; 'The Friends' Provincial School, Mountmellick' in *Journal of the Royal Society of Antiquaries of Ireland*, lxxxix (1959), pp59–89; 'Quaker schools in Dublin' in *Journal of the Royal Society of Antiquaries of Ireland*, xciv (1964–5), pp47–68; 'Ballitore School' in *Journal of the Kildare Archaeological Society*, xiv, 2 (1966–7), pp174–209; 'Zelva School, Valentia Island' in *Journal of the Cork Historical and Archaeological Society*, 2nd ser, lxxii, (1967), pp10–19; 'The Diocesan Schools 1570–1870' in *Journal of the Cork Historical and Archaeological Society*, 2nd ser, lxvi, (1961), pp26–49; 'The Hibernian Marine School, Dublin' in *Dublin Historical Record*, xxi (1967), pp67–8; 'The Royal Hibernian Military School, Dublin' in *Dublin Historical Record*, xviii (1962–3), pp15–23, 45–55.

7. Harriet Butler and Richard Butler (eds), *Black Book of Edgeworthstown and Other Memoirs 1585–1817* (London 1927), p164.

8. National Library of Ireland, Ms 11,470, no 6.

9. T U Sadlier (ed), 'The Diary of Anne Cooke 1761–1776' in *Journal of the Kildare Archaeological Society*, viii, 1 (1915), pp104–32.

10. Olive Goodbody, 'Anthony Sharp, a Quaker merchant of the Liberties' in *Dublin Historical Record*, xiv, 1 (1955), p19.

11. W M Wyse, *Notes on education reform in Ireland during the early part of the 19th century: compiled from the unpublished memoirs of Sir Thomas Wyse by his niece* (Waterford 1901), p16.

12. Sir W R Wilde, 'Memoir of Gabriel Beranger and his labours in the cause of Irish art, literature and antiquities, 1760–1780' in *Journal of the Royal Society of Antiquities of Ireland*, xi (1870), p236.

13. William Carleton, *Traits and Stories of the Irish Peasantry* (new edition, London 1843), pp293–302.

14. Anne Crookshank and the Knight of Glin, *The Painters of Ireland* (London 1978), p182.

15. Eva Bell, *The Hamwood Papers* (London 1930), pp182, 323.

16. P C Williams, 'Pestalozzi, John: A Study of the Life and Educational Work of John Synge with special reference to the Introduction and Development of Pestalozzian Ideas in Ireland and England', PhD thesis, Trinity College, Dublin, 1965, p60.

17. Edward Nicholson, *A Method of Charity Schools* (Dublin 1712).

18. Edward Nicholson, *Supplement to a Method of Charity Schools* (Dublin 1714).

19. Nicholson, *A Method of Charity Schools*, p25.

20. Nicholson, *Supplement*, p278.

21. Nicholson, *A Method of Charity Schools*, p40.

22. [Henry Maule] *Pietas Corcagiensis* (Cork 1721), p19.

23. *Methods of Erecting Supporting and Governing Charity Schools* (Dublin 1721), p11.

24. *Freeman's Journal*, 2–5 November 1765, p71a. I am indebted to Mairead Dunlevy for this reference.

25. Peadar McCann, 'Cork city's eighteenth-century Charity schools' in *Journal of the Cork Historical and Archaeological Society*, lxxxiv (1979), p108.

26. For example, Mr and Mrs S C Hall, *Ireland: Its Scenery and Character* (3 vols, London 1841–3), ii, p298.

CHAPTER 12 (PP185–206)

The author wishes to record her indebtedness to the Electricity Supply Board, in particular to the chairman, Pádraig Ó Muircheartaigh, and to Jack Wylie, Colm Healion and Donal O'Sullivan. She is especially grateful to John O'Connell, P F Wallace and John Teahan.

1. *Observations on Modern Gardening* (Dublin 1770).

2. Fergus D'Arcy, 'An age of Distress and Reform 1800–1860' in Art Cosgrove (ed), *Dublin Through the Ages* (Dublin 1988), p97.

3. *Freeman's Journal*, 7 July 1804.

4. Application of David Cooke at Mr Binns, Dame Street, on 2 October 1828, for the invention of a 'sort of boat and machine' that 'can sink underwater any depth and man can walk upon the bottom 20 feet under water with great safety and see, hear, etc as above'.

National Archives, Dublin, State Paper Office, OP Carton 588, no 770/2.

5. Patent applied for and sworn by George Malam of Stephen's Green on 8 September 1824. National Archives, State Paper Office, OP 588/765.

6. In her journal, Louisa Beaufort mentions a Gothic tripod in the drawingroom of Killymoon Castle, County Tyrone, in 1807, Trinity College, Dublin, Ms 4034.

7. Sale notice of James Donovan's china establishment, *Saunders' News-Letter*, 13 June 1829, p4 a.

8. *Saunders' News-Letter*, 1 April 1817, p2 cd.

9. Protest on 2 June 1820, Sir J T Gilbert & Lady Gilbert (eds), *Calendar of Ancient Records of Dublin* (19 vols, Dublin 1916), xvii, p316.

10. 'An account of the Corporation of the City of Dublin and expenditure of the pipe water and metal main establishments for one year ended 28th September 1816 and 1817.' National Archives, State Paper Office, OP 571/495/1–10.

11. Anthony Edwards, *Cork Remembrances or Tablet of Memory* (Cork 1792).

12. For example, *Saunders' News-Letter*, 2 February 1820, p4 c.

13. *Saunders' News-Letter*, 1 January 1820, p2 d.

14. For example, advertisement of Thomas Jones, *The Cork Gazette*, 17 September 1791, p3, and advertisement of John O'Neill, floor cloth and house painter, 49 Capel Street, Dublin, in *Saunders News-Letter*, 1 April 1785, p3.

15. Mrs H G Leask [Longfield] has written much on wallpapers in Ireland, but probably the most relevant here is her article 'Old wall-papers in Ireland' in *The Journal of the Royal Society of Antiquaries of Ireland*, lxxxvii (1957), pp141–6.

16. Second Annual Exhibition of Articles of Irish Manufacture and Invention at the RDS House, May 1835, Lots 42 and 46; *The Public Gazetteer*, 24 August 1771, p3.

17. The Knight of Glin, 'Early Irish trade-cards and other eighteenth-century ephemera' in *Eighteenth-Century Ireland, Iris an Dá Chultúr*, ii (1987), pp118–19.

18. Allied Irish Bank Archives, Ms 170, Isaac Morgan & Sons Sale Book. I am grateful to Dr David Dickson for guiding me to this, and to Mr A Lambkin for allowing me access to it.

19. Thomas Humphrys, *The Irish Builder's Guide* (Dublin 1813).

20. J C Loudon, *An Encyclopaedia of Cottage, Farm and Villa Architecture and Furniture* (London 1834), pp1014–16.

21. National Library of Ireland, Ms 9314, Mary Shackleton's diary, November 1789.

22. National Archives, State Paper Office, OP 588 AAE/983/1.

23. Margaret Boyle Harvey, *A Journal of a Voyage to Cork in the Year of Our Lord, 1809* (Philadelphia 1915).

24. Loudon, *An Encyclopaedia*, p345.

25. Account of Col Pratt, 6 March 1833, AIB Archives, Ms 170, ff 150–51.

26. *Saunders' News-Letter*, 1 April 1817, p4 a.

27. *The Freeman's Journal*, 19 January 1847, p2 a.

28. *Saunders' News-Letter*, 12 February 1796. I am grateful to Donal O'Sullivan for this reference.

29. *Saunders' News-Letter*, 8 March 1809, p2.

30. Mr & Mrs S C Hall, *Ireland: Its Scenery and Character* (3 vols, London 1842), ii, pp317–21.

31. Mr & Mrs Hall, *Ireland*, iii, p63.

32. Loudon, *An Encyclopaedia*, pp707–15. Advertisement for Slater's Celebrated Patent Steam Kitchen Range for Cooking by Steam and hot air, *Saunders' News-Letter*, 3 April 1817, p3.

CHAPTER 13 (PP207–230)

1. F S L Lyons, *Culture and Anarchy in Ireland 1890–1939* (Oxford 1979).

A basic guide to Irish architectural history is Maurice Craig, *The Architecture of Ireland From the Earliest Times to 1880* (London 1982), and for an excellent bibliography, see Edward McParland, 'A bibliography of Irish architectural history' in *Irish Historical Studies*, xxvi, (1988–9), pp161–212. For Irish buildings, see Lord Killanin and Michael Duignan, *The Shell Guide to Ireland*, revised and updated by Peter Harbison (London 1989), and the published volumes of the ongoing Penguin 'Buildings of Ireland' series, Alistair Rowan, *North West Ulster* (London 1979), and Christine Casey, Alistair Rowan, *North Leinster* (London 1993). See also D S Richardson, *Gothic Revival Architecture in Ireland*, (2 vols, New York 1983), Peter Costello, *Dublin Churches* (Dublin 1989), Peter Galloway, *The Cathedrals of Ireland* (Belfast 1992).

The religious history of the nineteenth century in Ireland is little explored. For an overview of the Irish Catholic Church, see chaps 7 & 8 of P J Corish, *The Irish Catholic Experience* (Dublin 1985), which also provides a guide to further reading. The most important ideas are those of Emmet Larkin in his *The Historical Dimensions of Irish Catholicism* (Washington 1984), especially the first essay for its discussion of the funding of church buildings. For the Church of Ireland, D H Akenson, *The Church of Ireland: Ecclesiastical Reform and Revolution* (New Haven 1971) provides a useful introduction, supplemented by the essays of Fergus O'Ferrall and Kenneth Milne in 'The Church of Ireland: a critical bibliography 1536–1992' in *Irish Historical Studies*, xxviii (1992–3), pp369–84. For the Nonconformists, David Hempton, Myrtle Hill, *Evangelical Protestantism in Ulster Society, 1740–1890* (London 1992).